Black Radicals and the Civil Rights Mainstream, 1954–1970

Black Radicals and the Civil Rights Mainstream, 1954–1970

HERBERT H. HAINES

THE UNIVERSITY OF TENNESSEE PRESS / KNOXVILLE

Copyright © 1988 by The University of Tennessee Press / Knoxville.
All Rights Reserved.
First Edition.

LIBRARY OF CONGRESS CATALOGING-IN-PUBLICATION DATA

Haines, Herbert H.
   Black radicals and the civil rights mainstream, 1954–1970.

   Bibliography: p.
   Includes index.
   1. Afro-Americans—Civil rights.   2. Afro-Americans—
Politics and government.   3. United States—Politics and
government—1945-   . 4. Radicalism—United States—
History—20th century.   5. United States—Race relations.
I. Title.
E185.615.H25   1988   305.8'96073   87-25518
ISBN 0-87049-563-1 (alk. paper)

To the memory of Hadley H. Haines

Contents

Preface	xi
Introduction	1
Radical Flank Effects as Features of Complex Social Movements	3
Varieties of Radical Flank Effects	5
Scope of the Study	11
1 The Shifting Spectrum of Black Collective Action	15
The Pre-War Years	17
World War II–1954: Legalistic Integrationism as Radical	20
1955–1963: Direct Action Integrationism as Radical	29
1964–1970: The "New" Radicalism	46
Conclusion	74
2 Radicalization and Resource Mobilization	77
Resources, Third Parties, and Collective Action	77
The Data	79
Exogenous Income Trends, 1954–1970	81
The Sources of Financial Support for Black Collective Action	99
Conclusion	126
3 Radicals, Moderates, and the Federal Government	129
The Structure of Federal Civil Rights Politics	134
Federal Responsiveness across Three Eras of Protest	137
The Kennedy Administration and Racial Crisis, 1961–1963	149
Conclusion	166

	4 **Radicals, Crises, and Concessions**	172
	Summary of Findings	172
	Other Factors	173
	Radical Flanks and Social Interests	178
	Toward a Theory of Radical Flank Effects	180
	The Consequences of Reactive Support by Elites	183
	Movement Success as Stepwise Change	185
Appendix: Supplementary Tables		187
Notes		197
Bibliography		207
Index		217

Tables and Figures

TABLES

1	White Approval of Types of Racial Integration, 1942	29
2	White Approval of Racial Integration: 1942, 1956, 1963	45
3	Percent of Whites Disapproving of Nonviolent Protest Tactics, 1963	47
4	Nationwide White Approval of Racial Integration: 1942, 1956, 1963, 1968	72
5	White Opinion on Effectiveness of Black Leaders, 1966	73
6	White Attitudes toward Pace of Integration, by Category, May 1965–April 1968	74
7	Expected Radical Flank Effects in the Financial Support of Black Collective Action	79
8	Total Exogenous Income of Major Black Organizations, 1952–1970	84
9	Rate of Yearly Exogenous Income Growth of Major Black Organizations, 1952–1970	88
10	Distribution of Exogenous Income among Major Black Organizations, by Year, 1957–1970	89
11	Individual Contributions to Selected Black Organizations, by Year, 1952–1970	102
12	Labor Contributions to Selected Black Organizations, by Year, 1952–1970	108
13	Corporate Contributions to the National Urban League, 1961–1972, 1980	113

TABLES AND FIGURES

14	Foundation Grants to Selected Black Organizations, by Year, 1952–1970, 1980	116
15	Foundation Grants to Selected Black Organizations, Reported in *Foundation News*, 1960–1970	117
16	Foundation Grants for Black-Related Issues, Reported in *Foundation News*, 1960–1970	118
17	Total Foundation Grant Funds, Grants to Movement Organizations, and Other Black-Related Grants	123
18	Federal Funding of the National Urban League	125
19	The Achievement of Major Black Claims	130

APPENDIX TABLES

A-1	National Urban League (NUL): Sources of Funding	188
A-2	National Association for the Advancement of Colored People (NAACP): Sources of Funding	189
A-3	Legal Defense and Educational Fund, Inc. (LDEF): Sources of Funding	190
A-4	Southern Regional Council (SRC), General Fund: Sources of Funding	191
A-5	Southern Regional Council (SRC), General Fund and Special Projects: Sources of Funding	192
A-6	Southern Christian Leadership Conference (SCLC): Sources of Funding	193
A-7	Congress of Racial Equality (CORE): Sources of Funding	194
A-8	Student Nonviolent Coordinating Committee (SNCC): Sources of Funding	195

FIGURES

1	Distribution of Black Organizations, 1945–1954	27
2	Distribution of Black Organizations, 1955–1963	42
3	Distribution of Black Organizations, 1964–1970	71
4	Total Exogenous Income of Major Black Organizations, by Year, 1957–1970	83
5	Number of Foundations Contributing to Racial and Antipoverty Activities, 1960–1970	120

Preface

In a sense, this book had its origins in April 1968—the month the racial crisis became real to me. Before then I had been dimly aware of Birmingham and Selma and Watts and what they meant for America. But like most other white teenagers living in white neighborhoods, I had no reason to pay much attention to such things.

In the days after the murder of Martin Luther King, however, I could not avoid paying attention. Racial turmoil was no longer just something shown on the television news—now it was something happening in the corridors outside my high school classrooms. It was also something happening on the black East Side of Kansas City, several miles from my home but close enough that I could see smoke from the fires if I went to the top of a nearby hill. By the standards of the 1960s, the Kansas City rioting wasn't very serious: only six people died in three days of warfare. Nonetheless, it had a lasting effect on my way of looking at the society I had been born into. Years later, I began to think that the turmoil of the 1960s and the massive changes in the nature of black protest must have had a similar effect on other people's ways of thinking, that many white people must have found it harder to see mere racial equality as an unreasonable idea after having heard demands for reparations, black control of ghetto institutions, and the like. Further, I began to think that at least some who called themselves "leaders" must have seen in the eruptions of 1964 through 1968 a grim indication of the costs of moving slowly or not at all. The investigation that culminated with this book began as an effort to test this hunch. But as time went by it became less a study of what people *thought* than what people *did* in response to the black revolt. And it is offered not simply as a description of the civil rights movement alone but rather as a theoretical exploration of an aspect of modern social movements in general.

ACKNOWLEDGMENTS

I have many people to thank for their contributions to this book. The largest measure of my gratitude goes to Joane Nagel, without whose encouragement and guidance it would literally never have been started. Norm Yetman, Anne Schofield, and Jack Weller provided not only insight and criticism but an enthusiasm for the project that made it seem all the more worthwhile. My intellectual debts to Bob Antonio are not limited to his role in this book; whatever merits I can claim as a scholar or a teacher bear his mark.

Aid in various phases of the data-collection process was provided by Gary Bloom, Louise Cook and the staff of the Martin Luther King Library and Archives, Clayborne Carson, Minnie Clayton, Megan Floyd Desnoyers and the staff of the John F. Kennedy Library, Jack Greenberg, Doug McAdam, Ruth McKeever, and Steve Suitts. The research was supported by grants from the National Science Foundation and the Faculty Research Program of the State University of New York at Cortland. David Garrow, Craig Jenkins, Gary Marx, August Meier, Joan Roelofs, Elliot Rudwick, and two anonymous reviewers read portions of the manuscript and gave helpful criticism and advice. The editors at the University of Tennessee Press, especially Cynthia Maude-Gembler and Bettie McDavid Mason, have my gratitude not only for their technical expertise and assistance but for their patience with this inexperienced author. Gilda Mason, Janet Dauley, and Mark Wheeler assisted in the preparation of the manuscript. Figures in Chapters 1 and 2 were prepared at the Learning Resources Center, State University of New York College at Cortland. Cynthia Moy, Evan Moy Haines, and Colin Moy Haines put up with it all, and I am especially grateful for that.

Introduction

> I want Dr. King to know that I didn't come to Selma to make his job difficult. I really did come thinking that I could make it easier. If white people realize what the alternative is, perhaps they'll be more willing to hear Dr. King.
> —*Malcolm X, 1965*

This is a study of "moderates" and "radicals." It inquires into the role of militant groups in social movements and the impact of their activities on the capacity of moderate organizations to pursue their goals effectively. It focuses upon black collective action, mostly during the tumultuous period between 1954 and 1970. During those years groups of black activists adopted increasingly militant goals, rhetoric, and tactics, and this process of radicalization led to an almost constant concern over the threat of a "white backlash." Withdrawal of white support or the mobilization of white opposition, it was feared, would be devastating to minority interests. Hence Martin Luther King's prediction that "[t]he more there are riots, the more repression will take place, and the more we face the danger of a right-wing take-over, and eventually a fascist society."

Perhaps King's concerns were exaggerated, but they revealed a point of view that was widespread during the escalation of protest in the 1960s. Even now the most common interpretation of that decade of black protest maintains that black militants impeded progress by spawning a backlash. It is undeniable that many whites turned against the cause of civil rights in the midst of the struggle. That a decrease in white sympathy for civil rights was at least partially a response to racial violence and "black power" is also beyond debate. This book, however, presents evidence that such an understanding of the years of black protest is one-sided and inadequate: the turmoil which the militants created was indispensable to black progress, and indeed, black radicalization had the net effect of enhancing the bargaining position of mainstream civil rights groups and hastening the attainment of many of their goals.

While the focus of this book is black protest in both its civil rights and nationalistic forms, it has implications for any social movement which is composed of moderate and radical factions.[1] Thus, since ideological and tactical unanimity are so exceptional as to be virtually nonexistent, it has implications for nearly all sustained episodes of collective claims-making. Schisms between radicals and moderates, between "extremists" and "responsible leaders," have been noted in the abolitionist movement against slavery (Nye 1963), the American labor movement (Dick 1972; Garraty 1969; Zieger 1986), the women's movement (Freeman 1975), the antinuclear movement (Barkan 1979), and the conservative resurgence of the 1970s (Crawford 1980), to name only a few. In each of these cases, moderates have expressed fears that the behavior of the "radical fringe" would undermine the legitimacy of more reasonable leaders. And not uncommonly, the radicals have portrayed themselves as the "muscle" without which established leaders would be reduced to impotence. In the pages which follow, the consequences which radicals and their actions have for moderates—be they helpful or damaging—are termed *radical flank effects*.[2]

Little attention has been paid to radical flank effects as recurrent features of social movements. Thus, this inquiry cannot add to a distinct and specialized literature on such phenomena, for no such literature yet exists. On the other hand, the study is closely linked in a number of ways to recent developments in social movement theory. During the 1970s resource mobilization and political process theorists began to deemphasize the personal motivations and psychological states of movement participants as critical variables for understanding collective action. Instead, they have stressed such social and political variables as participation by external groups, fluctuations in the social control activities of the state, increases and decreases in monetary and other resources at the disposal of formal movement organizations, changes in opportunities for mobilization and claimsmaking by powerless groups, and the importance of organizational infrastructure.

This book focuses upon many of the same variables in black collective action. It concentrates upon the formal and informal organizational features of the movement. It treats the goals pursued by black organizations and other collectivities as crucial independent variables to be taken seriously rather than as dependent variables to be explained as by-products of the personal characteristics of their membership. It examines the all-important roles of outside groups as financial supporters and as key decision-makers in civil rights politics, emphasizing interorganizational processes in movement analysis.

RADICAL FLANK EFFECTS AS FEATURES OF COMPLEX SOCIAL MOVEMENTS

It has been suggested by activists and scholars alike that the emergence of radical activists and organizations in a social movement can undermine the position of moderates (and sometimes that of the movement as a whole) by discrediting movement activities and goals, by threatening the ability of moderates to take advantage of resources supplied by supportive third parties (Barkan 1979; Killian 1972; Nye 1963; Scott and Brockriede 1969), or by otherwise rendering favorable responses to moderate claims less likely. In the following pages this general pattern, process, or outcome will be called a *negative radical flank effect*. Moderate abolitionists of the early nineteenth century, for example, predicted that the actions of antislavery extremists would discredit the cause and delay emancipation (Nye 1963). Similarly, groups opposed to nuclear power plants have feared that their cause would be hurt by violent or obstructionist tactics and by efforts to expand the movement's focus to include nuclear disarmament and various sorts of corporate misbehavior (Barkan 1979).

Others have suggested, conversely, that a strengthening of the moderates' hand may result from the activities of radical groups (Drake 1968; Elinson 1966; Freeman 1975; Golden 1964; Killian 1972; Oberschall 1973). Radicals may thus provide a militant foil against which moderate strategies and demands can be redefined and normalized, i.e., responded to as "reasonable." That is, they may play a boundary-setting role in a social psychological process not unlike the phenomenon of relative deprivation (Merton 1967). It has been argued, for example, that moderate, reformist women's organizations of the late 1960s and early 1970s would have been dismissed as "too far out" had it not been for the existence of more extreme groups (Freeman 1975). Lesbian and socialist feminists appear to have improved the bargaining position of the moderates by making the demands of the latter appear rather mild. It has also been suggested that radicals may enhance the bargaining position of moderates by creating crises which come to be resolved by means of limited concessions to moderate groups. This appears to have happened in the labor movement during the Progressive Era (Ewen 1976; Ramirez 1968) and following World War II (Bowles and Gintis 1982; Bowles, Gordon, and Weisskopf 1983); the rights of trade unions to exist and to bargain for higher wages and better working conditions were granted largely as a means of neutralizing more fundamental demands—demands for a greater measure of control over the productive process itself. Such a pattern, in which radicals enhance the positions of moderates in some manner, will here be called a *positive radical flank effect*.

Though many scholars have referred to radical flank effects in passing, these phenomena have received virtually no systematic attention. In fact, the only direct investigation of the effects of moderate/radical factionalism on the outcomes of protests is found in Gamson's research on "strategies" of protest (1975). Gamson explained the conditions under which protest groups became recognized spokespersons for a set of constituents and managed to gain "new advantages"—i.e., various collective gains—for those constituents. Among the conditions examined was the existence of multiple challengers, representing both moderate and radical alternatives. Using a subsample of thirty groups which had competitors of greater or lesser radicalism, he tested the hypothesis that the more militant organizations enhanced the success of less militant ones. This hypothesis he rejected. On the surface, Gamson's analysis would seem to close the book on radical flank effects as significant features of social movements. Several characteristics of his research, however, make such a conclusion premature. First of all, the sample which he used was too small. From the total sample of 53 American challenging organizations, he picked 30 which had been faced with a competing movement organization during their heyday. In only seven of these cases were the competitors more radical. Not only was the sample too small to justify a firm conclusion, but it was composed primarily of labor unions; fully two-thirds of the subsample and six of the seven groups designated as more moderate than their competitors were of this category. To generalize so broadly from such a narrow range of types is dangerous. Moreover, Gamson's coding strategy has been criticized, as have his measurement and analytic techniques (Goldstone 1980). Consequently, further research is necessary before the issue of radical flank effects can be considered settled.

Because social movements are frequently composed of both moderate and radical factions and there exists a good deal of anecdotal evidence of both positive and negative outcomes resulting from the presence of radical flanks, an understanding of radical flank effects would contribute greatly to current social movement theory. Such an understanding would, for example, be relevant to the debate between the resource mobilization model of protest and that of Piven and Cloward (1977). The resource mobilization perspective stresses the dependency of protest groups on the resources obtainable from third parties (Jenkins and Perrow 1977; Lipsky 1968). Implicit in this model is the notion that protest groups must refrain from tactics and statements which would alienate prospective supporters. Piven and Cloward, on the other hand, suggest that reliance on such resources only undermines protest goals and that protest groups can succeed through tactics of mass disruption. *Positive* radical flank effects serve as a link between these competing theories. Under certain circumstances, moderate groups might well be able to maintain good relations with supporting groups by distancing themselves from the disruptive activities of radicals while at the same time profiting from the crises those same radicals create.

VARIETIES OF RADICAL FLANK EFFECTS

As I have noted, various movement participants and movement scholars have suggested that radical flanks can exert either a damaging or an enhancing influence on the chances for successes by moderates. What is meant, however, by "success" in this context? Given the complexity of social movements and contemporary political processes, it is necessary to identify the specific nature of the gains or setbacks which might occur for moderate organizations as a result of more militant activities. There are five levels on which such gains and losses might be identifiable: (1) public awareness and recognition; (2) public definition and redefinition; (3) outside resource support; (4) access to decision-makers; and (5) goal attainment.

Awareness and Recognition

Although protest groups and movement organizations differ in the degree to which they are dependent on public opinion as a resource, most do require at least some public awareness of their existence (Lipsky 1968). Claims-makers usually find it in their best interests to become as widely known as possible and to turn their concerns and goals into public issues; radical flanks can play important roles in this regard. For one thing, militant groups often engage in activities which cannot be ignored, such as disruptive protests, damaging boycotts, or violence. The use of such tactics sets them apart from "quiet" moderates who stick by gradualist, noncontroversial, "acceptable" activities. Thus, the actions of radical flanks may bring movement claims to center stage, engaging the attention of the public and/or the elites who may have ignored them until a crisis emerged. This was antiabortion activist Joseph Schneidler's meaning when he insisted that "no social movement goes anywhere without going to the streets." When moderates and their claims receive more attention as a result of such crises, we may say that a positive radical flank effect has occurred at this level. For instance, events such as the occupation of Alcatraz Island by militant Native Americans, the uprising on the Pine Ridge reservation, and the emergence of the American Indian Movement helped to transform the problems of the Indian people into public issues.

On the other hand, the often outrageous and shocking character of militant actions can threaten to steal the show from moderates. The complaint is frequently heard, for example, that the news media treat bizarre or unusual events as more newsworthy than those which are more typical but undramatic. There is always the danger, then, that a small but extreme fringe can upstage the more restrained mainstream. Radical flanks may also divert attention to a whole new set of issues not on the agenda of moderates (Killian 1972). When such patterns appear, we may say that a negative radical flank effect has occurred at the level of awareness and recognition.

Such a negative effect might be especially damaging to the interests of moderates in situations where audiences and target groups fail to make accurate distinctions between the various segments and organizations operating simultaneously. When militant tactics attract media attention, audiences unfamiliar with the range of ideologies within the movement, with the range of issues being raised, or with the tactical disputes within the social movement may come to view the actions of the radical flank as indicative of the movement as a whole. Such seems to have been the case during the earliest years of the women's movement, when many uninformed observers defined feminism only in terms of media images such as "bra burners." The *initial* effect of militant feminists may thus have been, ironically, to elicit public disapproval not only of themselves but also of other feminist groups employing other types of tactics.

Definition and Redefinition

Moderation and radicalism are troublesome, relative terms; they mean different things to different people. Moreover, both terms may be applied to the same actors or organizations at different times. Killian (1972) takes note that "extremist" leaders of social movements may come to be redefined as "moderate" not because of any real ideological shift but rather because of the emergence of other leaders who make more fundamental claims. In other words, the positions of a particular spokesperson or movement organization may *seem* to be truly radical until a more radical spokesperson or organization appears. At that point, an intersubjective shift may occur on the part of audiences, and those activists previously thought to be extreme or outlandish become redefined as relatively reasonable and tame. Killian argues that this sort of transformation has taken place again and again in the history of the black revolt in America (also see Meier and Rudwick 1976: ch. 7). Such redefinitions may or may not be associated with concrete gains by the newly-defined moderates; this is an empirical question. At the level of definition and categorization of movement organizations, however, such a pattern may be designated a positive radical flank effect.

It is likewise possible, though, that the emergence of more militant actors may lead to the redefinition of existing spokespersons and organizations as *more* radical than previously thought. The actions of emerging militants might, for example, lead audiences to see threatening implications in moderate agendas and tactics which had not been apparent before. In similar fashion, militants' deeds may lead to popular outrage which spills over onto less extreme groups, thus diminishing their stock of moral capital. Recent waves of abortion clinic bombings may have had this effect for the Right to Life movement. When such patterns appear, we may say that a negative radical flank effect has occurred at the level of definition and redefinition.

Outside Support

The central contribution of the resource mobilization approach to social movement analysis has been its focus on the tremendous importance of accumulating funds and other resources for initiating and maintaining claims-making activities (for example, see Jenkins and Perrow 1977; McCarthy and Zald 1973, 1977; Oberschall 1973; Zald and McCarthy 1979).[3] Discontent and moral fervor can go only so far in sustaining collective challenges in the modern context; concrete resources like money, manpower, and facilities are at least as important.

If it is true that the emergence of militant actors can affect the definition and categorization of other spokespersons and organizations, as has been suggested, then there is also good reason to suppose that it may affect the ability of moderates to mobilize resources. On the one hand, external groups as well as movement constituents may react to growing militancy by increasing their levels of support for more moderate movement factions and organizations. Where this occurs, we may speak of a positive radical flank effect at the level of support. On the other hand, the emergence of growing militancy may be interpreted as a threat and moderates blamed in some manner. Under such circumstances, it is likely that levels of outside support will decline. Similarly, where militants succeed in upstaging moderates—or stealing the show entirely—defections or shifts in monetary contributions may take place among members and constituents. When such patterns occur, we may speak of a negative radical flank effect at the level of support. Radical flank effects on outside support will be the subject of Chapter 2.

Access to Decision-Makers

At least as important as a favorable climate of public opinion, and probably much more so, is the degree of access to key decision-makers that movement organizations and their leaders are able to maintain. The attainment of goals is typically dependent upon a group's ability to have an input into political policies or other decisions. Militant groups may either increase or decrease the openness of power centers to moderate influence.

All in all, it appears that militant political tactics are more useful for creating crises than for resolving them, but as we shall see in our analysis of collective action among blacks, crises can be useful for moderates. Moderates, likely to have at least some access to decision-makers (even if it is more symbolic than real), have to be concerned lest rocking the boat jeopardize what may be a very marginal bargaining position. Militants, generally lacking the connections necessary for negotiating with decision-makers, are not constrained by the need to protect their political influence. Consequently, militants may provide the useful service of generating crises which lead elites to negotiate "mild" ameliorative measures which are in the interest of moderate groups. Walker (1963) notes such a pattern in interracial politics in Atlanta, Georgia, and I shall show in Chapter 3 that similar processes were at work on the federal level in the early 1960s. Where moderates receive greater access to decision-makers as a result of radical pressure, we may speak of a positive radical flank effect at that level.

If moderates are to benefit by gaining increasing access, it is of critical importance that they are not *blamed* for the militants' crisis-generating activities. If they do receive part of the blame, it is likely that their access to the decision-making process may be at least temporarily diminished. Even if they are not blamed, the crisis generated by militants may become so severe that claims of moderates are reduced to a low priority by the besieged elites. Either pattern would constitute a negative radical flank effect at the level of access to decision-makers.

Goal Attainment

Finally, the activities of militant organizations and groups in a movement may lead to greater or lesser attainment of the goals of moderates. At this level, the issue is not merely access but *outcome*, not merely a hearing for claims but policy responses. We might safely assume that elites, who by definition have a vested interest in maintaining the status quo, will very likely try to avoid dealing with the demands of *any* change-oriented organization if they can afford to. But in a situation in which the elites have no choice but to deal with some set of demands and are faced with two or more movement organizations which are making distinct claims, they may choose to act upon the demands of whichever organization they believe least threatening to the status quo (Piven and Cloward 1977: xxi–xxii; Zald and McCarthy 1979). A positive response to the demands of moderate groups may come to be seen as an effective way to give up as little as possible and simultaneously to diminish the viability of other organizations. For instance, as was noted earlier, the eventual acquiescence of corporate leaders to the rather tame agenda of "business unionists" has been attributed to a concern over rising labor radicalism during both the Progressive Era (Ewen 1976; Ramirez 1978; Spring 1972) and the postwar years (Bowles and Gintis 1982; Bowles, Gordon, and Weisskopf 1983; Fones-Wolf 1986).

Conversely, a negative radical flank effect might become evident at the level of outcome. Such a pattern involves a decrease in the likelihood of policies, programs, or laws reflecting moderate interests or a slowing of the pace of such accomplishments. Negative radical flank effects may occur in situations in which elites, considering the moderates culpable in some way for the actions of the militants, come to view further accommodations of the moderates' demands as counterproductive. The most negative of all possible outcomes occurs when powerholders use crises generated by militants as a license not merely to ignore but to repress the whole range of groups in a movement. This is most likely to occur under authoritarian structures, such as those Latin American regimes which have lumped even moderate leftist and centrist opposition groups together under the umbrella of "communist subversion" so as to justify eliminating them.

In summation, radical flank effects are patterns of gains or losses, successes or failures experienced by moderate organizations which can be directly attributed to the activities of more radical organizations or other groups. These gains or losses may involve the degree to which audiences are aware of moderates and their claims, the manner in which moderates are defined by various audiences, the levels and types of support granted to moderate factions by external parties, the degree of access to decision-making elites which moderate activists enjoy, and the degree and pace at which moderates attain their goals (i.e., target group responses). This list of varieties of radical flank effects is by no means exhaustive. Moreover, there is no reason to suppose that radical flank effects must occur in only one direction at a time. When social movements mobilize and act collectively, many different groups respond, including not only the general public but diverse interest groups, various subgroups within the private and public sectors. Each audience and target group has its own interests, its own range of ideologies, and its own set of constraints within which it must operate. It is quite possible, even probable, that *simultaneous opposing radical flank effects* may occur. Some sort of backlash might take place at the level of public definition, for example, even as a positive effect is appearing at the levels of access and outcome. Similarly, factions within a single responding group or audience may react differently to the emergence of new forms of militancy. Both the Congress and the federal bureaucracy have always included competing factions which have responded to black radicalization in different ways. In other such circumstances, the issue of whether or not a radical flank effect has occurred can be somewhat complicated.

SCOPE OF THE STUDY

Although a number of researchers have investigated the growth of militancy and the emergence of violence in the black revolt, none has attempted to study the effects of these developments upon public and governmental responses from the standpoint of an intramovement division of labor. Nor has there been an investigation of possible connections between radicalism/violence and patterns of resource mobilization by major black organizations during the 1950s and the 1960s.[4] This study investigates three areas: shifts in black radicalism, trends in resource allocation, and effects of radicalism on policy responses.

Shifting Black Radicalism

Chapter 1 describes the changing character of black protest during the years following World War II. It is not intended to be a complete narrative of black collective action; many outstanding histories of the civil rights movement have been written already.[5] Rather, it will be concerned with tracing the escalation in movement goals, rhetoric, and tactics as well as the shift in the focus of black collective action from the rural South to the urban North. A particular concern is to identify critical periods of escalating radicalism. A wide range of secondary sources will be employed in this process, and public opinion data will be used to gauge changing attitudes about specific organizations, goals, and leaders. Greatest emphasis will be placed upon the following organizations, the major national proponents of black claims during at least part of the 1954–1970 period:

Congress of Racial Equality (CORE)
National Association for the Advancement of Colored People (NAACP)
NAACP Legal Defense and Educational Fund, Inc. (LDEF)

National Urban League (NUL)
Southern Christian Leadership Conference (SCLC)
Southern Regional Council (SRC)
Student Nonviolent Coordinating Committee (SNCC)

For the investigation of radical flank effects, the American civil rights movement of the 1950s and 1960s, along with the urban violence of the latter decade, makes an excellent case study. This extraordinarily complex movement involved a variety of organizations, ideologies, and strategies. In addition, it was characterized by a rapid tactical and rhetorical escalation between 1954 and 1970.

Resource Allocation Trends

Chapter 2 involves the analysis of longitudinal financial data. These data reflect trends in resource allocation by financial supporters of each of the seven major black organizations listed above. The principal emphasis will be upon contributions from outside the organizations themselves.

The role of third parties in social movements has been recognized for some time. Lipsky (1968) argues that "the essence of political protest consists of activating third parties to participate in controversy in ways favorable to protest goals." The need to do so, however, can sometimes lead to characterizations of protest leaders as "sellouts," as was the case when militant black activists began to criticize coalitions with whites during the mid-1960s. Lipsky (1968) has suggested that one way in which such tensions can be minimized "is by dividing leadership responsibilities. . . . Protest leaders can, in effect, divide up public roles so as to reduce as much as possible the gap between the implicit demands of different groups for appropriate rhetoric, and what in fact is said. Thus divided, leadership may perform the latent function of minimizing tensions among elements in the protest process by permitting different groups to listen selectively to protest spokesmen" (1153).

The importance of third parties for the mobilization and maintenance of social movement organizations has been given particular emphasis in the resource mobilization perspective.[6] In their consideration of the changing nature of social movements in the United States, McCarthy and Zald (1973) point out that the decade of the 1960s was "a period in which institutional support for social movement organizations became increasingly available and in which . . . organizations not usually thought of as social movement supporters . . . began to support social movement activities" (12).

This change has obvious implications for our understanding of contemporary social movements, but what does it have to do with radical flank effects? It was noted earlier that *support* is one level at which such effects might be expected to manifest themselves—i.e., the statements and actions of emerging militants might be expected to lead to changes in the willingness of various third parties to support moderates. Previously reliable supporters might either become disillusioned with the inability of moderates to control the character of the movement or become convinced that the cause which they had been supporting had gone too far. On the other hand, various third parties might become convinced that support for moderate organizations is the best way to channel the movement into "safe" and reasonable issues or to forestall any further radicalization of the movement's constituency. Along these lines it has been suggested that reliance upon institutional funding can lead to the co-optation of social movements and an alteration of what would otherwise become radical programs of collective action (McAdam 1982; Piven and Cloward 1977). In short, the patterns of involvement of such groups as foundations, corporations, labor organizations, and churches might be seen as suggestive of their response to militant challenges; in fact, patterns of external support might be a better index of a particular organization's relative "acceptability" than public opinion data, at least for certain groups and in certain circumstances.

Oberschall (1973: 217–18) offers an overview of the sources of funds upon which various black organizations relied during the peak of civil rights movement activity. Unfortunately, his discussion is not detailed, is inaccurate in places (Morris 1984: 281), and fails to deal with changes in the movement's support structure over time. In a more recent study, McAdam (1982) has constructed a longitudinal data set which describes the externally-derived income of several major civil rights organizations over time. While some of this information is used in Chapter 2, it nonetheless suffers from three drawbacks: (1) it is taken largely from incomplete secondary sources; (2) much of it is estimated; and (3) it is not broken down by source. Though not without problems of their own, the data which I employ in that chapter are, I believe, significant improvements on McAdam's in each of these regards.

The analysis of these data has been guided by the working assumption that shifts in the amounts and sources of financial support indicate the presence and direction of radical flank effects. More specifically, positive radical flank effects are expected to produce increases in the total amount of financial support for moderate organizations during periods of increasing radicalism, while negative radical flank effects are expected to produce decreases or a leveling of previous increases. The absence of significant changes in resource mobilization patterns or inconsistent fluctuations in external funding would suggest the absence of radical flank effects. In Chapter 2 analysis will show that resource mobilization patterns for seven major black organizations are generally consistent with the evidence for positive radical flank effects.

Radicalism and Policy Responses

Chapter 3 deals with the effects of black radicalization on federal policy. There I shall summarize the temporal correspondence between levels and types of movement activity on the one hand and major legislative and executive branch concessions on the other. In addition, I shall take a closer look at a selected administration—that of John F. Kennedy—and provide evidence from primary sources as to the specific motivations behind shifts in federal policies. My goal: to determine generally the impact of black radicalization and violence and to delve into the interpretation of these historical episodes by specific decision-makers. Needless to say, the process by which federal civil rights and social welfare policy was made during the 1960s was exceedingly complex, and no single factor can be given exclusive causal significance. But radical flank effects were central among the considerations that shaped many of the government's actions during those times.

1

The Shifting Spectrum of Black Collective Action

Collective action among black Americans during the twentieth century has been characterized by great diversity, especially since the 1950s. Various leaders called for strategies ranging from accommodation and self-help, to legislated integration, to the creation of a separate black nation. Forms of collective action have included litigation, peaceful demonstrations, civil disobedience, and violent confrontation. Numerous formal organizations have participated. Some of these organizations burst upon the scene and captured the attention of the nation, only to disappear after a few years. Others became institutionalized features of black life and have survived in the rapidly changing milieu of racial politics. Contradictory ideologies and claims have been advanced and bitter internal disputes have arisen over proper and effective means for attaining ends.

The range of formal organizations was not the only source of diversity in black collective action. Relatively spontaneous protests have played important roles as well, and the urban disorders of the 1960s, while not formally orchestrated or controlled, were of tremendous importance in shaping America's responses to racial themes.

The complexity of black protest in the 1950s and the 1960s creates certain problems of terminology for a study of this sort. Is it properly approached as a single social movement? If so, what is this movement to be called? Scholars have disagreed on the question of whether black collective action from 1945 through the 1960s should be seen as a single "civil rights movement" or as a series of overlapping movements with varying ends and means (Jackson 1976). For present purposes, it is not essential to settle this argument. It is essential, however, that attention be directed to the interconnectedness of the events which have made up the whole. For this reason, I will generally speak of "black collective action" or "black protest" rather than the "civil rights movement," the "black revolt," and so forth. In short, I shall approach civil rights, black power, black nationalism, etc., as integral phases of a larger totality, and leave the question of boundaries to others.

Conceptual problems aside, the complexity of black collective action and the rapidity with which its goals and tactics changed between World War II and the late 1960s make it an excellent case for the investigation of radical flank effects and the conditions under which they occur. In this chapter I shall review some of the main features of black collective action which are relevant to the study at hand. I am not attempting a comprehensive history of black activism, for several have already been written (for example, Blumberg 1984; Brisbane 1974; Brooks 1974; Killian 1968; Muse 1968; Powledge 1967). My purpose here is to describe how the nature of black "militancy" or "radicalism" has changed over the years from the end of World War II to the early 1970s.

Before proceeding further, it is necessary to define "radicalism." I have already noted that the term means many things to many people. For our purposes, however, *ideological* radicalism shall be defined in terms of the degree to which a given set of collective goals (a) departs from those goals conventionally deemed appropriate or legitimate at a given time, and/or (b) is perceived as threatening to the values or interests of various audiences, and/or (c) would require fundamental and sweeping social change to achieve. The demand that several southern states be ceded for the purpose of creating an independent black nation, voiced by the Republic of New Africa during the later 1960s, is an example of such a radical ideological position. *Tactical* radicalism shall be similarly defined in terms of the degree to which a given tactic or set of tactics (a) departs from those tactics conventionally deemed appropriate or legitimate as means for pursuing group goals at a given time, and/or (b) is perceived as threatening to the values or interests of various audiences, and/or (c) requires alterations in institutionalized mechanisms for dealing with and responding to group claims. According to such a definition, direct action tactics are more radical than litigation and lobbying, while organized violent attacks on dominant group members or their property are more radical than direct action.

From World War II through the mid-1950s, the vanguard of black "radicalism" was made up of organizations seeking racial integration through legal channels, i.e., by means of litigation and legislation. During the late 1950s and especially from 1960 through 1963, however, such ends and means were much less commonly seen as characteristics of militancy or radicalism, because advocates of civil rights were turning increasingly to a new style of collective action. While racial integration remained the dominant goal of black organizations of this newer type, they chose nonviolent direct action techniques over legalistic strategies. Still another form of radicalism emerged after 1964. During this period, black radicalism or militancy came to imply some degree of racial separatism and a refusal to reject categorically the legitimacy of violence.

THE PRE-WAR YEARS

Black collective action from the early 1950s through the end of the 1960s is the focus of this chapter. Nevertheless, a brief examination of earlier leaders and issues will contribute to an understanding of the ideological background of this period.

The National Urban League

Blacks migrated into northern cities in large numbers during the late nineteenth and early twentieth centuries, often encountering conditions which were different from those in the South but hardly better. To this situation the National Urban League owes its creation and long life. Founded in 1911 by conservative blacks and white philanthropists, it was originally called the National League on Urban Conditions. Although the NUL has functioned as both a social service agency and an activist organization, the emphasis was clearly on the former role during the early years.

The orientation of the League's founders differed little from that of Booker T. Washington, who rose to prominence by preaching a doctrine of accommodation and black self-help. Similarly, the NUL stressed improving employment opportunities for urban blacks through appeals to the economic self-interest of white employers (Meier 1963: 438; Laue 1970; Meier and Rudwick 1976: 242). Black newcomers to the city were advised to conduct themselves in a manner appealing to whites so as to improve their chances of finding employment and to speed their acceptance into the white-controlled urban world. Since the NAACP, then more concerned with issues affecting middle- and upper-class blacks, was not actively involved in issues of employment until much later (Meier and Rudwick 1976: 243), the Urban League was in fact filling a void in those days.

The National Urban League and its local affiliates also functioned as social service agencies, attempting to deal with the problems of urban blacks on a one-to-one basis. Local and national surveys were conducted to gather and publicize information on their economic condition, and a major emphasis was placed on job placement. In the nine years following its formation, for example, the League placed over 64,000 persons directly in jobs, though many of them were menial in nature (National Urban League 1980: 16). Through its housing bureau, the League also fought for stricter local housing standards and assisted individuals in finding a decent place to live (Parris and Brooks 1971; National Urban League 1980). In the 1930s it lobbied organized labor to eliminate discrimination, struggled to gain black representation on agencies distributing general aid, and opened "survival centers" in cities to help urban blacks deal with the difficulties of the depression (Parris and Brooks 1971).

The NUL has had a reputation as the most conservative of the major groups through most of its history. In certain respects, however, this view is misleading. Some of the League's programs reappeared in later years in the programs of groups labeled "extremist" or "radical." For example, while the Urban League often did take a conciliatory approach, it nevertheless focused on the day-to-day economic problems of the urban poor many years before such issues moved into the forefront. Even before the NAACP came to be criticized by militants for focusing on caste issues of the black bourgeoisie, Urban Leaguers were working in the ghettos on jobs and housing. But in spite of some forward-looking activities, the *ways* in which the League worked in those years marked it as conservative.

The National Association for the Advancement of Colored People

The major organization of the pre-War years was the National Association for the Advancement of Colored People (NAACP). Founded in 1910, the NAACP was in its youth a small interracial organization. In fact, its highest office was not occupied by a black until 1920, when James Weldon Johnson became secretary (Hughes 1962: 56). The Association's black membership was drawn primarily from urban business and professional people (Howard 1974:

23), and the middle-class characteristics of its membership led the NAACP, in contrast to the Urban League, to focus upon *caste* issues such as discrimination in public accommodations rather than such *class* issues as employment and welfare. From the beginning, the NAACP relied primarily upon lawsuits and lobbying to fight discrimination and segregation. It proceeded in a gradual and methodical fashion, earning a designation as the "long-distance runner" of civil rights. From its founding through the years of the Great Depression, most of the legal work that the NAACP instigated might be labeled "separate-but-equal legalism"; it was aimed not at attacking segregation directly but rather toward enforcing the Fourteenth and Fifteenth Amendments to the Constitution and ensuring the equality of provisions under the separate-but-equal doctrine laid down in *Plessy v. Ferguson* (Howard 1974; Killian 1972).

During the 1930s, the focus of NAACP activities changed from separate-but-equal to integrationist. Under the leadership of Charles C. Houston and Thurgood Marshall, the NAACP began a long and calculated legal campaign against the separate-but-equal doctrine and the legal segregation which it condoned (Hughes 1962; Meier and Rudwick 1976: 264–65; St. James 1958). The transition to legalistic integrationism ultimately led to victory in the landmark Supreme Court case, *Brown v. Board of Education*, which reversed the separate-but-equal doctrine and created the basis for the most active phase of black collective action.

Though the methodical and gradualist nature of NAACP activities through its early years seem moderate today, this was not always the case; through most of its development, the Association has been widely perceived as radical. In 1919, for instance, the Justice Department defined as radical any organization which denounced the Washingtonian ideology of self-help (Tuttle 1970: 227–28). In the South racists continued to harass and intimidate NAACP members years after the Association's militancy had been surpassed by that of the newer organizations. As late as February of 1959, newsman Chet Huntley suggested during a national broadcast that the NAACP might do well to step aside in order to let "moderates" guide the desegregation effort (NAACP 1959: 67–68).

Within the community of black leaders and strategists, however, the spectrum of radicalism often looked quite different. A. Philip Randolph, a socialist and the *"enfant terrible* of Negro journalism" in the 1920s, criticized the NAACP for moving too slowly and even called W. E. B. DuBois a "hat-in-hand" Negro (Meier and Rudwick 1976: 245). The Association also engaged in public sparring with the black nationalist Marcus Garvey, accusing him of extremism and in turn being accused by Garvey of seeking racial amalgamation and of being ashamed of the black race (Meier and Rudwick 1976: 246–47).

In the period of the 1950s and 1960s, the ideology and strategy of black collective action was to change very rapidly. As will be seen later in this chapter, the goal of integration would achieve virtual hegemony among black activists, only to be questioned and rejected by many a short time later. As the preceding discussion demonstrates, the conflicts of these decades have appeared before, if not in so visible an arena. The black nationalists of the 1960s were not the first black Americans to entertain a separatist outlook or to encourage the development of "black capitalism." The radicalism of recent decades has a history, although it is often forgotten. But "radicalism" can be a transitory label that is applied to a given group, only to be revoked later and reassigned to a new batch of socially-designated "extremists." One might be able to understand intuitively how the NAACP could be thought radical in an era which lacked a Black Panther Party or a Republic of New Africa. But why did the presence of Marcus Garvey, who urged racial separatism and anticolonialism, not temper the views of Americans toward the Association during the 1920s? The answer would seem to lie in *visibility*. Although the NAACP was hardly a flamboyant organization, and although the problems of blacks were not yet viewed as one of the nation's pressing social issues as in later decades, the radical critics of the NAACP were even less known throughout white America. Moreover, many of the more extreme black voices were not making demands upon the white society at all, as in the case of Garvey's call for a return to the African homeland. As a result, a white audience unaccustomed to black protest lacked a point of reference further along the scale of extremism which might have served to soften its judgement of milder claims. It was in this context that the NAACP's arduous struggle, first for truly equal conditions of life and later for racial integration, appeared radical.

WORLD WAR II–1954: LEGALISTIC INTEGRATIONISM AS RADICAL

The nation's attention from 1940 through 1945 was monopolized by the war in Europe and the South Pacific. Civil rights for blacks were not high on America's list of priorities. Yet the racial front was not totally quiet. On the one hand, the NAACP intensified its legal campaign for the elimination of segregation and discrimination. It was the largest and, in the end, probably the most important civil rights organization of the period; its methodical legal battles would set the stage for the explosion of civil rights activities in the 1950s and for the redefinition of black radicalism accompanying that explosion. On the other hand, strategies were being contemplated during the war years and the late 1940s which would eventually displace the NAACP's legalism in the spectrum of black radicalism.

The NAACP was unquestionably the preeminent black organization during the period. Although a rise in membership fees caused the total membership of the organization to decline from nearly 400,000 in 1948 to less than 200,000 in 1950, it remained by far the largest organization of black Americans. Local NAACP branches in the North were active during the late 1940s and the early 1950s in the areas of fair employment practices and fair housing. Branches in the border states and the Upper South concentrated on litigation for the fair use of public recreation. In the Deep South, local branches engaged in voter registration (Meier 1963: 437–38).

Through the Supreme Court the NAACP was successful on the national level in whittling away much of the legal basis for segregation and discrimination. In 1944 its victory in *Smith v. Allwright* finally invalidated the white primaries that had effectively blocked black participation in candidate selection in Southern states (Lawson 1976: 37–42). In 1948, the NAACP scored another landmark victory in *Shelley v. Kraemer*, which ruled that restrictive covenants in housing were unenforceable (Hughes 1962: 119). Favorable decisions in *Sweatt v. Painter* and *McLaurin v. Oklahoma State Regents*, both in 1950, paved the way for nondiscriminatory treatment of blacks in graduate and professional education (Hughes 1962: 136–37; Kluger 1976: 260–84; Meier 1963: 438) and set precedents which would prove critical in the *Brown* victory.

Meanwhile, the National Urban League and its local affiliates continued their activities in housing and employment. Not a mass movement or a membership organization like the NAACP, the League continued to be plagued by financial difficulties and by a paucity of dramatic, visible successes. When race riots broke out in several American cities, the NUL campaigned with some success for the establishment of "human relations commissions" on the municipal level (Parris and Brooks 1971: 302). Long-standing efforts to secure decent housing for urban blacks and to obtain housing standards in the cities were formalized in 1951 with the establishment of a specialized housing committee (Parris and Brooks 1971: 324). League officials also buttonholed builders, developers, and mortgage financiers and lobbied at the federal level for improved housing policies (Parris and Brooks 1971: 325–27).

A major focus of the Urban League during the 1940s and the early 1950s was, as always, employment. League officials were active in the effort to secure fair employment practices in the Civil Service and in war-related industries. NUL activities in the field of employment, however, were mostly particularistic. Rather than following the legal route of litigation and lobbying against discriminatory practices in employment, its local affiliates functioned as job placement agencies. Local Urban Leagues often placed overqualified blacks in entry-level or menial jobs just to get their feet in the door of white-owned companies. The purpose behind such efforts was the gradual assimilation of black workers into American society through concrete demonstrations of their worth. From the standpoint of the individual black worker who may have been successful in gaining entrance through such a strategy (such as the black chemist working his way up from laborer), it is difficult to fault the approach; indeed, there were many whose lives were immeasurably improved by the sponsorship of the League. But the image of the organization among black people was not uniformly positive. When compared to the NAACP, which was achieving seemingly spectacular results—including 34 victories in 38 cases argued before the Supreme Court by 1952 (Hughes 1962: 126)—the Urban League seemed markedly weak and conciliatory. As a result, it enjoyed little support among the majority of blacks and received little in the way of financial contributions from black communities. And while the NUL received most of its budget from white businesses and philanthropic interests, many potential white contributors shied away because of the visible lack of black enthusiasm for the organization. Except in the minds of the most virulent white opponents, the Urban League has occupied permanently the most conservative position at the conservative end of the black spectrum.

The Southern Regional Council

Among the new organizations which appeared during the war years was the Southern Regional Council (SRC). First established in 1919 as an antilynching organization called the Commission on Interracial Cooperation, it was renamed in 1944. Although its stated goals were "To attain, through research and action, the ideals and practices of equal opportunity for all peoples in the South" (Laue 1970; Southern Regional Council 1964: 27–28), it has not functioned as an activist organization. Rather, its emphasis has always been on research. In later years it became a respected source of reliable information on regional social problems, especially those of black people, and a key source of legitimacy for the civil rights movement in the South. It was and still is a nonmembership organization with a professional staff trained in law, economics, sociology, political science, and journalism. SRC staff members have served extensively on local and state human relations commissions (Muse 1968: 24–25).

The Emergence of Direct Action Tactics

Despite the predominance of litigation and lobbying during the period between the early 1940s and 1954, there were black leaders who advocated more dramatic techniques of collective action. One of the early proponents of what would later be popularized as "nonviolent direct action" was A. Philip Randolph, who, twenty years before the famous 1963 March on Washington, proposed that American blacks come together for a mass demonstration in the nation's capital. After President Roosevelt's refusal to desegregate the armed forces in 1940, Randolph set about to organize a mass march which would have brought 100,000 people to Washington. The demands behind the march included both the desegregation of the armed services and the elimination of racial discrimination in defense industries. The threat of such a demonstration proved to be sufficient. FDR relented, creating the first Fair Employment Practices Commission on June 25, 1941—seven days before the planned march (Blumberg 1984: 32–33). Though lacking powers of enforcement, this commission was symbolically important, for it represented the first presidential accommodation to a threatened protest by blacks.

The Congress of Racial Equality

Randolph's March on Washington "movement" was a fleeting episode in the annals of black collective action, but the formation in 1942 of the Congress of Racial Equality (CORE) turned out to be of more lasting significance. Emerging as a spinoff of a Christian pacifist organization called the Fellowship of Reconciliation, CORE became a pioneer of neo-Gandhian nonviolence and civil disobedience. It began as a small interracial group made up primarily of white activists (Bell 1968; Jezer 1977; Meier and Rudwick 1973).

The height of CORE's influence and popularity was not reached until the 1960s, but its first tiny bands of committed activists were among the chief architects of direct action militancy. During the 1940s, however, CORE activists tended to confine themselves to fighting discrimination in hiring and in public accommodations.

CORE was markedly different from the NAACP. The NAACP stressed working through the court system; CORE favored direct, face-to-face confrontation. The NAACP was organized along bureaucratic lines; CORE activists distrusted hierarchy and preferred a network of local cells bound together by an extremely weak national headquarters. And while the NAACP required only the payment of a small fee to become a member, CORE demanded a high degree of commitment to the organization's goals, the philosophy of nonviolence, and a willingness to put one's body on the line. During the period CORE's central tenet, consonant with the tradition of religious radicalism out of which it had emerged, was that victory must ultimately be achieved by appealing to the enemy's latent sense of morality.

From 1942 through the end of the decade, CORE organized demonstrations in many northern and western cities, including Chicago, New York, Denver, and Kansas City. Some actions involved picketing and negotiation. Others involved sit-down protests, a technique that the Fellowship of Reconciliation had borrowed from the labor movement and infused with Gandhi's philosophy of *satyagraha,* truth through love and right action (Meier 1963: 439; Peck 1968: 4). In its early years, CORE activists introduced still another tactic which would reappear in the tumultuous 1960s: the "Freedom Ride." In 1947 members of CORE organized a "Journey of Reconciliation" to test compliance with a Supreme Court decision against segregation in interstate transportation. Eight whites and eight blacks braved threats and arrests to journey through the upper South by bus (Meier and Rudwick 1973: 34–37; Peck 1968: 49–60).

The NAACP was hesitant to embrace such tactics. Naming CORE explicitly, Thurgood Marshall spoke of "well-meaning radical groups" that had sought his advice about testing the compliance of interstate bus companies with the desegregation decision of the high court. Although the Association was openly skeptical about the use of nonviolent direct action in the South in 1947 and refused to help finance the Journey of Reconciliation, it did provide contacts along the route. Some legal services were also provided to the CORE defendants by NAACP lawyers, although they ultimately declined to carry the North Carolina convictions to the Supreme Court (Meier and Rudwick 1973: 35, 38).

Following the Journey of Reconciliation, CORE entered a period of decline. By 1954 the group was in a state of organizational and financial disarray owing to its loose structure. A convincing argument can be made, however, that the decline of CORE was also due to its being ahead of its time. Many of the manifestations of racism that the organization sought to confront in the streets were not yet illegal. Consequently, their tactics did not yet have a solid legal footing. In addition, there was not yet an organizational infrastructure sufficiently developed to coordinate protest campaigns on a regional basis; CORE's protests, though courageous, remained isolated and underpublicized. For these reasons, the times were not yet ripe for CORE's style of protest, and the organization was unable to establish a national image, a dependable resource base, or a coherent national strategy.

In the meantime, the NAACP was approaching its greatest victory, the school desegregation decision in *Brown v. Board of Education*. As of 1954, 15 states had statutes mandating racial segregation in public schools, while four other states and the District of Columbia permitted such segregation (Brisbane 1974: 23). Although earlier decisions in the *Sweatt* and *McLaurin* cases had invalidated discriminatory treatment in postgraduate professional education, segregated public schooling still enjoyed the protection of the separate-but-equal doctrine. The plaintiff's argument in the *Brown* case was that it was impossible to acquire a truly equal education in segregated schools, and NAACP attorneys introduced the results of studies by psychologists and sociologists to support this contention (Kluger 1976: esp. 555–57). Earlier cases made it practically inevitable that the Supreme Court would decide for the plaintiffs (Newman et al. 1978: 15).

Strictly speaking, *Brown* established a rather limited legal principle: It invalidated only *de jure* segregation in tax-supported educational facilities. Discrimination in private schools, public accommodations, and other spheres, as well as *de facto* segregation deriving from residential patterns, were left untouched. NAACP officials hastened to emphasize these limitations so as not to encourage unreasonable expectations among blacks. Still, the "revolutionary" implications of the decision were clear; subsequent history would show that racial segregation supported by law had been dealt a serious blow. To many blacks, it seemed that a second Emancipation Proclamation had been issued.

But this reaction was tragically naive. Although the *Brown* decision withdrew the legal basis for racial segregation, it produced no sudden improvements. Blacks were not the only Americans to read a spirit of revolution into the words of Chief Justice Warren; southern whites also saw the writing on the wall. The *Brown* decision and their collective reaction to it set the stage for the turbulent period that is the major focus of this book.

World War II–1954: A Summary

From the war years through the school desegregation decision of 1954, who were the "moderates" and who were the "radicals" in the struggle to improve the lives of black Americans? The answer is partially dependent upon whose perspective is used. The problem of perspective will be discussed presently, but it is useful to take note of the broad progression of black goals and tactics that has occurred during the twentieth century. From the closing years of the last century through the 1960s, the guiding philosophy of black liberation has evolved from (a) gradual assimilation through the acceptance of segregation, to (b) more immediate assimilation through the aggressive pursuit of racial integration, to (c) the preservation of racial integrity through the acquisition of political and economic power. Not all black organizations have proceeded from the first of these to the last, to be sure, but the long sweep of history has seen the sequential rise and fall of each of these positions.

A similar process has occurred in the realm of tactics. This century has witnessed the waxing and waning of several tactical repertoires, beginning with (a) black self-help; followed by (b) legalism; (c) nonviolent protest ranging from peaceful, nondisruptive demonstrations through intentionally disruptive actions; (d) violent self-defense; and, among a few groups, (e) urban guerrilla skirmishes. All but the last two have enjoyed a degree of hegemony for a time. Given this broad historical pattern, one way to establish an organization's position on a scale from moderation to radicalism is to consider the *timing* of its progression (or lack of progression) along these ideological and tactical scales. Using such an approach, it is possible to categorize the organizations which were active between World War II and 1954 as to their relative radicalism for that period (Figure 1).

The least radical of the organizations was the National Urban League, which stressed the delivery of social services and the assimilation of blacks on an individual-by-individual basis. Clearly more conservative than either the NAACP or CORE, the NUL

FIGURE 1. Distribution of black organizations, 1945–1954. CORE is shown in parentheses because most whites during the period were unfamiliar with the organization.

approached the full integration of blacks into American life as a long-range goal to be achieved through the mechanism of the marketplace. Thus, its agenda—very much in line with the conventional American "bootstraps" ideology—represented relatively little threat to established interest groups, especially in the context of the post-War economic boom. A major representative of black "militancy" during the period was the NAACP, which had worked since the late 1930s for state-enforced racial integration. Its methods—lawsuits and campaigns of civil rights legislation on the local, state, and federal levels—were far more aggressive than those of the League. More militant still was CORE, whose goals were identical to those of the NAACP but whose strategy called for direct, face-to-face confrontation of discriminatory institutions. Most whites during this period, however, were still quite unfamiliar with CORE; thus, for practical purposes, the NAACP might best be thought of as representing the radical endpoint. The Association, ruffling the feathers of many whites, called for legal actions affecting a whole social category rather than a pursuing particularistic, case-by-case approach. The Southern Regional Council is also somewhat difficult to classify, as it was not a action group, strictly speaking. Nevertheless, it was directly concerned with the problems of southern blacks. Because its work was much in line with the integrationist philosophy of the NAACP but its activities did not involve direct challenges to discrimination, I have classified it as more moderate.

Moderation and radicalism, however, are relative properties of organizations, strategies, and ideologies. That is, they are labels which are applied to groups, at different times, by different audiences. Two such audiences during the period from 1940 through 1954 were Northern white liberals and the politically aware, active black elite. For these groups there was nothing particularly "radical" about the NAACP; from their perspective, the Association was

28 demanding nothing that was inconsistent with basic American values and it was pursuing its quest strictly within the confines of cherished legal traditions. Some members of the black intelligentsia, critical of the NAACP's "conservatism" as early as the 1920s, had treated the Urban League as virtually unworthy of discussion (Parris and Brooks 1971: 142–54, 198–204, 268, 317). Such groups, however, comprised only a small minority.

White southerners were another matter. Most of them had lived their lives—like their parents and their grandparents before them—in the context of a taken-for-granted system of southern apartheid and white supremacy. From such a cultural perspective, and within the socioeconomic system that was both the basis and the product of such a system of beliefs, *any* serious effort to promote racial change was *by definition* radical. Public opinion researchers have consistently found the attitudes of southerners toward racial integration to be far less favorable than those of northerners. Indeed, as late as 1963, it was noted that "the average white Southerner accepts equal job opportunities and integrated transportation facilities, but he is doubtful about parks, restaurants, and hotels, and he still draws the line at school integration (Sheatsley 1966: 311). Even those southern whites who viewed themselves as relatively enlightened and well-meaning tended to see the NAACP and the Ku Klux Klan as the two primary forces of extremism stalking the land (Hough 1968: 224–25; Killian 1968: 69–70). And some blacks themselves, especially in the South, often feared the NAACP for its seemingly extreme intent to reverse centuries of oppression "overnight" (Killian 1968: 43). To blaze such a trail could, it seemed, be dangerous. Indeed, in many areas of the deep South, it could be a matter of life and death.

But what of the rest of the American population? How was the landscape of black collective action viewed by those who did not fall into the categories discussed above? Public opinion polls did not consistently include questions on racial issues until the sixties, and the capacity of such surveys to tap honest feelings is always suspect. Moreover, it is quite likely that most Americans outside of the South were quite uninformed and apathetic about these issues as late as 1963, it was noted that "the average white Southerner accepts equal job opportunities and integrated transportation facili-period was marked by relatively negative white attitudes toward the major goals of the NAACP and CORE, as data gathered in 1942 by the National Opinion Research Center (NORC) suggest (Table 1).

TABLE 1   White Approval of Types of Racial Integration, 1942

	Approval rate (percent)		
Region	Schools	Residences	Transportation
North	40	42	57
South	2	12	4
Composite	30	35	44

Source: Adapted from Sheatsley 1966: 305, 308.

Opinion researchers have also found that whites consistently disapproved of demonstrations and other protest tactics by blacks; this pattern lasted into the 1960s (Erskine 1967; Sheatsley 1966: 317; Skolnick 1969: 186). Such findings support the contention that the NAACP and CORE were widely viewed as radical during the period ending with the *Brown* decision of 1954, as do the observations of students of the movement. Unlike the Urban League, which tried patiently to "inch" the white society toward acceptance of blacks, the NAACP was trying aggressively to *force* that society to open itself—but through conventional legal procedures. Had CORE been larger and had its activities in the 1940s and 1950s extended farther south, it might have earned a reputation as *the* radical black organization of the period.

1955–1963: DIRECT ACTION INTEGRATIONISM AS RADICAL

Rather than an ending, the 1954 decision in *Brown v. Board of Education* turned out to be a new beginning for the black movement. It marked the point at which integrationist goals began to attain the official sanction of the federal government. The court had invalidated *de jure* segregation in an important and sensitive area, public education, and in its 1955 implementation decree had allowed states with legal school segregation a grace period of one year to comply.

The two years following the 1954 decision were filled with legal maneuvering on both sides. For its part, the NAACP sought to capitalize on the favorable decision by bringing antidiscrimination suits in areas other than education. It experienced some success. Meanwhile, southern politicians were mobilizing to resist.

The southern white countermovement against school desegregation grew rapidly and took several forms. One such form was the mobilization of White Citizens' Councils and state segregationist organizations to coordinate resistance to desegregation and to bring pressure to bear on the advocates of racial change in the region. During 1956 and 1957, eight southern states adopted doctrines of "interposition," derived from early political concepts of the right of states to nullify any federal law, in efforts to nullify the *Brown* decision. During the late 1950s, segregationists also initiated a massive legal campaign designed to stall the implementation of school desegregation. Some 226 suits were filed throughout the region, and the result was that the NAACP and other pro-integration forces found themselves in a quagmire of legal and administrative red tape (Brisbane 1974: 28–29). Of the laws which southern states passed to circumvent the Supreme Court's decision, many were directed specifically against the "radical" NAACP itself. For example, to scare black public employees in South Carolina and Mississippi away from the NAACP, they were suddenly required to disclose the organizations of which they were members. The NAACP was literally outlawed in five states during the mid-1950s (Brooks 1974: 129).[1] And finally, civil rights advocates in the South were targets of economic reprisals and violence.

The resolute southern resistance to desegregation and the expansion of civil rights clarified the limitations of legalism as a means for bringing about social change. Without question, the NAACP had been remarkably successful in upsetting the legal foundations of second-class citizenship, and they would have further successes in later years. But the South's reaction to the *Brown* decision made it abundantly clear that court cases won in Washington would not lead automatically to sudden improvements in people's daily lives. The oppressors could, if they wished, choose to ignore the law of the land. Consequently, many blacks determined that new strategies were necessary. Often it was not the strategies themselves that were new, but rather their use on a relatively wide scale. In any case, the focus of the civil rights movement during the mid-1950s began to shift from legalism to nonviolent *direct* action.

Direct Action Protest in the 1950s

"Direct action" refers to a number of related tactics which have the common characteristic of confronting the enemy in a direct but nonviolent manner. Its ideological roots are found in the Christian pacifist tradition and in the Gandhian philosophy of *satyagraha* (Jezer 1977; Peck 1968). The first widely publicized episode of direct action protest occurred in Montgomery, Alabama, in 1955 and 1956. It began on December 1, when Rosa Parks, a black seamstress, was arrested for refusing to comply with city code and move to the rear section of a city bus. The action set off a city-wide protest. During a meeting held at the Dexter Avenue Baptist Church, and attended by forty local blacks, it was decided to organize a black boycott of the city's bus system. Accordingly, an organization was formed among black clergymen and other professionals and named the Montgomery Improvement Association. Although Dr. Martin Luther King agreed only reluctantly to become its leader, his talents as a public speaker made him quite effective in the role and catapulted him to national fame.

The choice of a boycott was appropriate. Three out of four riders of the city buses were black, and the Chicago-based line stood to lose $3,000 a day from the withdrawal of their patronage. For its part, the city of Montgomery stood to lose a considerable amount of tax revenue. These economic stakes and the confrontational style of the protest created an atmosphere of racial tension. King's home was bombed, participants in the boycott were harassed and threatened, and dynamite was thrown onto the lawn of another boycott leader. The boycott also mobilized whites: the executive director to the Association of White Citizens' Councils of Alabama, a state Senator, claimed that his membership rose from 800 to 14,000 in Montgomery alone during the protest (Brooks 1974: 116).

In the end, the Montgomery crisis was "resolved" as much by legal means as by economic ones. In the midst of the year-long boycott, the NAACP filed suit in federal district court and won a ruling against segregated seating on buses. Although violence against King and other activists continued (Brooks 1974: 118–19), the successful outcomes of the Montgomery Bus Boycott and a similar episode in Tallahassee (Meier and Rudwick 1976: 275) illustrate how legal and direct action tactics so often complemented each other in the civil rights movement.

After the Montgomery victory, King formed the Southern Christian Leadership Conference in 1957. The SCLC was intended as a mechanism to coordinate nonviolent protest by blacks and their allies throughout the South. By the early 1960s it came to have about 100 affiliates in 30 states (Laue 1970: 272). The Montgomery boycott and the establishment of the SCLC set the pattern for civil rights tactics during the post-*Brown* period. It established King as the leading figure among the new militants, a position he held until the mid-1960s (Marx 1967: 26, 42; Meier 1965: 52; Walker 1963: 99).[2] To many old-line black leaders in southern towns and cities, however, he was a fanatic (Walker 1963).

In spite of the notoriety achieved by King and the SCLC, CORE had actually served as the true pioneer of direct action tactics. But the second half of the 1950s was a period of serious decline for that organization. Between 1954 and 1957, the number of CORE local affiliates wavered between seven and nine, and in 1956 the largest and most active chapter was in Hutchinson, Kansas—hardly a national center of civil rights activity. The dismal state of CORE is illustrated by the attendance at the organization's 1957 national convention: only seven persons, four of whom were national officers. Moreover, there was still no field staff which might serve to stimulate and coordinate activities of the chapters (Meier and Rudwick 1973: 73–79). But 1957 was also beginning of CORE's revival. The national staff began to grow in number and to engage in more active fundraising. Tens of thousands of copies of promotional literature, including *This is CORE* and *CORE Rules for Action*, were mailed out. In these and other publications, CORE attempted to take advantage of the publicity which the Montgomery Bus Boycott had received and the enthusiasm it had generated. By 1960 the organization was ready to assume a critical role in the southern drama of the early 1960s.

The Montgomery action was not the only instance of direct action protest during the late 1950s. Local NAACP chapters staged sit-in demonstrations during 1958 and 1959 in Oklahoma City, St. Louis, Louisville, and Baltimore[3] (Meier 1963). CORE chapters as well utilized sit-down protests and picketing on a few occasions during 1958 and 1959 (Meier and Rudwick 1973: 90–94; Wolff 1970: 12). But the level of direct action in the civil rights movement during the 1950s was minuscule when compared to that of the next decade. Rather than a period of widespread demonstrations, 1950s were years of intense *mobilization* for the explosion of direct action that was approaching (Morris 1984). Burstein (1979: 168–69) reports that only in 1956 and 1957 did more than five demonstrations occur. Using a much broader definition, McAdam (1980) determined that fewer than 160 "movement initiated events" took place during 1956 and that the level was lower during the remaining years of the decade. During the 1960s, on the other hand, yearly protest events numbered in the hundreds.

Direct Action in the Early 1960s

The tactical watershed of the civil rights movement, the "decisive break with the past" (Meier 1963: 441) took place in 1960 with the sudden eruption of student sit-ins across the South. On February 1 of that year, four black students at the North Carolina Agricultural and Technical College attempted to eat lunch at the whites-only lunch counter of the F. W. Woolworth store in Greensboro. When refused service, they remained seated until the store closed. The action was a startling display of defiance. Even a black woman working behind the counter openly disapproved, saying: "You're dumb! That's why we can't get anywhere today. You know you're supposed to eat at the other end" (Carson 1981: 10).

When the manager of the store directed his employees to ignore the students, they realized that this was an act of nonviolent protest that they were likely to get away with unmolested. Accordingly, they decided to continue the action. The next day the participants numbered thirty. The third day there were more still. The news media began to cover the emerging drama, generally giving favorable reports of the well-dressed protesters who ended their sit-in with a prayer (Carson 1981: 10). The only real resistance to the protest was by white youths who not only threatened and harassed the blacks but attempted to engage in a counter–sit-in, holding seats for whites. As the ire of the white community rose, the store was closed and the students agreed to postpone further sit-ins in Greensboro until local leaders could negotiate a solution. In the meantime, similar protests were organized at nearby black colleges, and by mid-April, sit-ins had occurred in every southern state and had involved an estimated 50,000 participants (Carson 1981: 10–11).

The sit-in movement was remarkable for its suddenness as well as for the broad support it achieved among black college students in the South, who had heretofore appeared apathetic. What is most important to our concerns here, however, is the manner in which the sit-ins affected the ideological and tactical spectrums of the larger civil rights movement. The goals of the protests were strictly integrationist, and in their statements to the press, participants were quick to stress how little they were really after. Of course, the right of a black person to come to a lunch counter and be served side by side with whites was not, in the context of the South, such a small matter, but the protesters sought to emphasize that it was consistent with American values. Some of the sit-in participants even employed Cold War rhetoric to legitimate themselves, implying that racial justice at home would enhance the nation's success against communism abroad. A Nashville student leader, for example, stated that if equal educational opportunities could be achieved, then "maybe some day a Negro will invent one of our missiles" (Carson 1981: 13).

As was noted above, direct action tactics had been used prior to 1960 and even, on rare occasions, before the *Brown* decision. But the student sit-ins marked the advance of nonviolent direct action to the cutting edge of civil rights activity. After the Montgomery protests and the sit-ins, the NAACP and the NUL became increasingly overshadowed. When the sit-ins became headline news all over the country, the NAACP's share of national press coverage declined and the public definition of the Association as the vanguard of civil rights militancy began to fade (Killian 1968: 48). This is ironic in certain respects. In terms of organizational income (see Chapter 2) and overall levels of activity, the NAACP continued to be the giant of the movement. Moreover, a Harris poll taken in 1963 found that nearly half of a nationwide sample of blacks viewed it as the organization that had accomplished the most for them (Killian 1968: 47). Nonetheless, a new wind was blowing.

Early in the first protest episode, the four original participants had contacted the president of the local NAACP branch, Dr. George Simkins. That same evening, the branch voted to back the students however it could. In addition, Simkins, lacking any first-hand experience in nonviolent direct action and having just read a CORE pamphlet, made contact with CORE leaders and asked them if they could help. CORE immediately sent representatives to Greensboro and began organizing sympathy demonstrations and pickets at dime stores in other cities (Chafe 1980: 117; Meier and Rudwick 1973: 103–12; Wolff 1970: 35–36). Simkins' decision to contact CORE was not a revolt against the national NAACP. It was simply based on his opinion that the sit-in was not large enough to be of interest to the Association (Wolff 1970: 36). But the decision was tremendously significant for CORE. It allowed the organization a foot in the door of a crucial series of events in the South, it stimulated chapter activity in northern cities, and it ultimately produced increased levels of contributions to the organization (Meier and Rudwick 1973: 109–12). Although the NAACP and the SCLC were naturally quite interested in events in Greensboro and other centers of student activity, neither was in the habit of jumping into controversial situations without considerable soul-searching. CORE, on the other hand, was bound by no such tradition of restraint. Thus, of these three civil rights groups it was CORE that profited the most from the sit-ins (Hodgson 1976: 185–86). Rather than being absorbed into any existing group, however, the student movement led to the creation of new and independent organization: The Student Nonviolent Coordinating Committee.

The Student Nonviolent Coordinating Committee

The person most directly responsible for the formation of SNCC was Ella Baker, the executive director of the SCLC. In order to ensure that the student activists would remain independent and free to act creatively, she brought their leaders together at a conference in Raleigh, North Carolina, in the spring of 1960 and arranged a contribution of eight hundred dollars from the SCLC to pay for it (Hodgson 1976: 187). From this conference, SNCC emerged.

Like the SCLC, the SNCC was not a membership organization. Rather, it was established as a coordinating unit for affiliated youth groups in the southern and border states. In practice, it came to consist of a small, autonomous activist group centered in Atlanta (Meier 1963) and another cohesive group in Nashville, Tennessee. Through its first five years, SNCC fought for goals which were virtually identical to those of the other civil rights groups. Its brand of collective action was built around grass-roots organizing of a nonelitist, noncondescending sort. SNCC activists believed in going out among the poor rural blacks of the South and serving as guides rather than leaders. Although the organization was created to be a vehicle for nonviolent protest, its focus after 1961 was voter registration and community organization. This change of focus, however, became a point of contention among SNCC activists as early as 1961. Many recognized the advantages of voter registration activities,[4] but others saw voter registration as an attempt by the Kennedy administration to divert the energy of the civil rights movement from direct action (Carson 1981: 31). In fact, the White House *was* attempting to exercise control over the tactical direction of the civil rights movement, as Chapter 3 will show in detail.

When compared to long-lived organizations such as the NAACP and the National Urban League, SNCC, with its brief life span and rapid transformation, is all the more remarkable. Within a few years of its founding, it became one of the most important, if not *the* most important, organization in the southern movement. Begun as a strictly integrationist group, it became in little more than half a decade a firebrand of black nationalism. This ideological transformation is illustrated by an episode at a second conference of 1960, when an invitation to Bayard Rustin to deliver an address was rescinded due to complaints about his "radical" reputation. A very few years later, the same organization would attack him for being overly moderate and firmly entrenched in the liberal establishment (Carson 1981: 29). Within a year or two of its founding, SNCC became the *enfant terrible* of the civil rights movement. From a loose organization of part-time activists, it was transformed into a federation of full-time, highly committed, and courageous workers. The organization was never large; at its peak its workers numbered no more than 150 (Hodgson 1976: 187). But the group made up in intensity what it lacked in size. SNCC was noted for its refusal to compromise, its frequent clashes with the federal government at a time when other organizations carefully courted political favor, and the willingness of its members to risk their lives for little or no pay.[5] As early as the summer of 1961, the public image of the organization changed from "respectable" to "revolutionary" (Carson 1981: 54). For this reason, the press tended to picture the group as too extreme to accomplish anything. Recent historical scholarship on the civil rights movement, however, has given SNCC its due; as the "shock troops" for the movement in the South, it deserves a large measure of the credit for the vast changes which occurred there during the 1960s.

The Freedom Rides

In addition to the student sit-ins and the emergence of the Student Nonviolent Coordinating Committee, the character of the civil rights movement of the early sixties was also significantly affected by the Freedom Rides of 1961. And, as with the lesser-known rides of 1947, the principal protagonist in these events was the Congress of Racial Equality. Once again, the precipitating event was a decision by the United States Supreme Court. In 1960 the Court ruled in *Boynton v. Virginia* that segregation in railway and bus terminal accommodations violated the Constitution. Clearly, the decision would be ignored in the South unless it were publicly tested through direct action. Accordingly, in March 1961, CORE advised President Kennedy that some of its members would ride buses throughout the South to challenge resistance to the order. On May 4 the first group of Freedom Riders—six whites and seven blacks—left Washington on two buses. Heading south they encountered little negative reaction in Virginia and North Carolina. In Rock Hill, South Carolina, however, the inevitable finally happened; two of the participants were beaten in the town's Greyhound terminal.

They did not press charges. As they proceeded still further south, the riders were not harassed in Georgia and were served at white lunch counters there. But outside of Anniston, Alabama, the first bus was burned by a mob; and when the second bus arrived in Anniston its riders were attacked and beaten with pipes and iron bars, one rider requiring more than fifty stitches (Brisbane 1974; Lomax 1968; Peck 1968).

The second Freedom Ride of 1961 was manned by SNCC workers from the Nashville group. In Birmingham, Alabama, they were arrested by Commissioner "Bull" Connor, kept in jail overnight, then warned to head north. They did not. The next day they were attacked and savagely beaten by a mob of Birmingham whites.

Throughout the spring and summer of 1961, groups of Freedom Riders from the North continued to undergo the ritual of challenge, assault, and arrest. Although it did not officially condemn the Rides, the Kennedy administration called for a moratorium on the demonstrations. Speaking for a newly formed "Freedom Rides Coordinating Committee," Martin Luther King promised to comply. The action was not taken well by the student activists, and King's compromise was one of the first instances in which his commitment was questioned by more militant participants and sympathizers (Brisbane 1974: 56–57). This episode also confirmed the belief of many—especially in SNCC—that the federal government was not to be trusted to protect civil rights workers from the ferocity of white supremacists. The issue would reach its maximum intensity following the murder of three activists in 1963.

For the NAACP the escalation of direct action protest in the early 1960s presented both opportunities and challenges. On the one hand, it increased public awareness of racial issues in a way that court cases alone could not. This was generally a positive development from the Association's standpoint so long as widespread resentment did not ensue. On the other hand, the rapidity with which direct action had spread and the tendency of politicians and much of the public to view such tactics as "extreme" put the NAACP in a difficult position. Should it endorse the escalation from legalism to direct action and even assist it in hopes that what King called "creative tension" (Brisbane 1974: 56–57) would expedite the Association's own program? Or should it attempt to channel the energies of younger activists back into the tried and true path and take a chance of losing its position as the established leader of black collective action? As noted previously, the NAACP's reaction was complex. While some local branches and Youth Councils became involved in direct action protests, the national headquarters tended to remain in the background and provide moral and legal support on a selective basis. A fact too often overlooked is that the supportive activities of the NAACP and its close relative, LDEF, the Legal Defense and Educational Fund (established in 1939 and an autonomous organization after 1955), were indispensable to the protests of the early 1960s. Without the bail money and legal representation provided by these organizations, protesters would have succumbed to legal and quasi-legal repression. Nevertheless, the NAACP paid a price for its less than total embrace of direct action and for its cumbersome, bureaucratic structure: it lost its preeminence among civil rights groups and tarnished its image among more militant blacks.

The frequency of civil rights demonstrations fluctuated during the first half of the decade. According to one rather conservative estimate (Burstein 1979: 169), the total number of demonstrations in 1961 dropped to about 150. There appear to have been fewer than 100 in 1962, slightly fewer than 300 in 1963, nearly 200 in 1964, and about 300 in 1965. After 1965 the frequency of demonstrations entered a precipitous decline which lasted into the next decade. But though the sheer frequency of civil rights demonstrations may have peaked during 1960, their size and intensity did not. In these respects, the high point of nonviolent direct action came in 1963. According to estimates by the Southern Regional Council, about 20,000 persons were arrested in protests in southern states that year. Moreover, ten persons died in circumstances directly related to protest activities during 1963 (Carson 1981: 90). Nowhere, however, was the heat of racial crisis more intense than in Birmingham, Alabama, during "Operation C" (for "confrontation"), a large-scale boycott organized by Martin Luther King and the SCLC in 1963. Aimed at the many forms of discrimination against blacks for which the city was infamous, the campaign mobilized Birmingham blacks to use their collective buying power as a weapon in much the same way that Montgomery blacks had done in 1955. Demands included the desegregation of public accommodations, the improvement of hiring practices in the business and industrial communities, the creation of a biracial committee to work on the desegregation of other areas of life in the city, and the release of demonstrators jailed for disobeying a court order banning demonstrations and marches. After a long stalemate, numerous jailings, the use of high-pressure fire hoses by police to break up marches, and the deaths of four young black girls at the hands of a white bomber, two crucial factors—the economic clout of blacks and the adverse national publicity about official mistreatment of demonstrators—led to concessions from the city.

The Birmingham offensive was significant because it was the first time that a nonviolent protest had been accompanied by *black* violence. After the bombings and beatings, black people took to the streets, setting fires and causing other property damage. Thus, even as nonviolence was reaching its zenith, it was becoming clear that blacks would not remain nonviolent forever. As Chapter 3 will show, this realization played an important part in speeding political concessions on civil rights.

Although Birmingham provided a preview of the violence that was soon to become commonplace, the era of nonviolent protest had not yet reached its symbolic climax. That came on August 28, 1963, when 250,000 people participated in the March on Washington. The march was originally conceived in 1962 by A. Philip Randolph and Bayard Rustin. As all the major civil rights organizations became involved and plans were concretized, the concerns of President Kennedy and his aides grew. They feared—and secretly planned for—the possibility that the march would turn into a riot. But after White House negotiations led to certain rhetorical compromises by the planners, the administration agreed to cooperate. The March on Washington became less a demonstration *against* the federal government than a demonstration *for* the civil rights bill that later passed as the Civil Rights Act of 1964. The March on Washington was an impressive symbol of the civil rights movement as a whole, and no part of the event was more so than Martin Luther King's "I Have A Dream" speech, in which he addressed the changes that were in the offing:

> We must forever conduct our struggle on the high plane of dignity and discipline. We must not allow our creative protest to degenerate into physical violence. Again and again we must rise to the majestic heights of meeting physical force with soul force. The marvelous new militancy which has engulfed the Negro community must not lead us to a distrust of all white people, for many of our white brothers, as evidenced by their presence here today, have come to realize that their destiny is tied up with our destiny and their freedom is inextricably bound to our freedom. We cannot walk alone. . . . You have been the veterans of creative suffering. Continue to work with the faith that unearned suffering is redemptive (quoted in Friedman 1968: 111–12).

Why direct action did sometimes succeed has been examined before (Bell 1970; Colaiaco 1986; Fairclough 1986; Garrow 1978; Hare and Blumberg 1969; Hubbard 1968; Jezer 1977; Von Eschen et al. 1976), but the answer is complex. For one thing, nonviolent direct action tactics fit nicely with general American values. The rhetoric of direct action was highly moralistic, and its practitioners, like King, represented themselves as highly committed fighters for justice. Moreover, direct action required a great deal of courage. The willingness of nonviolent protestors to risk themselves physically to further a principle gained them the admiration of many otherwise unsympathetic observers.

But equally important was the fact that, despite its frequent ornamentation with talk of the "power of love" and "creative suffering" and its mildness (compared to later forms of collective action), nonviolent direct action was an effective means for creating crises. Direct action generally worked *only* when it disrupted "business-as-usual" and threatened the interests of businessmen and politicians (Barkan 1985: 55–57; Bell 1968: 101–3, 173; Colaiaco 1986; Fairclough 1986; Meier and Rudwick 1976; Von Eschen et al. 1976; Walker 1963). Disruption was no guarantee of change, but it was often a necessary precondition. So long as a state of normalcy could be maintained, reform could be put off; direct action, however, could force issues to center stage.

The ability of direct action protest to elicit racial crises was most obvious in larger southern cities. Business and political elites in these cities tended to have an interest in the creation of a "New South," fully modern and capable of wooing industrial development. In such cities as Dallas, Memphis, Atlanta, and Charlotte, white leaders recognized that the highly publicized events in their streets were bad for business. Thus, they often sought out blacks with whom they could work, created committees which really did *act* rather than just talk and delay, and tried to forestall trouble (Powledge 1967: 98–119). Sometimes this created tensions within black leadership. SNCC workers often complained with some justification that other organizations and leaders waited for SNCC to create a crisis, then stepped in and grabbed the attention of the press and federal officials as though *they* were in charge.

As noted previously, organizations such as the NAACP and the National Urban League did not make it their practice to jump headfirst into direct action; in fact, they greeted the rise of direct action protest with some trepidation. But when local and, in some cases, national elites began to look for blacks with whom they could deal, these two groups were frequently the ones to which they turned. In the South it was often the NAACP that fulfilled this role. And as direct action protest began to appear in northern cities, industrialists under pressure to hire more blacks often turned to the National Urban League—which would be waiting patiently with lists and résumés in hand (Powledge 1967: 82; Parris and Brooks 1971: 417–18).

Still another feature of nonviolent direct action that was especially significant, particularly in terms of influencing northern opinion, was the contrast between its restrained character and the frequent viciousness of the reaction to it (for example, see Barkan 1985). The brutal treatment of civil rights activists by mobs, Klansmen, and especially police officers often backfired. To television audiences and newspaper readers throughout the nation, the dignified and reserved appearance of the demonstrators was heightened by the behavior of those who were arresting, beating, and killing them. Thus, a key to the impact of nonviolence was the ability of its practitioners to *construct* a sense of moral superiority; opponents could be made into a radical flank of a different sort. The importance of this factor can be seen, for example, in the fact that in Birmingham (1963) and Selma (1965), where law enforcement officials set upon the demonstrators and brutalized them in full view of television cameras, King's civil rights forces were victorious. In Albany, Georgia (1962), however, where police behaved with intentional restraint, a similar campaign ended in failure (Garrow 1978: 2–3, 221–22; Garrow 1986: 173–230; Hubbard 1968: 7).

1955–1963: A Summary

In summarizing the 1945–1954 period, I suggested that black collective action had been grounded in three general styles which have risen and fallen during the twentieth century: (a) gradual assimilation through accommodation; (b) immediate assimilation through aggressive integration; and (c) the preservation of racial integrity through the acquisition of political and economic power. During the period from 1955 through 1963, the second of these remained dominant. I also argued that several tactical shifts have occurred during this century, from (a) self-help, through (b) legalism, (c) nonviolent direct action, and (d) self-defense, to (e) a guerrilla orientation. During the late 1950s and the early 1960s, there occurred a significant shift in black collective action from legalism to nonviolent protest. Because of this tactical shift, legalistic groups were no longer the most radical units of black collective action (Figure 2).

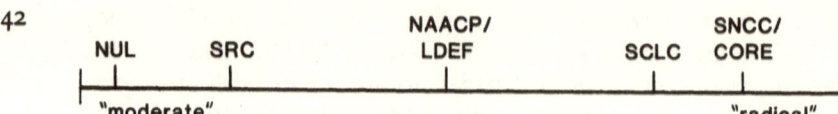

FIGURE 2. Distribution of black organizations, 1955–1963.

So far as the major black organizations were concerned, no significant transformation of official goals took place. With the partial exception of the Urban League, which will be discussed below, civil rights organizations called for racial integration and an end to all discrimination. It may be argued that the activists of the early 1960s were even more immediatist in their demands than their predecessors had been, but the goals were still strictly integrationist. In tactics, however, the character of the movement had changed greatly. Before the *Brown* decision, the methodical legal approach characteristic of the NAACP was the most militant tactic employed on a large scale. During the late 1950s and especially during the period from 1960 through 1963, the level of direct action protest skyrocketed. Litigation and lobbying, though no less important, were no longer the most radical means in the repertoire of black collective action and, for all practical purposes, ceased to be characteristic of black radicalism as it was perceived by most observers.

The National Urban League. NUL activities from 1955 through 1963 were, generally speaking, continuations of its earlier style. The strong emphasis on employment continued, with much of the effort devoted to placing blacks in jobs on an individual basis. League officials also became more involved in housing issues, training programs, and various welfare reforms (Parris and Brooks 1971: 390). In all of these activities, the Urban League continued its preference for gradualism rather than aggressive collective action. It did not "demand" things; it "negotiated" and "consulted." As Whitney Young put it: "You can holler, protest, march, picket, demonstrate, but someone must be able to sit in on the strategy conferences and plot a course. There must be the strategists, the researchers and the professionals able to carry out a program. That's our role" (quoted in Parris and Brooks 1971: 409).

The NAACP and the LDEF. During the period between 1955 and 1963, the NAACP continued to emphasize a strategy that was primarily legalistic and integrationist. Attorneys of both the Association and the Legal Defense and Education Fund fought court battles against southern evasion and nullification of the desegregation decision, pressed for open public accommodations laws on the state level, and provided legal defense and bail money for jailed demonstrators from other organizations (Meier 1963; Meier and Rudwick 1976). Although some local branches of the NAACP became rather heavily involved in direct action protests, they were not representative of the national office or of the branches as a whole. It would be incorrect, however, to claim that by 1963 the NAACP was truly unsupportive of direct action as a matter of basic policy. But it continued primarily to work behind the scenes and in the halls of power rather than in the streets. According to Executive Director Roy Wilkins, the NAACP served to pay the bills while the SCLC and CORE furnished the "noise" in the streets (*Newsweek*, September 21, 1981: 52). And when the noise got so loud as to constitute what the national board considered a threat (as just prior to the 1964 Johnson-Goldwater election), the NAACP did what it could to rein the protesters in. Thus, the Association was closer to the radical end of the spectrum than the Urban League, but it had been displaced as the cutting edge of black collective action by the practitioners of nonviolent protest and southern grass-roots organizing.

The Southern Christian Leadership Conference. The SCLC and its leader, Dr. Martin Luther King, shared with CORE the task of popularizing nonviolent direct action. Its specialties were boycotts, peaceful marches, and the "staging" of mass arrests. King quickly became the single most charismatic leader of the civil rights movement, and in some ways it might be said that the SCLC was little more than "the organizational embodiment of this preeminent symbol of the Negro movement" (Muse 1968: 22). The goals of the SCLC during the early 1960s were not very different from those of the NAACP, but King stressed nonviolent confrontation in which the justice of his cause stood in stark contrast to the injustice perpetrated by the enemy. King's talent for talking to whites without alienating them was among the organization's greatest strengths—he was capable of casting himself as a "conservative militant" (Meier 1965: 54). In the early 1960s, King proved less willing than certain CORE and SNCC leaders to jump headlong into potentially dangerous confrontations with southern racists or with administration officials. He was more willing to "cooperate" with authority under certain situations as well. Thus, although the radicalism of the SCLC and its leader fell short of that of CORE and SNCC (Meier 1965), its reliance on direct action and the "politics of crisis" (Colaiaco 1986) certainly made it more radical than the NAACP.

Congress of Racial Equality. In its goals and preferred means, CORE continued through the late 1950s and the early 1960s in much the same way that it had functioned during the war and postwar years. The greatest change in CORE after 1960 was an increase in size, strength, and visibility in the black struggle. And with its increase in activity came an advance in status for CORE, now one of the two leading radical groups of the era of direct action.

Student Nonviolent Coordinating Committee. The other leading radical group was SNCC, which quickly became one of the most militant civil rights organizations. In the time between its founding and 1963, SNCC's strategy drifted from nonviolent protest to voter registration. Given President Kennedy's open advocacy of voter registration over direct action, this might be taken a change in the direction of greater moderation. Such was not the case. SNCC's registration drives did not involve the inculcation of a blind loyalty to the national Democratic Party or to the Kennedy or Johnson administrations. In fact, the relations between SNCC and the federal government grew progressively worse during the early and mid-1960s owing to a dissatisfaction with the pace of change and with the unwillingness of the government to assure the safety of civil rights workers in the South. Moreover, SNCC activists sought to do more than put names of blacks on registration lists. They sought to mobilize southern black communities under indigenous leadership and to organize them in such a way that they might bring about sweeping changes in the region (Carson 1981: 298–99).

As the various organizations redefined their strategies for action, public opinion about them also shifted. Clearly there are several problems with public opinion data as an index of changes in the legitimacy imputed to black groups. There are certain limited and incomplete data from opinion surveys, however, which relate to black *issues*, black *tactics* of collective action, and individual black *leaders*, which are useful in shedding light on how whites viewed the movement. In general, opinion survey data show that a striking increase in white support for racial desegregation occurred over the

TABLE 2   White Approval of Types of Racial Integration:
1942, 1956, 1963

	Approval rate (percent)		
Region	1942	1956	1963
SCHOOLS			
North	40	63	75
South	2	14	30
Composite	30	49	62
HOUSING			
North	42	58	70
South	12	38	51
Composite	35	51	64
TRANSPORTATION			
North	57	73	88
South	4	27	51
Composite	44	60	78

Source: Adapted from Sheatsley 1966: 305, 308.

years from the 1940s through the 1960s (Skolnick 1969: 181). Surveys conducted in 1942, 1956, and 1963 show that white opinion on the acceptability of integrated schools, residential integration, and integrated public transportation increased rather steadily (Table 2). This trend toward greater white approval appeared in both the North and the South, although southern whites consistently were less favorable toward racial integration than northern whites. In Gallup Polls of 1957 and 1958, for instance, only a slim majority of whites agreed that "the day will ever come in the South when whites and Negroes will be going to the same schools, eating in the same restaurants, and generally sharing the same public accommodations." By 1961, three-fourths of whites agreed with the statement, and by 1963 the proportion had grown to five-sixths. Only 13 percent disagreed with the statement by 1963 (Sheatsley 1966: 309).

A similar pattern in greater approval of equal employment opportunity was found by Skolnick in his review of opinion survey data (1969: 181). NORC data also indicate that the proportion of whites who felt that blacks should have an equal chance at jobs increased from approximately 42 percent in the mid-1940s to more than 80 percent in 1963 (Erskine 1968a: 139).

At the same time, however, whites continued to express their disapproval of the *means* employed by blacks to attain their goals (Erskine 1967; Sheatsley 1966: 317–18; Skolnick 1969: 186). A Harris poll conducted on October 21, 1963, for example, found widespread disapproval of four basic forms of direct action (Table 3). In addition, nearly two-thirds of whites who were familiar with the Freedom Rides in June 1961 disapproved of them. A nearly identical proportion disapproved of the March on Washington (Erskine 1967).

It is tempting to conclude that the increasingly favorable attitudes among whites toward the basic *goals* of the civil rights movement was at least partially due to the increasing pressure of escalating tactics. This conclusion would be premature, however, and opinion survey data taken alone are not sufficient to support it. Increasingly favorable white attitudes about the integration of social institutions, however, does at least suggest that the tendency to view the goals of the major black organizations as unreasonable and radical was decreasing during the period of direct action militancy. And given the descending rate of disapproval as one moves down the list of direct action tactics in Table 3, it is at least quite plausible to suggest that a popular redefinition of *tactical* radicalism was also taking place in the early 1960s. Had "pursuing lawsuits for redress of civil rights grievances" been added to the list by the pollsters, we might speculate that disapproval rates would have been lower than for direct action tactics.

1964–1970: THE "NEW" RADICALISM

In 1963 and 1964 fundamental changes were occurring in black collective action. These changes, like those during the years following *Brown*, were based on a crisis of faith. In the 1950s the crisis of faith had to do with the capacity of legal change to bring about concrete alterations in social relations; in the mid-1960s, however, the crisis was related to both the effectiveness of nonviolent protest as the primary means for bringing about change and the nature of the changes required. Several more specific issues were involved: violence, the relationship of organizations in the movement to both the federal government and the national Democratic Party organi-

TABLE 3 Percent of Whites Disapproving of Nonviolent Protest Tactics, 1963

Tactic	Region	
	Nationwide	South
Lie down in front of trucks on construction sites to protest hiring discrimination?	91	94
Conduct sit-ins at lunch counters?	67	84
Go to jail to protest discrimination?	56	75
Boycott products whose manufacturers don't hire enough Negroes?	55	66

Source: Adapted from Erskine 1967: 659.

zation, and the desirability of coalitions with white liberal supports. Ultimately, disagreements over these issues led to the emergence of new forms of black radicalism.

I have designated 1964 as the birthyear of the "new" black radicalism, but many of the schisms out of which it evolved had appeared by 1963. The first instances of black collective violence, for example, occurred that year; it was, in a limited sense, the first of the "long hot summers" (Hubbard 1968). Compared to the disorders of 1964 through 1968, the post-Birmingham riots were quite mild, but they were extremely significant because they indicated to all who were paying close attention to black collective action that there were cracks in the nonviolent hegemony of the civil rights movement. In retrospect, it is perhaps remarkable that southern blacks remained as peaceful as they did for so long in the face of the violence of their opponents. In any case, 1963 was the year in which retaliatory violence against whites emerged as a really important part of black collective action.

The specter of blacks with guns had appeared before. In the late 1950s, for instance, a renegade local official of the NAACP named Robert F. Williams had organized a black rifle club in Monroe, North Carolina, which soon became an armed self-defense force. The confrontations in Monroe were somewhat isolated, however, and not well publicized compared to later episodes of real or threatened black violence. The erosion of the dominance of nonviolence over the movement became more widespread and public after

1963. In 1964 and 1965 rioting would become much more frequent and serious, and self-defense groups would begin to proliferate. A more detailed discussion of these developments will be reserved for a later portion of this chapter.

Mississippi Summer: The Federal Government as Enemy

During 1963 many within SNCC began to view the federal government's commitment to civil rights with skepticism. One source of the deteriorating relations with the government was what SNCC people saw as the administration's efforts to direct the movement toward voter registration without protecting those who participated in this dangerous activity. Accordingly, leaders of the organization made frequent requests for protection during the period from 1962 through 1964, even demonstrating at the Justice Department in Washington to dramatize this need (Carson 1981: 83).

The final split between SNCC and the administration came during the "Freedom Summer" of 1964. That year the Council of Federated Organizations (COFO), a confederation of civil rights groups active in Mississippi voter registration efforts, launched a registration project that was funded partially by the NAACP, SCLC, CORE, and the National Council of Churches, but manned mostly by SNCC workers. The major thrust of the project was to get voter registration efforts off the ground—after three years of frustration and intimidation (Hubbard 1968)—by importing large numbers of registration workers from the North. The project also had a less obvious purpose. Since violent reprisals against civil rights workers in the South had become common, the Summer Project was designed to force a confrontation with state officials in which the federal government would have no choice but to protect the volunteers (Carson 1981; Hubbard 1968). Before the summer ended, three project workers were kidnapped and killed. Even though the project attracted a great deal of national press coverage, the federal government still did not assume an active role.

Prior to the summer project, SNCC decided to create an alternative to the regular white-controlled Democratic party in the state. The new party, which came to be known as the Mississippi Freedom Democratic Party (MFDP), aimed to unseat the regular Mississippi delegation at the upcoming national convention in Atlantic City. More than 80,000 blacks registered as members of the party (Carson 1981: 124). In spite of a great deal of northern support for the MFDP, President Johnson opposed the effort. He hoped to avoid any weakening of his support among southern Democrats, worrying that their defection might lead to a Goldwater victory in the 1964 elections. After a series of convention-floor dramas and back-room negotiations, the Freedom delegation was denied seats on the floor.

The impact of the Mississippi Freedom Summer and the MFDP episode on SNCC members cannot be overstated. Their experiences confirmed what they had begun to suspect much earlier: that the Johnson administration was not the friend that it pretended to be; that white liberals in general were not trustworthy allies; that even some of the supposedly "activist" leaders like King lacked commitment and guts (see Meier 1965); and that the whole ideology of black civil rights required rethinking. After 1964, then, SNCC people were increasingly bitter and internally divided.

In 1965 a new issue was added to the conflict between SNCC and the Johnson administration: the Vietnam War. When Johnson announced on June 4, 1965, that American armed forces in Vietnam would perform not only advisory roles but also "combat-support" activities, the cause of civil rights fell somewhat in the administration's list of priorities. And from that point on, Johnson's increasing obsession with avoiding a military defeat contributed to the friction between the government and large portions of the civil rights movement (Meier and Rudwick 1976: 299; Parris and Brooks 1971: 434–35). Even Martin Luther King denounced the war, and it cost him part of his white support.

The Issues of White Involvement and Nonviolence

At roughly the same time, criticism of coalitions with white activists was growing in SNCC and CORE. The Congress of Racial Equality had been a biracial organization from the beginning, and it was not until 1963 that a majority of its convention delegates were black (Meier 1963: 444). By 1964 a group of militants began to rise in the organization—people skeptical about the usefulness of nonviolence and favorably disposed towards SNCC's techniques for organizing communities. They were also less than fully committed to the established doctrine of interracialism (Rudwick and Meier 1970: 17–18). In 1965 and 1966 this group began to dominate CORE conventions. The new CORE constitution, adopted in 1965, declared that a majority of the officers in any chapter must be black (Rudwick and Meier 1970: 18). From that year, the role of whites in CORE declined, and in 1968, they were excluded from the organization altogether.

Although whites had been instrumental in founding SNCC and continued to play critical roles in it, by 1964 concerns came to be expressed about the abilities of whites to contribute meaningfully to the organizing of black southern communities. And by 1966 some black SNCC members were claiming not only that the mere presence of whites at meetings of blacks tended to change the tone and discourage black participation but that whites were inherently incapable of identifying with black people's problems (Carson 1981: 196–97). White activists, even those who had been involved in the founding of SNCC, were being made to feel uncomfortable.

The ambivalence and even outright opposition to white involvement in the black movement that was growing in CORE and SNCC was a harbinger of the rapidly changing mood. That changing mood was closely related to the emergence of black separatism as a replacement for the older integrationist philosophy within the militant flank of the movement. And as separatism was popularized and publicized, racial integrationism became transformed into a hallmark of *moderation*. Racial pride and the rejection of "whiteward mobility" emerged as symbols of black radicalism. Tactically, the adherence to nonviolent direct action was becoming part of civil rights moderation; even the NAACP and the National Urban League were overcoming their reluctance to participate more fully in such protests. As early as 1963, nonviolent resistance had attained a considerable degree of legitimacy within American society as a whole (VanderZanden 1963). But gradually, many blacks were now rejecting nonviolence as a moral imperative or even as a fruitful strategy. The transformation of radicalism did not occur suddenly and does not lend itself to a simple chronological description. However, its major elements can be readily identified: the early urban riots and the place of violence in black ideology, the emergence of black power as an organizing principle for collective action, and the later riots of 1967 and 1968.

Urban Riots of 1963–1966

It was in Birmingham in 1963 that blacks first took their rage to the streets. In 1964, however, racial violence exploded in the North as well as the South. People in the northern urban ghettos, and poor blacks generally, had gained little more than unrealistic expectations from the hard years of nonviolent protest. It has often been stated that the goals of the southern movement were the goals of a black middle class—voting rights and the right to eat at the same lunch counter as whites, stay in the same hotel, ride the same bus or go to the same school. But beyond the symbolic value of such goals, they were of little immediate use to most lower-class black residents of inner-city neighborhoods in the North (Gregor 1970). For these people, it was more important to make enough money to eat than to have the right to spend it in a particular place of business.

So although northern blacks tended to approve of the goal of integration, they were naturally more concerned with *economic* issues. Civil rights and voting rights laws were good, but they did not deliver what these people needed most: a job, a decent place to live, and a share of the affluence that surrounded their ghettos. The question of why inner-city blacks took to the streets between 1964 and 1968 is a complex one that has attracted a good deal of attention (for example, Feagin and Hahn 1973; Fogelson 1971; National Advisory Commission on Civil Disorders, 1968; Skolnick 1969, 145–48). But the question of why the gradual successes of the southern movement failed to keep them out of the streets should puzzle no one.

During the summer of 1964, "major" riots occurred in six locations: New York City; Rochester; Philadelphia; Paterson-Elizabeth, New Jersey; Jersey City, New Jersey; and Chicago.[6] These first riots were commonly equated with simple street crime, differing from conventional predatory crime only in scale. Although there was an attempt to make "crime in the streets" an issue in the 1964 Presidential election, the landslide victory of the pro–civil rights incumbent over the states-rights challenger suggests that it met with little success.

Pessimists predicted that 1964 would be the start of a series of long, hot summers which would grow progressively worse. As it turned out, 1964 was only mildly indicative of things to come. Still, the summer of 1965 was not so severe as many expected. According to the Senate Permanent Committee on Investigations, only five "major" riots occurred during those months. In these, 36 persons were killed and 1,026 were injured. Arrests numbered over 10,000 and total property damage was estimated at over $40 million (Muse 1968: 245). One of the 1965 riots, however, was the first of the truly massive and catastrophic outbreaks. It occurred in the Watts section of Los Angeles, and it accounted for most of the deaths, injuries, arrests and property damage noted by the Senate Committee. It is very likely that at least 20 percent of the area's residents participated in some way in the riot (Sears and McConahay 1973: 9).

For many, the six days of lawlessness in Watts came as a "bewildering surprise," since it occurred only a week after the signing of the Voting Rights Act by President Johnson. Moreover, the rioting was unprecedented in its ferocity: white motorists were attacked, police were fired upon, widespread looting took place, and 977 buildings were damaged or destroyed. First reports in the media tended to exaggerate the events and the destruction and carnage they caused (Muse 1968: 206), adding to the feeling that a racial revolution was beginning. From the perspective of rather naive whites, one of the most surprising and frightening aspects was the inability of black leaders to stop the violence. Actually, few such leaders appeared in the streets to try to restore order. To do so would have been futile. Two of those who did, Martin Luther King and Dick Gregory, were jeered and told to "go back to the other side of town" (Killian 1968: 106).

As predicted, rioting continued in 1966. Although 21 "major" riots occurred that year (Muse 1968: 295; cf. Masotti et al. 1969: 124), the major indexes of riot severity were lower than those for the previous year: there were 11 deaths, 520 known injuries, 2,298 arrests, and property damage of only $10.2 million (Muse 1968: 295). Among the cities hit were Chicago, Philadelphia, New York, Cleveland, Atlanta, Oakland, Minneapolis, Milwaukee, Jacksonville, Omaha, and Des Moines. In character the 1966 riots were generally similar to those of the preceding years: the precipitating incident usually involved a police arrest of a black suspect and allegations of brutality, and there were always charges of "outside agitation" by officials. Unlike the earlier riots, however, fighting between black and white civilians was more common (Muse 1968: 248).

Much more could be said about the riots of 1963 through 1966, but their details do not concern us here. What is of direct importance is the reaction of civil rights leaders and organizations. The disturbances of this period, and the Watts riot in particular, created a dilemma of major proportions for the nonviolent civil rights movement. It was now obvious that established black leaders had little control over ghetto residents and enjoyed little real support among them. To elicit that support it was clear that the established leadership must become involved in issues affecting these people—jobs, housing, and welfare, for example.

The riots also intensified the leadership's concerns about negative radical flank effects. Of immediate concern was the possibility that their own opportunities for working within the system would be threatened. The ultimate blame for the riots of 1964 through 1966 was frequently heaped on civil rights leaders, as they allegedly had created a disrespect for the rule of the law (Killian 1968: 104). Polls taken during 1965 indicated even stronger public disapproval of civil rights demonstrations than two years earlier (Erskine 1967). Another poll indicated that whites saw blacks "pushing ahead too fast" as the third most serious problem facing the nation (Killian 1968: 88). All of this was beginning to take on the appearance of a white backlash, which is precisely what moderate leaders feared; accordingly, they viewed the 1964 riots as an "irretrievable disaster" (Hubbard 1968: 13). A moratorium on demonstrations was called in late 1964 pending the outcome of the November elections, but SNCC and CORE refused to endorse it (Brooks 1974: 237).

Although the riots presented the civil rights organizations with definite problems, some leaders also saw how to take advantage of the situation. In public statements established leaders typically stressed several common themes. First of all, they condemned the rioting and clearly distanced their own organization and factions from it. At the same time, however, they voiced an explicit recognition of the issues underlying the riots. Specifically, they interpreted the violence as the inevitable result of insufficient progress in resolving wrongs committed against black people. In addition, they linked their own organization to the "correct" position on urban ghetto concerns, as opposed to merely the concerns of *southern* blacks, and implied that these issues had been a part of their organization's agenda for some time. Furthermore, they stressed the ways in which they and their organizations had acted responsibly to prevent rioting or to stop it once it had begun. Finally, they predicted further and more severe violence unless authorities responded more favorably and quickly to their organization's claims.

Armed Self-Defense in the South

While the primarily northern urban riots were challenging the nonviolent dominance of the black movement, the issue of self-defense was doing the same in the South. Violent attacks on civil rights workers may have bolstered the legitimacy of the cause, but this was little comfort to those whose lives were on the line. Although they did not make a public issue of it, almost every SNCC worker in the field was carrying a firearm by the time of the Mississippi

Summer Project (Carson 1981: 164; Hodgson, 1976: 212). It is ironic that an organization born of the nonviolent student movement only four years earlier had become—of necessity—an armed group.

At about the same time (1964 and 1965), an organization called the Deacons for Defense and Justice appeared in Louisiana. Its purpose: to provide physical protection for civil rights workers. At that time CORE was the national organization that was most active in Louisiana, and there was considerable overlap between the two. Besides setting off a controversy of nationwide proportions, the alliance with the Deacons became a problematic issue within CORE itself. CORE was still officially a nonviolent organization, and it had always been assumed that nonviolence stood as a matter of principle rather than merely an expedient tactic. The attacks by segregationists, however, caused a debate over whether members were justified in using violence in self-defense. In 1965 a CORE worker in Ferriday, Louisiana, stated that self-defense in protection of one's home and person was "taken for granted" and that most of the organization's headquarters in dangerous areas of Louisiana and Mississippi had weapons on the premises to protect against night attacks. Most of the southern staff approved of this state of affairs, whereas many long-time CORE pacifists were less willing to compromise on the issue. Some chapter leaders in the North and West openly advocated moving away from nonviolence as a philosophy and advised that demonstrators should defend themselves when attacked. Although the members were not of one mind on the subject, CORE was not strictly committed to nonviolence after 1965 (Meier and Rudwick 1973: 397–400) and came very close to officially rescinding its official policy on nonviolence at the national convention that year (Meier and Rudwick 1973: 402).

King's famous voting rights campaign in Selma, Alabama, also raised the issue of violent self-defense during 1965 and 1966. The demonstrations in and around Selma met with violent white responses. After the spectacle of peaceful black demonstrators being beaten was transmitted over national television, the federal government finally intervened. And in August, the Voting Rights Act of 1965 was signed into law by President Johnson (Garrow 1978: 123–35). Meier and Rudwick (1976: 293) argue that "where Birmingham had made direct action respectable, the Selma demonstration, drawing thousands of white moderates from the North, made direct action fashionable." Among blacks, however, the demonstration contributed further to the principle of self-defense. In Lowndes

County, between Selma and Montgomery, a belief in armed self-defense was already widespread, in fact. A militant SNCC worker, Stokely Carmichael, who was soon to become a major firebrand of black realism, claimed that he actually exercised a restraining influence on the black farmers in the area during 1965 (Carson 1981: 164). Out of this tense atmosphere emerged another of the local organizations which openly acknowledged the rights of blacks in the South to defend themselves, the Lowndes County Freedom Organization (LCFO). Formed as a black political party, the LCFO took as its symbol the black panther—"an animal that when it is pressured it moves back until it is cornered, then it comes out fighting for life or death" (Carson 1981: 166). Although the LCFO failed to win any local offices, its rejection of nonviolence was symbolically significant (Brisbane 1974: 136; Hodgson, 1976: 221).

Self-Defense in the Ghetto

A rejection of the dictum "turn the other cheek" also occurred in northern inner-city areas. One of the earliest significant proponents of armed self-defense was Malcolm X, an official of the Black Muslims until he was expelled by Elijah Muhammad. Until shortly before his assassination in 1965, Malcolm rarely shrank from condoning violence by blacks. The Muslims preached a gospel which was the antithesis of assimilationist civil rights doctrine: it told blacks that they were the descendents of a superior original black race; the day would come, it claimed, when the black people would reassume their rightful place in the world and the rule of the white race would come to an apocalyptic end. Malcolm X preached this message for years until he was expelled from the Muslims, allegedly for making an undiplomatic remark about the assassination of President Kennedy. In the early 1960s he became fond of calling Martin Luther King "the Reverend Dr. Chickenwing" and the NAACP's Roy Wilkins a "Judas" to his people (Brisbane 1974: 113). As early as 1963 he attracted a great deal of attention for such remarks and became the object of much disdain among nonviolent civil rights activists. An admirer of King put it this way: "Malcolm X is many things. He is the face not seen in the mirror. He is the threat not spoken. He is the nightmare self. He is the secret sharer" (Brisbane 1974: 106).

His image in the ghetto, however, was less satanic. In years to come he became recognized along with Frantz Fanon as a prime theorist of the new black radicalism. Like Marcus Garvey, Malcolm foresaw the eventual return of American blacks to the African homeland. But in the meantime they would establish complete control over the black community, by way of armed force if necessary. Between the time of his pilgrimage to Mecca and his assassination in 1965, he softened his tone somewhat and explicitly rejected black racism. But he also became the most articulate spokesman for the spirit of the ghetto. The white press flocked around him in search of sensational antiwhite statements suggesting violence, even after such statements had ceased to be standard elements of his rhetoric. In the black world of the streets, he was a prophet of things to come.

Within months of Malcolm's death, there appeared in California a new group which owed much to his aggressive spirit: the Black Panther Party. The ideology of this group will be discussed later in this chapter, when I turn to the subject of black power. What is significant about the Panthers at this juncture is their position on weapons and self-defense. During 1966, the group's founders Huey Newton and Bobby Seale raised $170 by selling copies of *Quotations from Chairman Mao Tse-tung* to students on the campus of the University of California and used this money to purchase a small arsenal of firearms. Newton was sufficiently well versed in California state law to know that it was legal for any citizen to carry a loaded, unconcealed gun; in an automobile a citizen could carry a loaded handgun or a rifle, shotgun, or semiautomatic weapon without rounds in the chamber. The Panthers were soon familiar sights on the streets of Oakland's black neighborhood, dressed in striking all-black uniforms and carrying their weapons openly and proudly—including shotguns and M-1 carbines (Marine 1969: 40–41).

The Panthers' activities were varied and, contrary to the image created by the press at the time, largely of a rather "mild" nature: they established "liberation schools" and breakfast programs for ghetto children, for example. The activities which drew the most attention involved their militaristic posturing and their program of "policing the police," whom they viewed as an army of occupation in the black community. To keep an eye on the treatment of blacks by law enforcement officers, they set about—their weapons at the ready—following squad cars on their routine rounds. Confrontations were inevitable, and Newton was eventually jailed on charges of killing a police officer.

The Panthers appealed primarily to young, urban blacks. Their attractiveness was not based on instrumental successes, for their actual accomplishments were few indeed. Rather, it was based on *style*; the belligerence and pride of the group was pleasing to the "brothers and sisters on the block," and the Panthers spoke to the issues that were most relevant to ghetto residents.

After a number of well-publicized standoffs with law enforcement officials in California, the Panthers became well known to television audiences across the country. They presented a shocking and sometimes infuriating image to whites for whom black "radicalism" had previously meant marching through a southern town in a clean white shirt, demanding nothing more than constitutional rights. Fanon, not Gandhi, was the favored theorist of the Black Panther Party. And when confronted with the legal authority of the state, they drew guns, not hymnals.

Fanned by the urban riots, the rhetoric of black violence flamed higher. By 1966, said one member of SNCC, the organization's "naive and idealistic" founders were giving way to "a new generation who believed that nonviolence did not work" (Carson 1981: 237). Owing to this change, and to the inflammatory statements by such SNCC leaders as Stokely Carmichael during speaking engagements in the North and the South, the organization was blamed for the outbreaks of violence on a number of college campuses during 1967 (Carson 1981: 250). Carmichael's successor, Hubert "Rap" Brown, also became a favorite of the press for such statements as "if America chooses to play Nazis, black folks ain't going to play Jews" (Carson 1981: 254).

Black Power and Black Separatism

The split within the ranks of American blacks during the mid-1960s was ideological as well as tactical. The experiences in the southern struggles and the less-than-harmonious relations with their nominal supporters had led many, especially the SNCC and CORE, to reexamine the integrationist goals of the civil rights movement and to redefine the context in which they operated. They began to question whether the assimilation of black people into white America was really what they should be fighting for, whether close alliances with white activists and supporters were really worth maintaining, and whether the white-dominated power structure of the society was amenable to change.

The questions that were being raised by these radicalized veterans of collective action, though more articulate in expression, corresponded closely to the misgivings of the black urban underclass in the North—especially those who had been *born* in northern cities (Aberbach and Walker 1970). Though they were generally sympathetic with the broadest motivations and goals of the civil rights leaders and organizations, it was not *their* movement; it did not reflect *their* day-to-day problems in a direct manner. Accordingly, it is significant that when urban blacks vented their rage over the murder of Martin Luther King, it was the first time that many of the rioters had shown any sense of allegiance to the man. And even then, the "tribute" they paid was, ironically, a direct contradiction of what he had said and done for the last thirteen years of his life.

In the latter half of the 1960s, the ideological void felt by radical civil rights veterans and ghetto-dwellers alike came to be filled by a vague though powerful cause: black power. The term "black power" dates back to the 1950s, but it was not until 1966, when it was employed by Harlem Congressman Adam Clayton Powell and by SNCC workers in Mississippi, that it became part of the standard vocabulary of black political action (Marable 1980: 66). During the Mississippi Freedom March, carried on by King and others after James Meredith had been wounded by a white gunman, it emerged as a militant alternative to the integrationist slogan "Freedom Now" (Garrow 1986: 481–89). The news media were covering the march and, as was by then their habit, actively sought out evidence of disagreements between major activist organizations. Their chance for a good story came when Stokely Carmichael addressed the crowd at a rally. He announced that since blacks had been demanding "Freedom Now" for six years and had achieved nothing, from now on they would shout "Black Power!" The audience of over six hundred took up the chant (Carson 1981: 209–10).

The black power slogan became a major issue both within the Mississippi march and in the national press. For Dr. King and other established leaders, it was undesirable because it seemed to imply an antiwhite orientation and the threat of violence. But the crowds were ready for it and they reacted with enthusiasm whenever it was used. And thanks to the press reaction, "black power" was popularized in black communities nationwide.

But what was the precise meaning of "black power," either as a slogan or as a program for action? Benson (1976: 109–10) argues that the popular interpretation of black power eventually came to comprise (1) the view that the American social and political system is an interlocking and self-maintaining system of white advantage;

(2) a conflict model of society which saw the social order as held together by the coercive power of privileged groups over subordinate groups; (3) the rejection of racial integration; (4) the rejection of coalitions with white liberals and other such groups; and (5) the view that violence is justified under certain circumstances.

Specific spokesmen and organizations, however, came to espouse different versions of black power, and the reactions of elites varied accordingly (Allen 1969, ch. 5). Malcolm X, who died before the term "black power" was popularized, had himself developed an ideology which belongs in the same category. He called for black consciousness and pride in black culture. He argued that blacks must gain control over their own organizations and communities and that they should feel free to use violent self-defense when necessary. Moreover, toward the end of his life, Malcolm saw the roots of racism in the capitalist system (Allen 1969: 32). The capitalist system and racism were linked, he came to believe, by the economic necessity of exploiting colonized peoples. The plight of American blacks and that of the people of Africa, Southeast Asia, and Latin America were identical: all their woes were rooted in the imperialist dynamics of the capitalist order. Consequently, the struggle of American blacks must be *internationalized*, i.e., conducted in solidarity with other colonized peoples around the world. To this end, he forged contacts with the Organization of African Unity and attempted to arrange to have the United States charged before the United Nations with violations of the U.N. charter on human rights.

The Student Nonviolent Coordinating Committee. The inheritors of Malcolm's ideology included SNCC, which officially embraced black power in 1966. At the beginning of the year, SNCC's executive secretary was James Forman and its chairman was John Lewis. Forman had occupied his post with little opposition since 1961, and Lewis had served since 1963. But criticism had been growing among staff members in recent months, directed especially at Lewis for his involvement with the White House Conference on Civil Rights. The organization had become split into two opposing groups: one consisted of members who, though disillusioned, remained more or less loyal to the goal of an interracial movement for justice; the other, based in Atlanta, had become self-consciously separatist in orientation, stressing the development of black pride and a recognition of the common plight of colonized nonwhite people the world over. In addition, the Atlanta separatists considered it absolutely essential that whites be expelled from SNCC. Although Carmichael did not agree with many of these positions at the time, he did see the need for change in the organization and accordingly decided to run against Lewis for the position of chairman. Carmichael was elected at the May meeting (Carson 1981: 200–3).

Since Carmichael had been labeled as the most radical SNCC member by the press for his role in the Lowndes County Freedom Organization in Alabama, SNCC attempted to downplay the significance of the coup. But his election proved to be a monumental event in the history of the organization. During his first few weeks at the helm, Carmichael sought to reassure white supporters that their role would not be terminated and that SNCC was not moving in the direction of violence. Simultaneously, the New York office attempted to counter the impression presented in the media that the organization had gone off the deep end and adopted a revolutionary "racism-in-reverse" (Carson 1981: 207).

The next two years saw SNCC thrust itself into the center of attention, only to decline rapidly because of repression and internal disputes. Carmichael became known as a fiery orator and radical spokesman for the impoverished black masses. He helped further in shifting SNCC's emphasis from southern-oriented caste issues to economic and political ones. At speaking engagements in England, Africa, and Cuba, Carmichael stressed the necessity of overthrowing the capitalist order. But at other times, Carmichael's ideology seemed less revolutionary, as in his 1967 definition of black power:

> It is a call for black people in this country to unite, to recognize their heritage, to build a sense of community. It is a call for black people to begin to define their own goals, to lead their own organizations and to support those organizations. It is a call to reject the racist institutions and values of this society.
> The concept of Black Power rests on a fundamental premise: *Before a group can enter the open society, it must first close ranks.* By this we mean that group solidarity is necessary before a group can operate effectively from a bargaining position of strength in a pluralistic society (quoted in Carmichael and Hamilton 1967: 44).

Politically, SNCC worked through the mid- and late-1960s for the establishment of a black political party. The "freedom organizations" it set up in the South were parts of the effort but yielded few concrete results. Later in the decade, SNCC established ties with the Black Panther Party in hopes that the BPP could become such a mechanism. Such hopes died quickly, however, as violence nearly erupted between the two groups (Allen 1969: 262–63; Carson 1981: 278–86). Economically, SNCC's version of black power was vague. Though it called for the establishment of black cooperatives, collective ventures in such areas as banking (Allen 1969: 52), these efforts never truly got off the ground.

Carmichael's successor was H. "Rap" Brown, who was initially chosen for the post because it was believed that he would be less abrasive and less vulnerable to charges of irresponsibility and extremism. These charges and the harassment they provoked had made Carmichael quite happy to relinquish the office (Carson 1981: 244). Such hopes notwithstanding, Brown became at least as notorious as his predecessor. Charged with inciting riots, he became the subject of intense official repression.

Between 1964 and 1968, then, SNCC underwent a remarkable transition. Already defined as a spearhead of radicalism in its youth, it had rapidly embraced a brand of black power that surpassed any but the most revolutionary groups—the Black Panthers, the Republic of New Africa, the Revolutionary Action Movement, and later the Black Liberation Army. SNCC had rejected the use of white organizers, accepted self-defense, and replaced the goal of integration with that of black pride and separatism. Some of SNCC's workers even spoke of guerrilla warfare against the white power structure. By 1967, SNCC was part of the most radical wing of the black movement, and by 1971, it had all but disappeared.

The Congress of Racial Equality. Like SNCC, CORE officially adopted the concept of black power in 1966 after having undergone several years of radicalization. As a result of the Freedom Rides, the organization had expanded rapidly in the South, becoming a major civil rights organization. But northern chapters had also continued to develop, and their members had begun to take an interest in issues affecting poor blacks in the ghettos (Meier and Rudwick 1973: 182–94). In some localities the erosion of early CORE principles of interracialism and absolute nonviolence began as early as 1961 and 1962, but a crisis did not occur until the mid-1960s. By 1964 the old consensus over these matters had disintegrated (Meier and Rudwick 1973: 313). Also by that year CORE had become increasingly involved in community organizing in urban ghettos, where money for projects was being made available by the Johnson administration's War on Poverty programs (Bell 1968).

The issue of white involvement came to a head in 1965. At the

CORE convention of that year, a new constitution was drawn up which required that a majority of the officeholders in any chapter be black. This decision was a turning point in the subsequent development of the organization (Rudwick and Meier 1970: 17–18; Meier and Rudwick 1973: 414). Carmichael's black power slogan was given official endorsement. According to a unanimous resolution,

- Black Power is effective control and self-determination by men of color in their own areas.
- Power is total control of the economic, political, educational, and social life of our community from the top to the bottom.
- The exercise of power at the local level is simply what all other groups in American society have done to acquire their share of total American life (quoted in Allen 1969: 65).

Addressing the convention as a guest, Carmichael said, "We don't need white liberals. . . . We have to make integration irrelevant" (Meier and Rudwick 1973: 413–14). After the convention, the spirit of Carmichael's statement was expressed in the distribution of a poster that read "Support Black Power—send $1 to CORE" (Bell 1968: 190). CORE tried to shift its financial base from whites to blacks in ghettos, but as will be seen in chapter 2, serious monetary crises resulted and powerful white groups became involved in funding the organization—for purposes of their own.

CORE's brand of black power differed from that adopted by SNCC, and in ways that, perhaps ironically, proved attractive to private charitable foundations. SNCC by and large called for totally independent political action, including the establishment of black political parties. Riots were interpreted as rebellions, and eventually the notion of black guerrilla warfare in the cities was endorsed. CORE, on the other hand, clung to the hope that the Democratic party could still prove useful and sanctioned violence only in self-defense (Meier and Rudwick 1976: 310). To CORE, black power was equated largely with the entrance of blacks into decision-making positions. In the economic sphere, this meant *black capitalism*. Such an attitude differed from the government view that economic development of the ghetto meant luring white investment to create jobs. True black power would require *black* capital accumulation and investment. Roy Innis, the head of CORE after 1968, continued to make radical statements suggesting that violence and disruption were the black man's trump cards (Allen 1969: 188). But CORE's "bourgeois approach" to black power marked it as a *"moderate" within the black power sphere,* a designation which would prove useful in coming years.

The Black Panther Party. At the other end of the black power spectrum were the Panthers. Unlike CORE, the BPP was both nationalistic and leftist. Though it stressed racial pride and paid particular attention to the strictly *racial* issues among ghetto youth, it nevertheless grounded its program in a critique of capitalism and internal colonialism, viewing itself as part of a worldwide anticolonialist revolution. Huey Newton wrote the Panther program in 1966:

1. We want freedom. We want power to determine the destiny of our Black Community.
2. We want full employment for our people.
3. We want an end to the robbery by the capitalists of our Black Community.
4. We want decent housing, fit for shelter of human beings.
5. We want education for our people that exposes the true nature of this decadent American society. We want education that teaches us our true history and our role in present day society.
6. We want all black men to be exempt from military service.
7. We want an immediate end to POLICE BRUTALITY and MURDER of black people.
8. We want freedom for all black men held in federal, state, county and city prisons and jails.
9. We want all black people when brought to trial to be tried in court by a jury of their peer group or people from their black communities, as defined by the Constitution of the United States.
10. We want land, bread, housing, education, clothing, justice, and peace. And as our major political objective, a United Nations-supervised plebiscite to be held throughout the black colony in which only black colonial subjects well be allowed to participate, for the purpose of determining the will of black people as to their national destiny (quoted in Brisbane 1974: 197).

Cultural Nationalism. As noted earlier, much of the tremendous appeal of the Panthers flowed from their *style*. The Black Panther did not seek assimilation into the melting pot of American society. Rather, he or she celebrated *blackness* in dress, demeanor, and values. The cultural trappings of the BPP, however, reflected a strictly

American form of blackness. A different and distinct form of black nationalism during the second half of the 1960s emphasized *African* culture. From the standpoint of the "cultural nationalists," the struggle to recover a positive racial identity came logically before political, social, or economic battles. Liberation was to be sought through the development of distinctly black forms of culture and art. According to Ron Karenga, a leading cultural nationalist and founder of a group called US, "The revolution being fought now is a revolution to win the minds of our people. If we fail to win this one, we cannot expect to win the violent one" (quoted in Allen 1969: 165–66).

Cultural nationalists explored the territory of black theater, African artistic motifs, and black poetry. They frequently Africanized their names, adopted "natural" hairstyles and African dress, and learned Swahili. This form of black nationalism was important in the drive for the Afro-American Studies programs which proliferated on college and university campuses during the late 1960s. Cultural nationalism was not especially threatening to elites. It did not make overwhelming demands of whites and rarely threatened violence. Even when the rhetoric became heated, the threat did not seem so serious as in the cases of other types of black radicalism. The *Wall Street Journal*, for example, characterized Karenga as "typical of many militants who talk looting and burning but actually are eager to gather influence for quiet bargaining with the predominantly white power structure." With the decline of black radicalism in the early 1970s, bitter disputes between political and cultural nationalists arose over just such matters (Marable 1980: 83–89).

Despite the differences among types of black power and black nationalism, all such perspectives rejected the mainstream civil rights orientation. A survey of citizens of Detroit in 1967 found not only that whites held overwhelmingly negative attitudes about the black power slogan (80.7 percent), but that in large numbers they tended to view it as implying black control over whites, black racism, rioting, disorder, and the like (Aberbach and Walker 1970: 370). Conversely, they found black residents of that city to be almost evenly divided in their feelings. Substantial proportions of the blacks saw the slogan as meaning little more than "a fair share for black people" or "racial unity" (368–71). Moreover, 86 percent of the black sample polled in 1967 were in favor of integration, including most of those who had positive feelings about black power (372–73). Other studies have shown that there was a substantial acceptance among urban blacks of a "riot ideology" which more or less justified ghetto violence as a political tactic (Benson 1976: 110). Black people, it appears, defined black power as they saw fit, just as Carmichael had said they would and should (Carson 1981: 222).

It is not surprising that the black power slogan became a popular one. The civil rights movement was not viewed as especially relevant to the daily lives of many ghetto-dwellers (Gregor 1970: 320–27; Howard 1974: 26), and black power offered an alternative which could be defined flexibly. Community leaders and black politicians could espouse versions of black power which implied economic development and political organization of black communities, as did CORE. Militants and their followers could speak of a black power which was revolutionary in its implications. In either case, the slogan offered an aggressively militant alternative to what was increasingly seen as a conciliatory and assimilationist attitude toward civil rights. This was at least more emotionally satisfying than merely *asking* the white man for rights. Both mild and aggressive versions of black power implied standing up to oppression and *taking* what was rightfully one's own, as well as refusing to accept the social, political, and cultural models of one's oppressor. These are the same characteristics that had made the ideologies of Marcus Garvey, Elijah Muhammad, and Malcolm X so appealing in urban black communities.

The spread of the black power slogan during and after 1966 was, like the riots, a touchy issue for civil rights moderates. Established leaders feared that the possibility of a backlash was increased by the attention being paid to its advocates; many whites apparently could not understand why blacks were acting so belligerently in times when so much progress was being made. More directly, many moderates were afraid of the damaging effect that the anti-white thrust of black power might have on their own relations with white supporters and allies. Thus, they were naturally quick to respond. Martin Luther King stressed that while it was hard to find fault with the idea of more legitimate power for blacks, the use of the slogan by the new militants threatened to lead to widespread misunderstandings (Scott and Brockriede 1969: 32). The NAACP's Roy Wilkins called black power "separatism . . . wicked fanaticism . . . ranging race against race, . . . and in the end only black death" (Muse 1968: 243). Bayard Rustin argued that black power "diverts the movement from any meaningful debate over strategy and tactics, it isolates the Negro community, and it encourages the growth of anti-Negro forces" (Muse 1968: 244). A group of mainstream civil rights leaders took out a large advertisement in the *New York Times* which stated in part: "We repudiate any strategies of violence, reprisal or vigilantism, and we condemn both the rioting and demagoguery that feeds it" (quoted in Muse 1968: 243–44).

Later in the decade some of the moderates' criticism of certain forms of the black power ideology softened. The National Urban League incorporated a toned-down concept of black power into its own program of black community development (Parris and Brooks 1971: 454–71). The NUL chief, Whitney Young, addressing the 1968 CORE convention, gave CORE a surprising endorsement, especially in light of the historical gulf between the two organizations. Young praised CORE's "frontal attacks" on the problems of black people and credited the organization with making a "negotiable or legislative solution possible." He received a standing ovation at the end of his speech, and CORE delegates reportedly shouted, "The brother has come home; the brother has come *home!*" (Parris and Brooks 1971: 462–63).

The apparent rapprochement between the Urban League and CORE was a reflection of the fact that the two organizations were moving in the direction of the same sort of black power. Like CORE, the "New Thrust" adopted by the NUL called for neither guerrilla warfare nor the reconstruction of American society along socialist lines, but quite the opposite. According to James A. Linen, president of Time, Inc., and a participant in the NUL,

> The UL pledges its all-out support to the creation and support of black groups which can speak for a united community, and who will be able to bring about a "dialogue of equals" with the representatives of the power structure outside the black community. We pledge our help in giving a voice and a structure to the just demands of the ghetto. . . . We will build the economic institutions of the ghetto through the development of black-owned businesses, cooperatives, consumer unions, and black-owned franchises. . . . As we intend to devise the means by which white involvement replaces guilt and fear, we intend to devise the means whereby black involvement replaces bitterness and despair. The emerging black middle-class will be called upon to aid their brothers in the slums, for here is a vast untapped strength within the black community. The resources, expertise, and know-how of these brothers who have made it have to be applied to solving the problems of the ghetto (Parris and Brooks 1971: 464).

The Riots of 1967 and 1968

Even as concepts of black power were being developed and popularized, the problem of urban violence was growing more severe. The summer of 1967 surpassed all the others in the frequency and severity of rioting. When it was over, the Senate Permanent Committee on Investigation determined that there had been 75 "major" riots, in which 83 persons lost their lives, 1,897 were injured, and 16,389 were arrested. Property damage was estimated at a record $664.5 million, almost 17 times greater than in the 1965 wave of violence (Muse 1968: 295; cf. Masotti et al.). The worst of the 1967 riots occurred in Newark and Detroit. The rioting in Newark lasted for three days: twenty-five persons were killed, all but two of them black; about 1,200 were injured, and over 1,300 arrests were made. Property damage was estimated by the Newark Office of Economic Development at $10.25 million (Muse 1968: 293), with over a thousand businesses damaged or destroyed (National Advisory Commission 1968: 116). Soon after the violence in Newark and a number of lesser disorders, the worst riot to date broke out in Detroit, smashing records in every category: 43 deaths, over 2,000 known injuries, over 3,800 arrests, and property damage estimated at $85 million. In both numbers and range, the law enforcement personnel called in also reached new peaks: 4,300 local police officers, 370 state troopers, 1,100 National Guardsmen, and 4,700 Army paratroopers were involved; another 8,000 National Guardsmen were placed on alert (Muse 1968: 294).

The last of the long, hot summers proved to be 1968 and then the violence was concentrated in the late spring and early summer. In April, while in Memphis to lend support to striking sanitation workers, Martin Luther King was shot and killed by a white assassin. Black people, some of whom had never felt a close identification with King, set out to avenge his death. During the first eight months of the year, 313 riots and disorders occurred, a large percentage of which took place in the immediate aftermath of the assassination, and 78 lives were lost (Masotti et al. 1969: 168–71).

Revolutionary Black Liberation

In addition to the later urban riots, the late 1960s saw the continued development of groups which preached one or another variety of revolutionary black nationalism or left-leaning radicalism. With the exception of the Black Panther Party, these were quite small in size and limited in impact.

The leading exponent of a nonracialist, Marxist-Leninist brand of black liberation continued to be the Black Panther Party. During the late 1960s the Panthers' reputation grew, especially after they disrupted a session of the California legislature in 1967. During 1968, twelve new chapters of the Party appeared in American cities and over a thousand new members joined. By 1969 the Panthers' newspaper, *The Black Panther*, had achieved a circulation of over 100,000 nationwide. But there were troubles as well. Due to their outrageous actions and their militaristic demeanor, a nationwide campaign of legal repression was initiated, quite possibly directed by one or more federal law enforcement agencies. Partly as a result of this campaign, Panther activities began to take on a less revolutionary character. Knowing that they would be blamed for any violence in the San Francisco Bay area following the King murder, for instance, Panthers patrolled the streets and attempted to prevent an outbreak. As one member put it, "Burning the 'motherfucker' to the ground" was simply "not a correct revolutionary tactic at that time" (Brisbane 1974: 212). Indeed, about the same time, Panther chapters across the country initiated various community programs of a less than inflammatory nature: free breakfasts were served to more than 20,000 children in 19 cities; Liberation Schools were opened for youngsters during the summer vacation, and a free health program was initiated. Chapters in a dozen cities unsuccessfully sought referenda to decentralize police forces.

During 1969 the Panthers became more explicitly leftist in ideology, breaking with strictly *black* liberationism and adopting a hybrid political philosophy that Minister of Information Eldridge Cleaver called "Yankee Doodle Socialism." But continued repression and internal divisions led the party to fluctuate wildly in its official ideology, and by 1971 it had virtually disappeared from view.

Another Marxist-Leninist group which received some notoriety during the period was Robert Williams's *Revolutionary Action Movement* (RAM). After being charged with kidnapping during the Monroe, North Carolina, episode described earlier in this chapter, Williams fled the country. He lived first in Cuba and then in the People's Republic of China, from where he served as the absentee organizer and leader of RAM. Formed in 1963, RAM intended to assassinate national leaders of both races, including Whitney Young and Roy Wilkins, and to instigate a campaign of guerrilla warfare in the cities. New York and Philadelphia police raids in 1967 turned up an arsenal of weapons, ammunition, electronic communication equipment, and drugs (Brisbane 1974: 182). Another 1967 raid yielded 300 grams of potassium cyanide, which RAM terrorists had allegedly intended to use to poison the Philadelphia water supply.

Soon after the demise of RAM, there appeared a regional separatist group called the *Republic of New Africa* (RNA). The RNA demanded that the states of Mississippi, Louisiana, Alabama, Georgia, and South Carolina be ceded by the United States government to form an independent black nation. Furthermore, in 1969 it demanded the payment of $200 billion in damages to the Republic for wrongs committed against black people. The RNA went so far as to set up a sort of government-in-exile with Robert Williams as President, supported by an official council of ministers and a military unit called the Black Legion. The strategy which emerged at the May 1969 conference called for using the ballot as the primary means by which to found the Republic. Blacks would progressively take control of county governments in Mississippi and install black sheriffs, who would in turn appoint Black Legionnaires as deputies. The same strategy would be employed in the other states of the RNA until all county and state governments had come under black control. If the federal government attempted to interfere with these activities in the South, urban guerrilla campaigns would be launched in cities across the nation. In the meantime, Williams returned from exile to fight the old kidnapping charge and resigned as president of the RNA. From that point on, the organization declined, and it was virtually destroyed after a shootout in Jackson, Mississippi (Brisbane 1974: 183–85).

This and similar gun battles between armed black revolutionaries and law enforcement officers added a new sense of urgency to the urban violence that had been sweeping the United States (Killian 1968: 171). Besides the Jackson battle, in which one policeman was fatally wounded, shoot-outs took place in New York, Cincinnati, Seattle, Peoria, Gary, and Cleveland during 1968. To many persons, these occurrences appeared even more ominous than the riots. Though small in scale, they appeared much more like organized revolutionary activity than did the more or less spontaneous ghetto disorders. Not surprisingly, "law and order" competed with the Vietnam War as the central campaign issue in the general elections of 1968.

In addition to the demands of the Republic of New Africa, the year 1969 also saw the development of James Forman's *Black Mani-*

festo "movement." Forman, still a member of SNCC and briefly the minister of foreign affairs for the Black Panther Party, was invited by the white Interreligious Foundation for Community Organization to take part in a National Black Economic Development Conference. After consultation with other black liberation groups, Forman decided to use the opportunity to demand reparations from white churches. In his address to the conference, he denounced the United States as incurably racist and capitalist, advised blacks to overthrow the government by force, and demanded that white churches and synagogues finance the revolution by paying $500,000,000 or "fifteen dollars per nigger" (Brisbane 1974: 186). On May 4, Forman disrupted services at a wealthy New York church, informing the congregation that it would be required to pay extra reparations due to its connection with the Rockefeller family. Needless to say, no such reparations were ever made. But a number of liberal white churches did express sympathy for the idea of the Black Manifesto and increased their aid to existing programs for blacks or set up new ones (Brisbane 1974: 190). As outlandish as some of the demands of the RNA or the Black Manifesto may sound, it appears that their challenges were taken seriously by various groups. And there were other challenges as well, such as Detroit's League of Revolutionary Black Workers and the Dodge Revolutionary Union Movement (DRUM) between 1968 and the early 1970s (Geschwender 1977), which were successful in achieving certain gains for black autoworkers in that city.

1964–1970: A Summary

At the beginning of the period extending from 1964 through 1970, the militant wing of the civil rights movement had been represented by CORE and SNCC. Both organizations sought racial integration and an end to all forms of discrimination, as did other black groups. SNCC's brand of radicalism, however, entailed an aggressive campaign of voter registration and community organizing in the South, a steadfast unwillingness to compromise or to defer to nominal supporters in the federal government, and an aggressive style of activity which combined courage with a reputation for creating crises in southern segregationist strongholds. Similarly, CORE was known for its tendency to force racial issues through the use of nonviolent direct action. Having greatly expanded its organizational membership and strength since 1960, it enjoyed an attendant increase in publicity. The SCLC in 1963 was less militant,

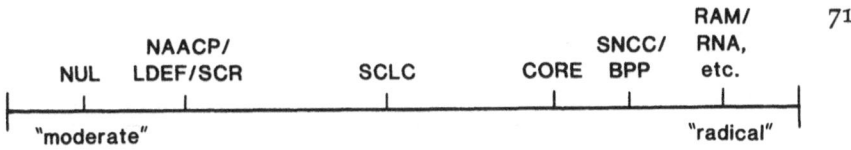

FIGURE 3. Distribution of black organizations, 1964–1970.

if only because of the personal charisma and somewhat greater willingness to compromise which marked its leader, Martin Luther King. The NAACP, though supportive of the direct action campaigns in which the more militant organizations engaged, retained its earlier character as a primarily legalistic group. In contrast to the newer and bolder groups, it was no longer a radical organization. The LDEF had also become part of the more moderate wing of the movement. So had the Southern Regional Council which, though not an activist group, was nevertheless associated with the goal of integration. The least radical of the major black organization in 1964 was the NUL: although the Urban League had become less gradualist in its orientation and more supportive—albeit indirectly—of direct action protest, it lagged behind the others in terms of the pace of the changes it sought and the directness of the means by which it sought to achieve them.

By the late 1960s the boundaries of black ideology and strategy had expanded farther than ever before. The goal of racial integration was challenged and rejected by SNCC, CORE, and the revolutionary nationalists. These groups, in contrast to the moderates, instead sought black *control* over the various institutions affecting the lives of blacks. These were *zero-sum goals*; i.e., the demands of the new radicals, if achieved, would involve absolute losses to dominant groups. The goals of moderates, on the other hand, were in most cases *variable-sum goals*; i.e., they generally did not imply direct losses to whites. This shift from variable-sum to zero-sum goals is part of the difference between the "old" and "new" radicals (Howard 1974: 12–14). Changes were also occurring on the tactical level. The techniques of nonviolent direct action—demonstrations, boycotts, picketing, sit-ins, and jail-ins, for example—were subjected to intense criticism. The farthest reaches of the tactical spectrum came to be occupied by a new array of black organizations (Figure 3), such "extremists" as the Republic of New Africa, the

TABLE 4 Nationwide White Approval of Racial Integration: 1942, 1956, 1963, 1968

Topic	Rate of approval (percent)			
	1942	1956	1963	1968
Schools	30	48	62	60
Housing	35	51	64	65

Source: Figures for 1942, 1956, and 1963 adapted from Sheatsley 1966: 305, 308; figures for 1968 adapted from Skolnick 1969: 192.

Revolutionary Action Movement, and the Black Panther Party, all of which advocated sweeping social, political, and even geographical changes, through armed insurrection if necessary.

How did white perceptions of black collective action change during the period from 1963 through 1970? In an era of increasing militancy, black separatism, and violence, what patterns are apparent in public attitudes toward integration, nondiscrimination, and nonviolent direct action? In general, public opinion data collected during those years indicate that the widely predicted white backlash did not occur. The trend of increasing white support for civil rights goals continued but slowed somewhat through the 1960s, while the long-standing pattern of white disapproval of the movement's tactics was sustained. As to integrationist goals, this pattern is apparent in white attitudes toward school and residential integration (Table 4).

Even as white support for integrationist goals was climbing slowly, however, approval for nonviolent methods continued to be low. The movement toward violent rhetoric and urban disorder did not soften opinions on the legitimacy or effectiveness of tactics like demonstrations and boycotts, and majorities of white samples continued to disapprove of such actions and to claim that they hurt the black cause (Erskine 1967: 656–60). Moreover, white views of the effectiveness of even moderate black leaders had not become overwhelmingly positive by 1966 (Table 5).

Perhaps the most striking aspect of the data is the large fraction of whites who had no opinion. It is apparent that as late as 1966 large numbers of white Americans had little knowledge of specific black leaders. The main exception was King, who half of the white

TABLE 5   White Opinion on Effectiveness of Black Leaders, 1966

	Percent of opinion		
Leader	Has helped Negroes	Has hurt Negroes	Other; no opinion
Martin Luther King (SCLC)	36	50	14
Roy Wilkins (NAACP)	31	16	53
Thurgood Marshall (NAACP)	11	7	82
Whitney Young (NUL)	8	12	80
Floyd McKissick (CORE)	7	22	71
Stokely Carmichael (SNCC)	2	45	53

Source: Adapted from Erskine 1967: 661–662.

sample still felt had hurt the cause of black rights. Although it seems likely that white opinion may have softened after the more intense rioting of 1967 and especially after his death, survey data is not available to test such a proposition.

White opinion on the *pace* of integration through the mid- and late-1960s showed an erratic pattern. Percentages of whites who judged the pace at which the Kennedy and Johnson administrations were "pushing" integration as too fast, too slow, or just right fluctuated considerably between 1962 and 1968 (Erskine 1968c: 514–15). The shifts seem to reflect reactions to short-term events. Of course, the period was one of tremendous change in the racial arena: in addition to changes in the ends and means of black collective action, three major civil rights bills were passed and a War on Poverty was launched. It is interesting to note, however, that the fractions of whites viewing the pace of integration as too fast swelled from 41 percent in May of 1963 to 58 percent in September of 1966, *only to decline rather rapidly by 1968*. By April of 1968, hardly a calm month in a quiet year, it was back to the 1963 level (Erskine 1968c: 514–15). We can only speculate about the reasons for this pattern—especially for the decline in expressed opposition to integration which appeared between late 1966 and the spring of 1968—but it certainly does not support the notion of an antiintegration backlash. It is not at all clear that white Americans in large numbers viewed rapid integration as a solution to the crisis in race relations during the peak of the new militancy. On the other

TABLE 6 White Attitudes toward Pace of Integration, by Category, May 1965–April 1968

	Percent viewing pace as too slow		Increase (percent)
	May 1965	April 1968	
Non-southerners	13	24	11
College-educated	12	33	21
Eastern states	17	27	10
Western states	16	29	13
Professional and business	9	28	19
Income above $10,000	8[a]	26	18
Income $7,000–$10,000	10	23	13
Residing in cities of over 1 million	12	21	9

[a] Surveyed during Sept. 1966.
Source: Adapted from Erskine 1968c.

hand, the fractions of whites reporting that the pace of integration was *too slow* underwent noteworthy increases during the period (Table 6).

These increases, to be sure, reflect the impact of short-term events and views of the policies of particular administrations at particular times. But it is reasonable to conclude that they may also reflect declines in resistance to integrationist goals during a time when more radical goals were being sought by portions of the black protest movement.

CONCLUSION

My goal in this chapter has been to demonstrate how, in the years from the early 1950s through the late 1960s, the black struggle has undergone rapid and profound changes. I have attempted to document the escalation of black radicalism during those years and to suggest that, among some audiences at least, conceptions of "extremism" and "radicalism" have been rethought.

During the period extending from the end of World War II to the Supreme Court decision of 1954, the benchmarks of black radicalism were, for all intents and purposes, immediate integrationism and legalism. The National Urban League was the most moderate of the few national black organizations. The NAACP and the Legal Defense and Educational Fund were marked as militant groups by their relatively aggressive pursuit of politically-enacted racial integration.

Following the *Brown* decision, integration remained the most radical goal of any major organization for several years. Tactically, the late 1950s were largely years of legalistic maneuvering. But this was also a period of ascendence for nonviolent direct action, which burst into prominence in the early 1960s. Then the NAACP and the LDEF came to occupy a less militant point on the scale. Among the new militants were Martin Luther King and his Southern Christian Leadership Conference.

With the deepening crisis in the movement during the mid-1960s and the entrance of the black urban underclass as a principal element, the spectrum of black radicalism shifted once more. The dominance of racial integration and assimilation as the guiding principle of black collective action was shaken, as was the moral imperative of nonviolence. Although the NUL, NAACP, and LDEF were pulled along to some degree by the new militancy, they remained the polite behemoths of black collective action, firmly and unflinchingly dedicated to integration, legalism, and negotiation. Neither did the SCLC significantly change in terms of its goals or strategies, except for a belated involvement in northern ghetto issues and the Poor People's Campaign. On the other hand, CORE and SNCC, by embracing their respective versions of the black power ideology and for refusing to rule out violence, retained their position as radical groups, surpassed only by the Black Panthers and a handful of small nationalist groups.

Thus it is apparent that major shifts took place in the character of black protest. Public opinion data and the accounts of other scholars suggest that these shifts seem to have caused at least some changes in white perceptions. That is, many whites—though certainly not all and perhaps not even most—moved toward a greater acceptance of certain black goals as these very goals were challenged by more radical and far-reaching claims:

> About 1953, I had my first conversation with [a southern friend] about race relations, and he and I agreed that while the Negro deserved a better chance in America, we must be careful to oppose two kinds of extremists—the NAACP and the Ku Klux Klan. In 1955, we had another conversation, and again we agreed that Ne-

groes ought to be able to attend desegregated public schools, but that we should oppose two kinds of extremes—White Citizen's Councils and Martin Luther King. In 1966, this same friend said to me, "If we could get the good whites and the good Negroes to support Martin Luther King, perhaps we could put the brakes on these SNCC and CORE people and also put a stop to this ridiculous revival of the Ku Klux Klan." I submit that this is evidence of some progress (Hough 1968: 224–25).

A truer test of this sort of "progress" requires the consideration of the degree to which changing black radicalism is associated with increases in the things that most of the black activist organizations wanted and needed: resources to make their organizations run and positive responses to their collective claims. In Chapter 2, I shall deal with the first of these. Patterns of financial contributions to major black organizations will be examined in light of the escalation of the movement as a whole in order to show how radical flank effects affected resource mobilization.

2 Radicalization and Resource Mobilization

Increasing militancy was not the only transition in black collective action during the two and a half decades after World War II. Ideological and tactical escalation were accompanied by major changes in the movement's structure of financial support and, as we shall see, these two developments were not independent of each other. This chapter will focus upon patterns of financial contributions to major movement organizations through the postwar period. First, we shall examine resource mobilization trends among the *recipient organizations* in order to assess a model of complex social movements that takes into account radical flank effects. Then we shall turn to the changing roles of several important categories of *contributors* in order to understand more fully the transformations which occurred in the funding of black collective action.

RESOURCES, THIRD PARTIES, AND COLLECTIVE ACTION

Why is it important or useful to examine levels and sources of financial support received by civil rights and other black organizations? From the perspective of resource mobilization theory, the answer is self-evident: financial support, especially that which flows into movements from the outside, is crucial to the very existence of sustained collective action. For our purposes here, however, the importance of resource mobilization lies in its suitability as an *index of radical flank effects*. In the introduction, levels of financial sponsorship were identified as one of five possible dimensions of such effects. Moderate groups, it was suggested, might experience gains or losses in resources as a result of the activities of radical groups in the same general movement. Supporters need not totally approve of an organization in order to contribute to it. Rather, they need only to have perceived a need to support the cause and to have accepted a given organization as a plausible vehicle for the support. The choice of financial support as an index of radical flank effects rests also upon the premise that "acceptability" is a *relative* concept. A movement organization's acceptability may be largely a function of the relative acceptability or unacceptability of other movement organizations. Thus, increases or decreases in levels of external financial support obtained by a given social movement organization may be taken as rough indicators of increases or decreases in the organization's acceptability to financial supporters.

We would expect *negative* radical flank effects—backlashes caused by radicals but damaging to moderates as well—to produce declines in exogenous incomes of moderate groups or a leveling of prior patterns of increased income for moderates following significant ideological or tactical escalations by more radical groups. We would expect *positive* radical flank effects, on the other hand, to produce increases in the exogenous income of moderate groups or a leveling of prior patterns of decreased income of moderates following such escalations.

Clearly, the perceived radicalism of an organization is not the only factor which affects its ability to attract exogenous support. (I shall return to this issue from time to time in discussing the specific case of black collective action and the events surrounding it.) In addition, the rapidity with which black collective action was radicalized introduces problems of interpretation. Had the major landmarks of escalation—the student sit-ins and the first of the long, hot summers of urban violence—been separated widely in time, then we might be better able to predict exactly when increases or decreases in funding would occur. In other words, a more gradual process of movement radicalization would permit us to test the model with little ambiguity. As it is, the close proximity of many of the relevant events makes it more difficult to identify clearly the roles of given movement and non-movement events.

Thus, we can speak of two senses in which the shape of the data might fit the model. At the general level, we might look for overall patterns of resource mobilization that are consistent with the expectations discussed above. In other words, given the more or less unbroken trend toward greater radicalism from the mid-

TABLE 7   Expected Radical Flank Effects in the Financial Support of Black Collective Action

Year[a]	Victim or beneficiary[b]	Precipitating event(s)
1955	NUL	*Brown* decision (major victory of legalism)
1956–57	LDEF, NAACP, NUL, SRC	Montgomery bus boycott (first major post-*Brown* protest event)
1961	LDEF, NAACP, NUL, SRC	Student sit-ins (transformation of protest into mass phenomenon)
1964–65	LDEF, NAACP,	Peak of non-violent protest/ early black violence
1967–68	LDEF, NAACP, NUL, SCLC, SRC	Rise of black power/peak of urban violence

[a] Lag times of about a year are built into the table.
[b] *LDEF* Legal Defense and Educational Fund, Inc.; *NAACP* National Association for the Advancement of Colored People; *NUL* National Urban League; *SCLC* Southern Christian Leadership Conference; *SRC* Southern Regional Council.

1950s through about 1968, we would expect negative radical flank effects to produce a long-term decline in overall movement income. Conversely, we would expect positive radical flank effects to produce a long-term increase in overall movement income and/or in the income of its more moderate organizations. On a more specific level, we would expect radical flank effects to impinge upon particular organizations at particular times as radicalization advanced (Table 7).

THE DATA

Ideally, an examination of the relationship between radicalization and resource mobilization by social movement organizations would require annual data on total movement income broken down by both recipient and source. Unfortunately, however, no such data set has as yet been compiled. The authors of organizational histories (Carson 1981; Meier and Rudwick 1973; Parris and Brooks 1971, St. James 1958) and of more general works on the civil rights movement (Brisbane 1974; Muse 1968) have provided limited information on the funding of particular organizations. None of these sources, however, contains data that are sufficiently systematic, detailed, and complete for an adequate study of radical flank effects.

The best set of data on movement income that was formerly available was compiled by McAdam (1980 and 1982). Since these data were collected not to study radical flank effects but to determine the usefulness of resource mobilization theory as an explanation of the civil rights movement,[1] he did not attempt to secure information on the specific *sources* of financial support. Moreover, since McAdam was unable to obtain much of his information from primary sources such as organizational files and records, he relied upon estimation and interpolation from incomplete secondary sources. In an effort to improve upon his data, I obtained financial data on major civil rights organizations during the period from 1952 through 1970, including two that he did not examine: the National Urban League and the Southern Regional Council. In most cases, it was possible to categorize contributions by donor type: (1) government agencies; (2) corporations and other business firms; (3) charitable foundations; (4) labor organizations; (5) churches and religious organizations; (6) other types of organizations; (7) members, chapters, or branches (i.e., endogenous sources); and (8) non-member individual contributors. These categories of donors accounted for the vast majority of the resources raised by black organizations during the period (Oberschall 1973). In the most general sense, such detailed financial data are not necessary in order to identify radical flank effects; changes in organizational and total movement income occurring at the predicted times are sufficient to indicate such effects. But the less information we have—on the sources of financial support for black collective action groups, the relative importance of various categories of supporters for the black movement, and the changes in the roles of those categories in underwriting black collective action—the less we are able to perceive the nuances and historical details of the radical flank effects that occurred.

Accordingly, data were sought for each of the following national black organizations that were active during the 1950s and 1960s: the Congress of Racial Equality; the Legal Defense and Educational Fund, Inc., the National Association for the Advancement of Colored People, the National Urban League, the Southern Christian Leadership Conference, the Southern Regional Council, and the Student Nonviolent Coordinating Committee.[2] My attempt to improve on McAdam's data, however, yielded mixed results. I found in some cases, as did McAdam, that even the total exogenous income for certain organizations in given years is unavailable. Some groups consider financial information to be sensitive and prefer not to divulge it to outsiders. Additionally, much financial information has been lost or has failed to find its way into archives.[3] And in most cases, breakdowns into donor-types have been impossible to obtain. Civil rights organizations often failed to maintain the sorts of careful records that would prove most useful in a study of this sort. SNCC, for example, was notorious for its spotty bookkeeping, and many other groups did not categorize donations in ways that are useful to scholars. In general, however, the organizations for which the richest data were located are those most commonly designated as "moderate": the Urban League, the Legal Defense Fund, the NAACP, and the Southern Regional Council. These, fortunately, are organizations whose incomes are most crucial in the analysis at hand.

The data on specific categories of donors, which will be discussed in more detail in the second part of this chapter, are also incomplete. I have taken the information from organizational financial reports where possible. In the case of foundations, however, the most authoritative available record of foundation grants, *Foundation News*, has been searched and coded. Secondary sources have also proved useful, especially for information on corporate support of black organizations and causes. Although the information about donors is insufficient to make firm conclusions for many categories, several clear trends emerge—especially a trend toward greater elite financing of black collective action.

EXOGENOUS INCOME TRENDS, 1954–1970

Before we examine the data, our major hypotheses bear repeating. If negative radical flank effects were present, we would expect a *decrease* in the total amount of financial support for moderate organizations—or a leveling of prior patterns of increasing income—during those periods characterized by escalating black radicalism. If positive radical flank effects were present, we would expect an *increase* in the total amount of financial support for moderate organizations—or the leveling of prior patterns of decrease—during the same periods. Either trend should be apparent in both the aggregate income of the movement and the individual incomes of particular moderate organizations.

During the years between 1954 and 1970, tremendous changes occurred in the financial base of the civil rights movement as well as in its ideological and tactical character. Examination of the major changes that took place will show that total levels of financial support of the black movement organizations by "third parties" (Lipsky 1968: 1145) rose dramatically, especially during the 1960s, and that this increase was largely a function of vastly increased incomes among moderate groups during periods of black radicalization. At a fairly general level of evidence, these findings strongly support the proposition that *positive radical flank effects* were important influences on the incomes of black organizations during the period under study. On the other hand, it will be seen that the most dramatic yearly changes in movement income did not necessarily occur during the expected years.

Findings

Of the basic data on resource mobilization by major black organizations during the period from 1952 through 1970 (Table 8), two features deserve special emphasis. First, the organizations varied widely in "wealth." The older, more established, and generally more moderate groups received far greater amounts of externally-derived income than did the newer and more militant groups. Second, the incomes of the former—the NUL, the NAACP, and the LDEF—were characterized by nearly unbroken patterns of growth during the 1960s. The incomes of the SCLC, CORE, and SNCC, on the other hand, grew rapidly during the early 1960s and then entered a period of rapid decline. Total movement income, however, increased after 1957. (Combined totals for 1952 through 1956 are unavailable due to the lack of Urban League income figures for those years.) With the exception of 1966, the combined income for the community of black organizations never failed to increase (Figure 4). Through the 1950s the trend line for total income remained rather flat.[4] During the early 1960s, however, and especially in 1963, it began to grow rather rapidly. The magnitude of this growth was especially dramatic in 1963, 1969, and 1970. The greatest rate of yearly increase, 114.5 percent, occurred in 1963 (Table

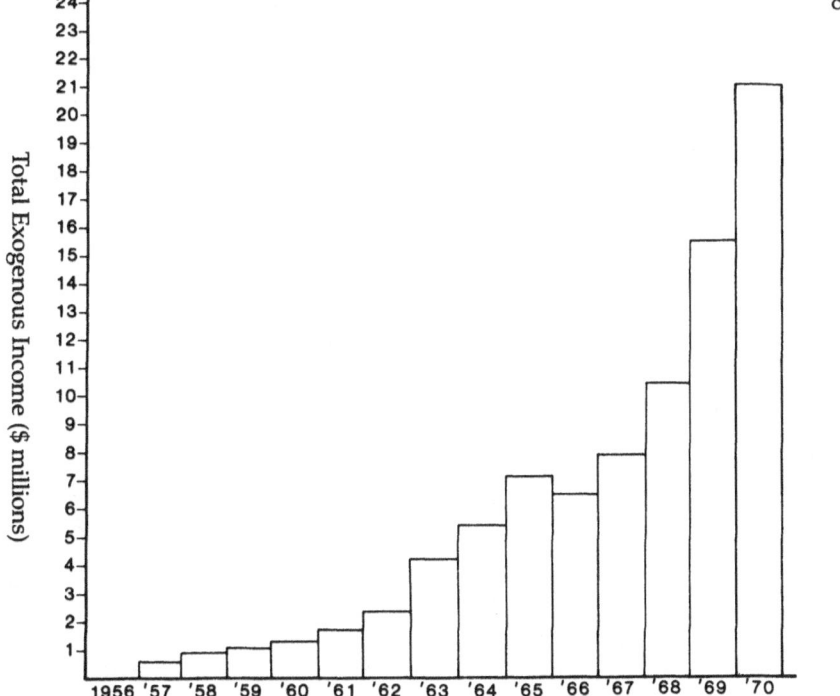

FIGURE 4. Total exogenous income of major black organizations, by year, 1957–1970. The organizations represented are the National Urban League, the Southern Regional Council, the NAACP, the Legal Defense and Education Fund, Inc., the Congress of Racial Equality, the Southern Christian Leadership Conference, and after its founding in 1960, the Student Nonviolent Coordinating Committee. No attempt is made to include income for years prior to 1956 due to the absence of any reliable estimate of the exogenous income of the National Urban League.

9). Aside from that watershed year, the greatest proportionate increases occurred in 1969 and 1970.

The Urban League and the Legal Defense and Educational Fund received the largest shares of exogenous income during the late 1950s and the early 1960s (Table 10). The LDEF was the richest of all the civil rights organizations in 1957 in terms of *externally derived* funds. By 1970 its share of these funds had declined considerably, but its gross income had not. Even though the NAACP's share of total outside contributions declined during the late 1950s and the

TABLE 8 Total Exogenous[a] Income of Major Black Organizations, 1952–1970

Year	NUL	NAACP	LDEF	SRC[b]	SCLC	CORE[c]	SNCC	TOTAL
1952			210,624[d]	27,495	—	4,604	—	
1953		16,436	244,321[d]	35,735	—	5,989	—	
1954		30,944	200,021	59,403	—	5,600	—	
1955		40,606		79,308	—	6,911	—	
1956	265,000[e]			31,369	—	10,115[f]	—	
1957	265,000[e]	103,907	346,947	109,062	10,000[g]	15,506	—	823,012
1958	265,000[e]	90,679	319,537	138,274	10,000[g]	22,936	—	841,970
1959	265,000[e]	93,703	315,081	126,285	25,000[h]	55,324	—	923,300
1960	265,000[e]	103,838	357,988	139,106	54,756	130,609	5,000[i]	1,187,849
1961	257,000	96,936	489,540	NA[j]	193,168	213,248	14,000[i]	1,475,160
1962	572,000	81,547	560,808	168,247	197,565	244,034	71,927[k]	2,004,567
1963	1,221,000	251,579	669,247	161,311	728,172	437,043	302,894	4,299,203
1964	1,539,000	292,738	1,197,204	180,005	578,787	694,588	631,439[l]	5,341,878
1965	1,824,000	388,077	1,425,321	101,105	1,643,000[m]	677,785	637,736[l]	6,933,496
1966	2,201,000	597,425	1,661,793	NA[n]	932,000	400,000[o]	397,237[p]	6,324,485
1967	2,812,000	1,294,909	1,695,718	138,670	932,000[q]	280,000[r]	250,000[i]	7,753,935
1968	3,921,000	1,904,512	2,046,356	269,112	1,000,000[s]	250,000[r]	150,000[i]	10,030,054
1969	8,619,000	2,418,000	2,535,430	204,591	500,000[t]	670,000[r]	50,000[i]	15,273,416
1970	14,542,000	2,665,373	2,811,825	174,321	400,000[t]	210,000[r]	25,000[i]	20,997,692

Note: empty cells (NA), data not available; —, organization not yet in existence.

TABLE 8 (continued)

ᵃ Somewhat different approaches to determining exogenous income are necessary for each organization. The *National Urban League* provided me with yearly totals of income derived from several categories of donors, including "affiliates dues," "special events," and "other." These three categories were eliminated, leaving only income derived from strictly external sources. Income for the *Southern Regional Council* was taken from the annual financial reports the organization provided to me directly and through the Atlanta University Archives. SRC figures appearing in Table 7 include "contributions from SRC members and friends" but do not include "members dues," fees, sales, subscriptions to *New South*, etc. Miscellaneous exogenous income, such as honoraria and overhead from project grants, is included. My procedures for calculating the exogenous income of the NAACP differ somewhat from those of McAdam (1981: 52), who merely subtracted regular branch memberships from total organizational income to arrive at an estimate for external income. I have used a much more restrictive procedure which excludes *all* receipts from branches and miscellaneous income such as interest and dividends. I believe that this more conservative approach yields a more accurate estimate of strictly *exogenous* resources.

Nearly all of the funds of the *Legal Defense and Educational Fund* over the years have come in the form of external contributions and grants. However, I have in all cases subtracted interest and dividends as well as the proceeds from the sale of securities. Because few financial records for the *Southern Christian Leadership Conference* survive and those which have been located (in Atlanta) are relatively unsystematic, it is extremely difficult to distinguish accurately between endogenous and exogenous income. The SCLC was not a membership organization, however, and from what is known about the group's methods of fund-raising, it can be safely assumed that little error results from treating all of its income as exogenous. I have done so for the most part, although funds of a clearly endogenous nature, when identified, have been eliminated from the data.

Congress of Racial Equality financial records are such that it is difficult to distinguish accurately between internal and external income. In most cases, for example, local CORE chapters were not set apart from other, non-CORE organizations, and their meager contributions to national CORE were simply lumped into the "organization" category. Nevertheless, CORE chapters were notorious for their reluctance to contribute funds to the national office, so little accuracy is lost from the procedure I have followed. Convention income, sales, and the like have been eliminated from the figure for exogenous income. SNCC records are even less specific than those of CORE, and a nearly identical procedure has been followed to determine the exogenous income of that group.

CORE operated on a fiscal year that ran from June 1 to May 31.

TABLE 8 (continued)

The SCLC's fiscal year fluctuated. Lacking any reliable procedure for transforming their fiscal year income data to calendar years, I have treated all income data in Table 7 as though it reflected calendar year income. This approach undoubtedly produces a good deal of error within adjacent years, especially for CORE.

^{b} Data on the Southern Regional Council in Table 7 relate to the organization's general fund only. Surviving financial reports prior to 1964 do not list information on special projects. Lacking a reliable procedure by which to estimate levels of income for special projects, I have excluded such income from the figures for 1964 through 1970. This is done for purposes of trend analysis only, and it seriously deflates SRC income during the mid- and late-1960s.

^{c} CORE reported on a fiscal year which ran from June 1 to May 31 of each year. My examination of monthly and quarterly CORE financial reports yielded no reliable manner in which to adjust these figures to a calendar year basis.

^{d} This represents *net* income after fundraising expenses were deducted. LDEF financial reports for 1952 and 1953 do not list either fundraising expenses or gross income.

^{e} No financial information was located for the Urban League prior to 1961. According to Parris and Brooks (1971: 394), NUL income during the mid- and late-1950s fluctuated between $209,000 and $315,000. In order to compute movement totals for those years, I have adopted the rather inelegant procedure of estimating yearly income midway between these two figures. The figure of $265,000 is a gross estimate only and should not be taken to mean that there were no changes in Urban League income between 1956 and 1960.

^{f} This figure is an estimate based upon the percentage of total CORE income for 1956 as reported by Meier and Rudwick (1973: 78): $12,000. The percentage, 84.3 percent, is taken from the endogenous/exogenous income ratio of the previous year.

^{g} This is an impressionistic estimate of SCLC exogenous income derived from various primary and secondary materials.

^{h} This figure is an estimate based upon an examination of all receipts for organizational contributions to the SCLC during 1959 which are located in the files of the Rev. Ralph Abernathy at the Martin Luther King Library and Archives in Atlanta. The total rests upon my estimate that no more than $4,500 in individual contributions were received. During its early years, SCLC received hundreds of individual contributions, most of which were in the two to five dollar range.

^{i} See McAdam 1982.

^{j} In order to derive a total movement exogenous income figure (far right column in Table 8), SRC exogenous income for 1961 is arbitrarily set at $140,000. This is probably somewhat lower than the actual figure, given the trend of preceding years.

TABLE 8 (continued)

k The SNCC income for 1962 is taken from a mimeographed pamphlet produced by SNCC (probably in 1964) entitled "You Can Help Support Programs for SNCC."

l These figures are estimated. External income for ten months of each year (all the data that has survived) is divided by ten to yield an estimated monthly average income. This is interpolated so as to yield the estimated yearly exogenous income which appears in Table 8. The partial exogenous incomes on which these calculations are based are: 1964—$526,198.85; 1965—$531,446.99.

m This figure is an estimate. Fiscal Year 1964–65 income data for the SCLC is available only for the first ten months (83.3 percent) of that fiscal year. The total income for the year as reported in the final audit was first reduced by 9.8 percent, which was the percent of the previous year's total income which was determined to have come from strictly internal sources. This yielded an amended FY 1965 estimated income of $1,409,335.40. This figure, in turn, was increased by 16.6 percent (i.e., the estimated income for the two remaining months was reflected in the official audit). This yields the estimated exogenous income for FY 1964–65: $1,643,308.30.

n SRC exogenous income for 1966 is missing. For purposes of producing a movement total, it is arbitrarily set at $101,105, the exogenous income for the previous year.

o See Meier and Rudwick 1973.

p This estimate is based upon the same procedures as was used for 1964 and 1965, except that 1966 financial data is available for only seven months of that year. Actual income for the first seven months is $231,721.32. It is quite possible that the interpolating procedure inflates the total SNCC income for 1966, since Stokely Carmichael's introduction of the black power slogan took place in the summer of that year.

q This figure is an estimate which was derived from various partial financial reports in the King Library and Archives. It includes all general contributions and appeals but may exclude a limited amount of income from benefit concerts, etc., for which data are unavailable.

r CORE income figures for 1967 through 1970 are based upon estimates by McAdam (1982). Each, however, includes foundation grants located in my analysis of *Foundation News*. Consequently, the numbers are somewhat higher than McAdam's estimates, especially that for 1969.

s This figure is an estimate.

t SCLC income estimates for 1969 and 1970 are adapted from McAdam (1982).

TABLE 9 Rate of Yearly Exogenous Income Growth of Major Black Organizations, 1952–1970[a]

				Organization				
Year	NUL	NAACP	LDEF	SRC[b]	SCLC	CORE	SNCC	Total
1952								
1953			16.0	30.0	—	30.1	—	
1954		88.2		66.2	—	−6.5	—	
1955		31.2		33.5	—	23.4	—	
1956				−60.5	—	46.4	—	
1957			−7.9	247.7	—	53.3	—	
1958		−12.7	−1.4	26.8	0	47.9	—	2.3
1959		3.3	13.6	−8.7	150.0	141.2	—	9.7
1960		10.8	36.7	10.2	119.0	136.1	—	28.7
1961	−3.0	−6.6	14.6		252.8	63.3	180.0	24.2
1962	122.6	−15.9	19.4		2.3	14.4	413.8	35.9
1963	113.5	208.5	78.8	−4.1	268.6	79.1	321.1	114.5
1964	26.0	16.4	19.1	11.6	−20.1	58.9	108.5	24.3
1965	18.5	32.6	16.6	−43.8	183.9	−2.4	1.0	29.8
1966	20.7	53.9	2.0		−43.3	−41.0	37.7	−8.8
1967	27.7	116.7	20.8	0		−30.0	−37.1	22.6
1968	39.4	47.0	23.9	94.1	7.3	−10.7	−40.0	29.4
1969	119.8	27.0	10.9	−24.0	−50.0	168.0	−66.7	52.3
1970	68.7	10.2	6.0	−14.8	−20.0	−68.7	−50.0	37.5

Note: Empty cells, data not available; —, organization not yet in existence.
[a] Based on data in Table 8. See notes to Table 8 for explanation.
[b] General Fund only.

1960s, it recovered somewhat during the middle part of the decade. The most astounding data of all, however, are the National Urban League's. The NUL's income climbed at a steep rate during the late 1960s in particular, causing it to become the financial giant of the movement. By 1970 it received nearly 70 percent of all the funds contributed to major black organizations by outside groups and individuals. Although all of the more radical organizations—the SCLC, CORE, and SNCC—increased their shares of total movement income during the early 1960s, they later entered a period of decline.

These, then, are the basic data upon which the following analysis of radical flank effects will be based. Later in this chapter, we

TABLE 10 Distribution of Exogenous Income among Major Black Organizations, by Year, 1957–1970[a]

	Organization							
Year	NUL	NAACP	LDEF	SRC	SCLC	CORE	SNCC	Total
1957	32.2	12.6	38.8	13.3	1.2	1.9	—	100
1958	31.5	10.8	37.4	16.4	1.2	2.7	—	100
1959	28.7	10.1	38.8	13.7	2.7	6.0	—	100
1960	22.3	8.7	41.2	11.7	4.6	11.0	0.4	100
1961	17.4	6.6	38.0	9.5[b]	13.1	14.5	0.9	100
1962	28.5	4.1	33.4	8.4	9.9	12.2	3.6	100
1963	28.4	5.9	27.8	3.8	16.9	10.2	7.0	100
1964	28.8	5.5	26.7	3.4	10.8	13.0	11.8	100
1965	26.3	5.6	24.0	1.5	23.7	9.8	9.2	100
1966	34.8	9.4	26.8	1.6[b]	14.7	6.3	6.3	100
1967	36.3	16.7	26.4	1.8	12.0	3.6	3.2	100
1968	39.1	19.0	25.3	2.7	10.0	2.5	1.5	100
1969	56.3	15.8	18.4	1.3	3.3	4.4	0.3	100
1970	69.2	12.7	14.2	0.8	1.9	1.0	0.1	100

Note: —, organization not yet in existence.
[a] The figures in Table 10, representing percentages of combined yearly exogenous income for all seven organizations, are derived from the raw data in Table 8.
[b] Based on estimated exogenous income.

shall look at exogenous income from another angle—its various sources—and the changes that occurred over time in the relative importance of particular sources of funds. First, however, let us see what the data tell us about the effects of growing black radicalism on the ability of moderate groups to mobilize resources effectively.

Discussion

The most immediate and significant aspect of the aggregate data on externally-derived resources is the *dramatic increase in the level of exogenous income for the movement as a whole during the 1960s* (Table 8 and Figure 4). Little increase in contributions to the civil rights movement took place during the 1950s, when black radicalism was largely equated with legalistic integrationism and when nonviolent protest was relatively sporadic. During the early 1960s, when nonviolent protest became much more frequent and intense, externally-derived contributions accelerated. The year during which nonviolent direct action reached its dramatic zenith, 1963, was also the year of the steepest climb in income (Table 9). External supporters, it seems, were "discovering" civil rights. Income continued to climb until 1966, when it dropped for the first time. Given that the overall trend of the 1960s was in the direction of ever-increasing support, this drop in income represents an anomaly. The slump of 1966 probably represents the withdrawal of some white support due to the black power controversy; still, on the level of total movement resources, it proved to be a temporary setback rather than a permanent backlash. For black organizations combined income from external sources returned to an upward spiral during the late 1960s. In fact, yearly proportionate increases surpassed all other years except 1963 (Table 9). In dollar amounts, these increases were unprecedented.

The rate of change in resource mobilization during 1969 and 1970 is somewhat unexpected. Assuming a consistent positive radical flank effect, we might have expected the end of serious rioting in 1968 to have reversed the trend. Nonetheless, it did not. A number of explanations might be offered. For instance, the movement's radical flank might have had a lasting impact upon resource mobilization through dramatizing the issue of black rights. Moreover, many financial supporters who had been "driven" to support moderate groups might have assumed that despite the lull in urban violence, the radical mood of the nation's blacks had not softened and there still existed a potential for renewed outbreaks. Later in this chapter, we shall also consider factors which, though unrelated to radicalization, may have affected the funding pattern of the times. However, understanding of overall trends in the resources made available to the movement (Figure 4) requires further analysis.

When overall data for black collective action are broken down (Tables 9 and 10), it becomes clear that *the greatest portion of the total increase in externally-derived resources during the 1960s, and especially after 1966, is accounted for by the increased exogenous incomes of three moderate organizations: the National Urban League, the NAACP, and the Legal Defense and Educational Fund, Inc.*, all of which saw their exogenous income rise rapidly during the 1960s. Not only did they suffer no financial backlash in the turbulent years of increasing black radicalism, but their outside contributions also rose more rapidly (in absolute terms) during the years of riots and nationalism than ever before. The *most* moderate of the groups, the Urban League, experienced a late-1960s windfall that was unprecedented in the movement's history. The NUL, the NAACP, and the LDEF together accounted for all of the increases in combined movement income by the closing years of the decade.

Those organizations which were parts of the radical flank of the mid- and late-1960s, on the other hand, were all characterized by rapid increases in exogenous income during the early 1960s followed by equally rapid declines during the era of the new militancy. It might be suggested that the increasing incomes of militant groups during the early 1960s are typical of newer organizations starting from scratch and of organizations whose goals or tactics have come into style among movement supporters.

McAdam (1982) argues that the funding pattern for black collective action depended heavily upon the relative acceptability of the various organizations involved in it. This, of course, is quite consistent with my argument that radical flank effects were among the critical dynamics of 1960s protest. He suggests that as movement goals and tactics shifted around 1965 and 1966, external support groups came to see the NAACP as virtually the only acceptable funding alternative. Consequently, the NAACP's income rose appreciably. Although my procedures for distinguishing between endogenous and exogenous NAACP income differ from those employed by McAdam,[5] my data support his contentions about that organization and its apparent acceptability. My data do suggest, however, that he is incorrect in his conclusion that the NAACP emerged from the fray of the mid-1960s as the *only* acceptable funding alternative. In McAdam's view, the Urban League did not qualify as a "civil rights organization" and consequently he did not examine its income trends. Regardless of how we might otherwise classify the League, it clearly satisfied a large number of potential contributors to movement organizations. The second half of this chapter will show that the main reasons for the steep increases in the incomes of the two organizations were rather different. For now, however, the essential point is that the shifting funding pattern after 1965 was *more than a mere zero-sum shift within the community of black organizations* (as a superficial reading of McAdam's analysis might imply). That is, it was not merely a case of reallocating a fixed sum of exogenous resources among a fixed set of recipients. Quite the contrary: the shifting funding structure of the movement involved *a vast expansion of aggregate resources* (Figure 4) as well as a reallocation of existing support. Recognition of both expansion and reallocation is vitally important. Had such moderate organizations as the Urban League, the NAACP, and the LDEF done no more than inherit the funds that CORE and SNCC—and to a lesser extent the SCLC—had forfeited because of their militancy, we would not have what could be considered a true positive radical flank effect. Rather, we would have simply a case of an intramovement transfer of funds. My data suggest that the radicalization of segments of the movement increased the pool of exogenous resources in a variable-sum manner. Again, this is *precisely* what a radical flank effect would be expected to do to the financial support structure of a movement.

Thus far I have been dealing with aggregated movement income and comparisons of the combined incomes of those organizations generally deemed moderate and radical. I have suggested that the general patterns which the data assume support the hypothesis about the positive radical flank effect. In later pages I shall turn to an examination of the more precise timing of the largest income changes in order to evaluate the correspondence between the aggregate data and the model further. Before doing so, however, I shall consider briefly the degree to which the exogenous incomes of specific organizations fit the radical flank effect model (Tables 7, 9, and 10).

National Urban League. It is not surprising that the NUL, always the least controversial of the seven organizations examined in this book, was among the first to experience truly significant increases in external contributions during the 1960s. A major portion of the credit for the League's improved fortunes during the early 1960s should go to Whitney Young, who became its Executive Secretary in late 1961. Under Young's leadership the NUL became much more visible on the civil rights scene (National Urban League 1980: 88). The greatest portion of the increased income came from "big money" sources: government agencies, corporations, and foundations. From the beginning, the NUL was quite dependent upon grants and donations from such foundations as the Rockefeller, Ford, and Rosenwald funds (Parris and Brooks 1971; Moore 1981). Between 1961 and 1970, however, foundation contributions to the NUL increased from $62,000 to over $5 million. Somewhat less dramatic was the increase in corporate contributions from $70,000 in 1961 to $1,973,000 in 1970. Governmental funds, however, made up the largest part of the League's windfall. During the mid-1960s the NUL became a "contractor" for social services (National Urban League 1980, 46). The first governmental funds in 1966 amounted to only $294,000, but by 1970 they had skyrocketed to nearly $7 million and made up 47.4 percent of the League's total exogenous income. Increases also can be seen in other categories of contributors, including United Funds and individual donations. But the bulk of the swollen League coffers, and hence of the aggregated exogenous income of the seven organizations, came from government, foundation, and corporate sources. From a radical flank effects perspective, the 1961 and 1962 increases in NUL income are not particularly surprising, but the tremendous increases of 1969 are more than might have been predicted.

Southern Regional Council. Like the Urban League, the SRC has always relied heavily upon charitable foundations for financial support. In 1952 foundations accounted for nearly half of its funds, while churches and individuals contributed 14.8 percent and 24.7 percent, respectively. By 1964 foundations were contributing over 90 percent, but the proportionate contributions of churches, labor unions, miscellaneous organizations, and individuals had all declined considerably.

The incompleteness of the data on the Southern Regional Council makes it somewhat difficult to identify short-term trends and to assess the quality of their fit to the radical flank model. Particularly troubling is the unavailability of income data for Special Projects prior to 1964. After 1964 *total* SRC income (including both General Fund and Special Projects) remained in the $650,000 range until 1968. In 1968 and 1969, however, it rose to $1,187,424 and $1,373,816, respectively. Then in 1970 it fell to $827,000. The brief rise during the late 1960s, of course, suggests a positive radical flank effect. But overall, the patterns in the SRC's exogenous income are less consistent than those of the other moderate organizations. This discrepancy may be largely a reflection of the Council's reliance on foundation grants, which are usually earmarked for specific projects and sometimes extend for only two or three years. Although SRC's income did expand in the 1950s, information from the early 1960s is so spotty that it is difficult to support a radical-flank interpretation firmly. Even the large increases for 1968 and 1969 are difficult to attribute to the impact of the riots and the rise of black nationalism, since a strictly southern group would not be expected to profit from what were largely northern developments. In sum, SRC exogenous income data are broadly consistent with the radical flank model, but are quite difficult to interpret.

National Association for the Advancement of Colored People. The NAACP's income patterns appear to reflect long-term radical flank effects on a general level. Unlike the other groups, the NAACP was self-supporting through most of its history; that is, it subsisted mostly on the dues of its many members. Unless this fact is understood, the relatively low levels of exogenous income may come as a surprise. Indeed, the Association has generally been the richest of all the black organizations when endogenous as well as exogenous income is taken into consideration. Still, outside contributions rose both in absolute terms and as a proportion of overall NAACP funds during the 1950s and 1960s. The NAACP enjoyed the long-term pattern of increased exogenous income that is predicted by the positive radical flank effect model. The increase was quite large over the two decades, though not so much as that of the Urban League. Although the precise timings of the largest annual increases do not correspond well to our earlier predictions, the Association seems in general to have done best during periods of increasing radicalism elsewhere in the movement (Table 10). Its biggest yearly increase occurred in 1963, the high point of nonviolent protest. The second largest came in 1967, the year of the most severe urban rioting and the year after the black power slogan was first introduced. After 1967 the sizes of yearly increases fell off. Exogenous income even began to fall somewhat during the more tranquil 1970s. This decline is in line with what could be predicted from the model, and it sets the NAACP apart from the Urban League.

As noted above, exogenous income became a more important part of the NAACP's budget as the years passed. In 1953 all but five percent of the organization's funds came from within its own ranks. By 1960 this proportion had risen to 15 percent. During 1967 exogenous income accounted for more than half (53.1 percent) of the NAACP budget for the first time, and by 1970 it made up 67 percent of all income. Thereafter, the ratio of endogenous to exogenous income began to revert to its older pattern, though not dramatically. This rise in outside support was essential to the NAACP's continued viability, for as Marger (1984: 24–26) has shown, it came at a time when the organization's membership and black support was declining.

Legal Defense and Education Fund, Inc. The LDEF also experienced steadily rising income during the 1950s and the 1960s. Again we see a pattern in which a moderate organization experienced a large increase in externally-derived income over the two decades. Moreover, we again see the largest proportionate increases during key years in the history of the civil rights movement. The greatest increase for the LDEF came in 1963, the year of the March on Washington and the peak of nonviolent direct action. The second greatest increase came in 1960, when nonviolent protest entered its mass phase. After those years, the greatest percentage increases occurred in 1967 and 1968, the final two years of summer rioting. These are not the specific years which were originally identified as likely for radical flank effects, but they are consistent with the general model.

Southern Christian Leadership Conference. The SCLC had a funding pattern unlike that of any other organization. Once the organization had become established, its levels of externally-derived contributions fluctuated wildly (also see Garrow 1986). The exogenous income pattern of the SCLC is difficult to interpret, and its meaning for the radical-flank-effect model is equally difficult to assess for several reasons. I have proceeded on the assumption that the Southern Christian Leadership Conference was a part of the radical flank of the civil rights movement until approximately 1964. In other words, King's stress on direct action still qualified as "militancy" well into the 1960s despite his integrationist agenda. Consequently, we would not expect a positive radical flank effect until 1964 or 1965, when something more radical appeared. But since King formed the organization in 1957, the large percentage of gains in income typical of newly-mobilized groups, appear as early as 1959. In a formal sense, this is contrary to the pattern predicted by the model. The small amounts of money involved in these large increases in percentage must be kept in mind, however.

The exogenous income patterns of the SCLC are also difficult to interpret because they seem to have fluctuated in an unpredictable manner after 1963. Although the organization reaped large numbers of new contributions in 1960 and 1961, its income rose only slightly in 1962. The year of the March on Washington it more than doubled as a result of King's starring role in the event, but it fell rather sharply the following year. In 1965, the second year of rioting, SCLC's exogenous income rose sharply again, only to fall in 1966.

Part of the apparent inconsistency of SCLC's fund-raising success during the 1960s may be due to the fact that the organization seems to have been affected more than others by particular events and by the activities of one person—Martin Luther King.[6] For its image the SCLC was almost totally dependent on that of King. Thus, when King alienated many erstwhile supporters by criticizing the country's early involvement in the Vietnam War, the SCLC's income for 1966 fell off. This interpretation of the 1966 decline seems more appropriate than the notion of a *negative* radical flank effect based upon the black power controversy and the continued rioting. Indeed, I strongly suspect that the declines in mid-decade income derived from the statements and actions of King himself—such as speaking out against the war before it had become widely acceptable to do so and attempting to bring the nonviolent civil rights struggle to the northern cities—not those of the radical flank on his left. Thus, while many observers were redefining King as a moderate, he persistently pushed out against the boundaries of this reputation.

It appears, in fact, that King's overwhelming persona continued to exert an influence on the SCLC's income even after his death: in 1968 outside contributions took a slight jump, almost certainly a reaction to his assassination. But this proved to be only a temporary pause in the downward spiral that all the smaller activist groups were experiencing in the late 1960s. All of the organizations that were part of either direct action militancy or the "new" black radicalism experienced the same income pattern—an initial climb followed by a rather rapid decline.

Congress of Racial Equality. This same pattern of early failure is apparent in the case of CORE, whose greatest success in fundraising came during the era of direct action integrationism. As was noted in Chapter 1, the organization was composed of small and scattered groups of committed activists during the 1940s and the 1950s. It was an "exclusive" group (Zald and Ash 1966: 330–31); i.e., unlike the "inclusive" NAACP, it preferred to limit its membership to small numbers of persons who satisfied high standards of direct involvement in protest activities. As a result, CORE neither needed nor achieved a high level of income. Its list of financial backers remained small, and its local chapters were reluctant to support a strong central office. But the character of the organization began to change somewhat in the late 1950s. Once a stronger national staff was established, more effective fund-raising and expansion of CORE activities became possible. Between June 1957 and March of the following year, 1,131 new donors emerged (Meier and Rudwick 1973: 81). By January 1960, the list of individual supporters had tripled to 12,000 (Meier and Rudwick 1973: 97). Exogenous income took a corresponding jump (Table 7). Although CORE was formed in 1942, trends in its income during the late 1950s were actually more characteristic of a newly-mobilizing organization, and in terms of national recognition, that was indeed the case.

CORE's income continued to grow until 1966, when it dropped precipitously, largely because of the group's shift toward the black power ideology. Curiously, CORE's exogenous income rose by more than 160 percent during 1969, strictly as a result of a sudden burst of foundation grants to CORE tax-exempt funds.[7] This sudden and short-lived influx was somewhat mysterious. According to Allen (1969), enlightened officials in large foundations picked CORE because it favored a "safe" form of black power—black economic development. As such, CORE was defined as less threatening than SNCC yet more likely than the NAACP or the National Urban League to succeed in helping to pacify the ghettos. (CORE's financial revival of 1969 will be discussed later in this chapter.) Overall, trends in CORE's exogenous income are not inconsistent with the radical flank model. While rather little can be said about the composition of CORE's outside contributions, it is clear that its ability to raise money was seriously impaired by the radicalization during the late 1960s.

Student Nonviolent Coordinating Committee. A similar abortive resource pattern was experienced by SNCC. In the five years after the group formed, the commitment of its young members caught the imagination of a great many northern civil rights sympathizers. Its income, which came mostly from northern whites, especially on college campuses, remained comparatively small but rapidly shot upward. As SNCC became radicalized by its experiences in the South, however, it entered a period of decline. The level of contributions followed suit, and by the beginning of the 1970s, the group was virtually defunct. As with CORE, the financial decline of SNCC began in 1965 and intensified in 1966. These were the years during which leaders of both organizations became recognized as spokespersons for the new brand of black radicalism that swore no allegiance to white liberals, racial integration, or nonviolence.

Two distinct patterns of funding thus emerged during the 1960s. Those organizations which emphasized either direct action integrationism or the "new" black power/nationalistic radicalism—the SCLC, CORE, and SNCC—were able to remain financially viable for only a short time. In the case of the SCLC, the financial decline seems, ironically, to have been largely connected to Martin Luther King—on the one hand, as a reaction against his opposition to the Vietnam war and, on the other, as a response to his assassination and the loss of King as the SCLC's primary fund-raiser and image-molder. For both CORE and SNCC, their financial decline was clearly a consequence of their embracing black power and alienating their supporters.

On the other hand, those organizations which assumed comparatively moderate postures—the Urban League, the NAACP, the LDEF, and to some degree the SRC—watched their exogenous incomes soar as other groups became more radical. When we compare relevant periods, the apparent link between black radicalism and income of moderate groups becomes all the more striking. In raw amounts, both the NUL and the NAACP increased their exogenous incomes far more during the riot-filled period of 1965 through 1969 than during 1960–1964. The LDEF saw its income rise by slightly less during 1965–1969 than during 1960–1964. This observation should be sufficient to put to rest the notion that the rising tide of violence set off a backlash among the financial supporters of civil rights.

Thus far, all of the data I have examined have pointed toward the accuracy of the positive radical flank model on a *general* level. Very large increases in the exogenous incomes of more moderate organizations occurred during the 1960s, the period when increasingly radical forms of black collective action were emerging. And as we have just seen, the most dramatic gains came during the period of the most intense racial crisis in American history, the late 1960s. But what about the *specific* timing of these gains? Earlier in this chapter, I attempted to predict precise years during which the largest proportionate changes would appear (Table 7), viz., 1958, 1961, 1964, 1965, 1967, and 1968. Although the basic trends through two decades support the hypothesis that black resource mobilization was shaped significantly by positive radical flank effects, nearly all of the tables presented thus far (especially Table 9) attest to the *failure of the model to predict accurately the precise years during which exogenous income changes would be most pronounced*. With the SRC excluded due to the incompleteness of its data, the average rate of growth for the moderate organizations during those years for which I predicted radical flank effects is only 25.7 percent. For those years in which no radical flank effects were predicted, the figure is 38.7 percent. Even if we exclude the year of 1963, during which an extraordinary and unpredicted increase in movement income occurred, the average rate of growth was 28.7 percent. A similar pattern emerges when rates of yearly income growth for individual organizations are compared: with the exception of the SCLC, no moderate group experienced greater average income changes during those years in which I predicted radical flank effects than in the years for which I did not.

None of this, of course, necessarily means that the model is fundamentally flawed. One distinct possibility is that the assumption of a one-year lag period needs to be revised. In other words, it is quite likely that radical flank effects would manifest themselves during the same year as the benchmark events of radicalization—the sit-ins or the most intense urban riots. If we examine the rates of exogenous income growth without assuming a lag period, the NAACP, the LDEF, and the SCLC all had greater rates of growth during the expected years. The NUL did not, even under these conditions. Clearly then, the model is not yet adequate for making precise predictions about *when* radical flank effects will appear.

THE SOURCES OF FINANCIAL SUPPORT FOR BLACK COLLECTIVE ACTION

In the first part of this chapter, we looked at trends in resource mobilization by the seven major black organizations of the two decades after *Brown*; the major emphasis was on trends in exogenous support and the distribution of that support within the movement over time. We found that levels of externally-derived support for black collective action increased dramatically during the 1960s, and especially during the intense racial crisis after 1963. We also found that the primary beneficiaries of these increased levels of support were the most moderate organizations in the movement. In fact, resource mobilization patterns among these moderate groups suggest that they profited immensely from the pressure created by more radical groups and rebellious ghetto-dwellers.

But what about the *sources* of increased external resources? Who were responsible for the millions of "new" dollars that poured into the civil rights movement during those years? Were they northern white liberals who dug deeper into their pockets to contribute to a cause they saw as increasingly righteous? Did the higher levels of support reflect a new commitment by long-time supporters such as churches or certain labor unions? Or was it a wealthy and powerful elite, awakened in the midst of a racial "revolution"? Unless we can provide some sort of answers to such questions, the resource mobilization patterns of the 1950s and 1960s will remain obscure. The remainder of this chapter will add detail to the picture. In learning *where* the money came from, we will come closer to knowing *why* it came.

Funds for civil rights and other black political activity have come from a variety of sources. Through most of its history, one organization, the NAACP, has depended largely upon the dues of its own members for financial support. But the other six organizations have always relied more upon various external sources of support. In the following pages we shall examine the changing roles of various types of donors, some of the factors which brought change about, and its consequences for black protest. The goal of the remaining portion of this chapter is more descriptive than analytic. The quality and detail of surviving financial information on major organizations and the sources of their income are too uneven to permit a very precise analysis of all categories of financial contributors. In gathering the basic data on which this chapter is based, I attempted to secure not only total amounts of income for each organization on a yearly basis, but also breakdowns by source. In the cases of the Urban League, the Legal Defense and Educational Fund, and the Southern Regional Council, these attempts were relatively successful. Each has maintained records on past contributors, although NUL data are available only for the period of 1961–1970 and SRC data prior to 1964 are limited to the SRC general fund. NAACP records permit the separation only of internal from external income. For the remaining groups (the SCLC, CORE, and SNCC), virtually none of the required decompositions has survived—if, indeed, any ever existed.

I have supplemented primary data on foundation grants by thoroughly searching *Foundation News*, a publication of the Foundation Library Center which is the best single source of information on foundation activity. But *Foundation News* is not without its problems: the publication almost certainly underreports grants information in a systematic manner.[8] Still, it provides a useful index of changing levels of contributions. The data coded from this source will be examined separately from that obtained from primary financial reports, however. For foundation, corporate, and other contributors, I have also made limited use of secondary sources which I shall describe as they are introduced.

The paucity of detailed information for any but the three organizations mentioned above creates obvious problems for the discussions that follow. Nevertheless, it is possible to make certain limited though reliable generalizations: (1) the larger and more moderate organizations, with the exception of the NAACP, have always relied more heavily upon "big money" funding sources, especially foundations and corporations; (2) the relative importance of these funding sources grew, along with the absolute amounts of their contributions, as radicalism expanded—and almost certainly *because* of this expanding radicalism and the intensifying racial crisis of which it was a part; (3) the smaller direct-action and "new" radical organizations (the SCLC, CORE, and SNCC) were always dependent primarily upon "small money" funding sources such as individuals, churches, and labor unions; and (4) the major change in the funding of black collective action over the course of the 1960s was the increased role of the powerful elites in underwriting black collective action and in responding to moderate black claims in other manners. The last of these points is especially important, for it suggests strongly that *the positive radical flank effect on moderate income consisted primarily of an accommodative response to moderate organizations by corporate, foundation, and governmental elites—elites whose interests were threatened by the black radicalism and violence of the late 1960s.*

Individual Contributors

One source of money for civil rights activism was the individual donor, stereotypically thought of as a liberal white living in the North. Such individuals did indeed have an important part in the movement (Muse 1968: 36–53; Oberschall, 1973: 214–15). Several of the major civil rights organizations began as integrated and sometimes largely white groups. And during the period of nonviolent integrationism, whites often participated in demonstrations, voting rights campaigns, and the like (Demerath, Marwell, and Aiken 1971; Pinkney 1968). The political importance of white activists in attracting attention to the southern struggles was great, as was the financial support of less active white supporters. The Legal Defense and Educational Fund, for example, which received a considerable proportion of its income from individual whites, used the money to pay for the legal defense of those arrested in southern civil rights and voting rights actions. Similarly, the SCLC, CORE, and SNCC were quite dependent upon white "conscience contributors" during the early 1960s.

To be sure, not all the contributions of white liberals came in the form of individual donations. Much of it came as the contributions of supportive organizations such as churches and labor unions. Moreover, the role of individual *blacks* in providing funds

TABLE 11 Individual Contributions to Selected Black Organizations, by Year, 1952–1970

Year	Organization							
	NUL		LDEF		SRC[a]		CORE	
	Amount (dollars)	Percent of year's income	Amount (dollars)	Percent of year's income	Amount (dollars)	Percent of year's income	Amount (dollars)	Percent of year's income
1952					6,781	24.7		
1953					2,718	7.6	3,580	77.8
1954					1,620	2.7	5,195	85.7
1955					3,694	4.7	4,972	88.8
1956					3,116	9.9	6,724	97.3
1957					4,815	4.4		
1958					1,042	0.8		
1959					6,730	5.3		
1960					28,871	20.8		
1961	70,000	27.2			1,729	1.0		
1962	106,000	18.5					318,722	72.9
1963	87,000	7.1			3,569	2.2		

TABLE 11 Continued

Year	Organization							
	NUL		LDEF		SRC[a]		CORE	
	Amount (dollars)	Percent of year's income	Amount (dollars)	Percent of year's income	Amount (dollars)	Percent of year's income	Amount (dollars)	Percent of year's income
1964	104,000	6.8	891,252	62.5	3,230	1.8		
1965	152,000	8.3	766,746	46.1	3,200 (est.)	3.2	435,054	64.2
1966	164,000	7.5	837,315	49.4				
1967	243,000	8.6	933,477	45.6	3,445	2.5		
1968	376,000	9.6	1,256,375	49.6	5,112	1.9		
1969	425,000	4.9	1,181,701	42.0	3,566	1.7		
1970	379,000	2.6	1,041,791	34.9	12,521	7.2		

Note: Empty cells, data not available.
[a] General Fund only.

for civil rights activism, particularly in its formative stages, is often overlooked (Morris 1984). In any case, levels of donations from individuals of either race can be but imperfectly gauged.

Several words of explanation are necessary before we proceed to a discussion of the trends in individual donations to those organizations for which even partial data could be obtained (Table 11). First, declining *proportions* of total exogenous income do not necessarily imply declining *amounts* in dollars. Thus, while the NUL, SRC, and LDEF show a declining role for individual contributions in the overall financing of these organizations, more money was actually being received from individual donors almost every year. Second, the SCLC has been excluded from the table because no reliable information on individual contributions to that organization could be located. It was, however, clearly quite dependent upon such supporters. The files of the SCLC contain boxes of hundreds of receipts for individual contributions of one to ten dollars. In addition, the Freedom Rallies held in northern cities and featuring Dr. King drew hundreds of thousands of dollars in personal donations over the years. The surviving records of specific yearly amounts, however, are so fragmentary that they could not be included.

Similarly, trends in individual contributions to SNCC are hard to tabulate because of their incompleteness. Although SNCC divided its income into the categories of "personal contributions," "Northern office and Friends" groups, and "organizations," much of the money raised by the northern (New York) office and the various "Friends of SNCC" groups around the country came in the form of individual donations. Therefore, SNCC was quite dependent upon individuals for funds.

The data in Table 11 illustrate something quite important about the financial structure of the various organizations included. The moderate organizations of the 1960s, including the largely self-supporting NAACP, were far less dependent upon the individual donations of nonmembers than were the more activist, protest-oriented groups. CORE subsisted almost entirely upon such resources, as well as upon the contributions of small groups such as student organizations, individual churches, and the like.[9] When CORE officially adopted black power, however, their financial situation deteriorated rapidly. The same held for SNCC.

Churches

Churches were a vital force in shaping the civil rights movement, particularly in the South. Christianity provided both a moral justification and a rhetorical framework for the struggle. Moreover, southern black churches served as mobilization centers and channels of communication which, compared to other institutions, were relatively immune to white social control (McAdam 1982: 135, 266; Oberschall 1973: 221). Accordingly, the Southern Christian Leadership Conference was able to make particularly effective use of the network of black churches throughout the region.

Churches and religious associations were also important in helping to finance much black collective action during the years between *Brown* and Birmingham. The Southern Regional Council, for instance, received between $3,800 and $4,190 from churches during each year of the 1950s. In 1952 churches accounted for 14.8 percent of the SRC's income, though the proportion fell thereafter. The SCLC also received considerable contributions from churches. Since these donations were often made in the name of ministers, however, they are difficult to distinguish from individual contributions. Moreover, churches and other groups often contributed money to King's Ebenezer Baptist Church which was in fact intended for the SCLC. Church contributions accounted for approximately 61 percent of the SCLC's exogenous income in 1959, and it appears that their absolute level in dollars remained relatively constant for the next several years. Because of the rising prominence of the organization and its increased income from other sources, the proportion of its income derived from churches decreased. Finally, SNCC received over $142,000 from churches in 1963, the only year in which the organization's financial reports include the category.

Unfortunately, data sufficient to make even reliable estimates of yearly amounts of church contributions are unavailable. Miscellaneous papers and correspondence of the SCLC, CORE, and SNCC suggest that church contributions remained at a roughly constant level in dollars through the late 1950s and rose slightly during the early 1960s. As a rule, churches were "small money" sources; they were not in the position to make large donations for civil rights activities. Although many individual churches donated funds, the total amounts involved were rarely large. And because the level of contributions from "big money" sources such as foundations and corporations increased, that of churches shrank proportionally. For example, throughout the 1960s church donations to the SRC remained in the range of $3,000 to $5,000, but by 1968 the flood of foundation grants to that organization reduced church gifts to less than two percent of total funds. It is in this relative sense, then, that the importance of church money in the financing of black collective action declined.

Labor Unions

In some ways, the pattern of relations between the black movement and organized labor has been quite similar to that between the black movement and churches. Labor organizations have tended to make official pronouncements in support of civil rights and have supported the movement both financially and otherwise, yet relations have often been strained. Civil rights organizations such as the NAACP and CORE frequently came into conflict with supposedly sympathetic unions over the issue of union discrimination (Foner 1974: 336–54; 368–70; Newman et al. 1978; 55–56).

As with the contributions of religious organizations to the civil rights movement, it is difficult to derive trustworthy information on the contributions of labor organizations from financial reports and other surviving information; some clues emerge, however (Table 12).

The figures suggest that labor organizations became a less important source of funds for black collective action as time went on. It can be seen that while union contributions were never very large in comparison to most other categories, they may have increased slightly through the 1960s (Donovan 1967: 57ff.; Hodgson 1976: 206). Civil rights groups simply became less dependent upon union money and more dependent—at least in the cases of the more moderate groups—on foundations and corporations. More important than the financial role of labor may have been its *legitimizing* role, and labor leaders such as Walter Reuther of the United Auto Workers were both outspoken advocates of the cause and active participants in civil rights activities (Carson 1981: 104; Foner 1974: 370; Lytle 1966: 285, 287; Meier and Rudwick 1973: 110–11, 126, 150; NAACP *Annual Report for 1963*: 31–32; Parris and Brooks 1971: 337).

Corporations

The business sector was rather late in arriving as a supporter of black collective action. This is not to imply, of course, that the business sector as a whole *ever* became a true ally. But portions of the corporate world did come to play a part in the movement.

Business support for pro–civil rights changes—which appears to have emerged first in southern urban areas—was brought about not by moral enlightenment but by the recognition that racial trouble damaged business interests. Turmoil disrupted the local economic climate, of course. But perhaps more important was that sustained conflict and the attendant bad publicity discouraged new investment in the South. Consequently, business leaders in southern cities often yielded to black demands when those demands were within their reach—as, for example, in the case of employment policies. But even with regard to those movement goals not *directly* within the businessman's domain, such as education, they sometimes pressured politicians, worked behind the scenes to bring public opinion into line with what they viewed as inevitable changes, and even took the dangerous step of publicly endorsing things like desegregated education (Patterson 1966). Not uncommonly, they sought out moderate blacks with whom they could work to sooth tensions and facilitate peaceful and gradual change (Powledge 1967: 98–119; Walker 1963: 122. In other words, a positive radical flank effect of sorts occurred in southern cities, and it sometimes yielded gains for more conservative blacks in terms of access to decision-makers.

The partial mobilization of southern businessmen as brokers of social change really began with the sit-in protests in 1960. With the wave of sit-ins, businessmen found that *they* were the targets of specific demands and that business was suffering more than it had ever suffered from purely legalistic attacks. But with the first outbreaks of violence, the incentive to act became even greater. After disorders at the University of Mississippi in 1962 and in Birmingham in 1963, more than a hundred biracial committees appeared in the Upper South. And quiet, voluntary desegregation of public facilities often took place: "Privately and publicly, the watchword was 'We want no Birmingham here'" (Patterson 1966: 71).

In the North as well as the South, business interest in civil rights and other black concerns lay dormant until the crises of the 1960s. It appears that the only black organization in which there was any appreciable business interest before 1960 was the Urban League. Through its Commerce and Industry Council, the League brought white business leaders into advisory positions in the organization; large firms such as General Motors, General Electric, Ford Motor Company, Standard Oil, and U.S. Steel participated (Parris and Brooks 1971: 337–39). With the advent of mass nonviolent protest after 1960, the incentive for business to deal with the League increased: "As businessmen came to fear demonstrations at their doorsteps or factory gates," report Meier and Rudwick (1976: 284), "they listened more carefully to requests and suggestions from the Urban League."

Surprisingly little research on corporate financial support of black collective action has been conducted. In fact, the only large-

TABLE 12 Labor Contributions to Selected Black Organizations, by Year, 1952–1970

Year	NUL Amount (dollars)	NUL Percent of year's income	LDEF Amount (dollars)	LDEF Percent of year's income	SRC[a] Amount (dollars)	SRC[a] Percent of year's income	CORE Amount (dollars)	CORE Percent of year's income
1952								
1953					3,700[a]	10.7		
1954					4,700[a]	8.1		
1955					4,350[a]	5.6		
1956								
1957								
1958					4,500[a]	2.8	695[b]	3.0
1959							1,347[b]	2.4
1960					3,425[a]	2.5	6,100[b]	4.7
1961	16,000	6.2			3,000[a] (est.)	2.2	13,500[b]	6.3
1962	18,000	3.1			1,200[a]	0.8	40,000[b]	16.4
1963	16,000	1.3			600[a]	0.4	40,000[b]	9.2

TABLE 12 Continued

Year	NUL		LDEF		SRC[a]		CORE	
	Amount (dollars)	Percent of year's income	Amount (dollars)	Percent of year's income	Amount (dollars)	Percent of year's income	Amount (dollars)	Percent of year's income
1964	27,000	1.8	455	0			40,000[b]	5.8
1965	27,000	1.5	3,355	0.2	5,000	0.7		
1966	31,000	1.4	3,225	0.2				
1967	0	0	1,700	0	0	0		
1968	25,000	0.6	5	0	5,000	0.4		
1969	24,000	0.3	0	0	0	0		
1970	30,000	0.2	0	0	0	0		

Note: Empty cells, data not available.
[a] General Fund only.
[b] Based upon Meier and Rudwick 1973: 82, 126, 149.

scale investigation of this issue is Cohn's 1970 analysis of corporate involvement in the "urban crisis." For this study of 247 major companies throughout the nation—including firms in the fields of banking, insurance, retail, transportation, manufacturing, and petroleum—interviews were conducted with top executives of most of the companies and supplementary information was collected by means of questionnaires. It was found that 201 of the 247 companies had established some sort of urban affairs program by 1970 but that only *five* of those programs had existed before 1965. They included (1) donations of money, staff, or facilities to groups and agencies dealing with aspects of the urban crisis; (2) special programs for hiring members of minority groups; (3) hiring programs aimed specifically at the urban hard-core unemployed; (4) programs for training and upgrading the hard-core unemployed; and occasionally (5) economic development programs for the ghettos.

Interviews with executives of the companies revealed a variety of motivations for the sudden increase of corporate involvement in urban problems. Nearly all claimed that a sense of social responsibility and a desire to improve their company's reputation were involved. Two-fifths stated that they had initiated their programs to satisfy government requirements for equal employment opportunity. A few expressed the hope that their urban activities might open up new markets among minority groups.

One-third of the respondents, however, initiated their urban affairs programs as a form of "insurance"; as a means to "discourage boycotts, violence, and other threats to company well-being" (Cohn 1970: 70). As one automobile executive commented, "It wasn't until after the Detroit riots that the automobile makers got busy. If their factories were in East Cupcake, they wouldn't be so energetic about the hard-core" (Cohn 1970: 76; also see Ginzberg 1968: 171–75).

It was also found that many of the urban affairs programs instituted during the late 1960s proved to be much more expensive than their parent companies had ever imagined. Thus, after the relatively peaceful summers of 1968 and 1969 had eased the immediate pressure to help ameliorate inner-city conditions, executives began to assume a more "reflective" posture about what had been done and what ought to be done in the future (Cohn 1970: 69).

Particularly relevant to the issue of radical flank effects are Cohn's findings on corporate contribution patterns. Of the 247 firms he studied, 70 percent had donated cash, staff, executive time, and/or facilities to some organization or agency active in minority/urban affairs. Although the corporate sector has always contributed resources to various recipients whose orientations have appeared acceptable, the events of the late 1960s were found to have brought about "significant changes in the patterns and styles of corporate donations" (70). Cohn discovered, for example, that of the 247 companies in the study, 175 have revised their annual donations lists since 1967 to include grants to national or local groups associated with urban affairs; at the same time, 45 of these companies have actually cut back on their donations to traditional charities" (21). Moreover, the average company donation for urban affairs after 1967 was approximately $175,000, an amount which no single company had set aside for such purposes before that year (71).

Cohn's findings suggest that black radicalization and urban rioting stimulated business to increase its involvement in issues directly affecting urban blacks. The information he provided on the *recipients* of corporate donations is also consistent with the radical flank effects model. Approximately 25 percent of the companies added the NAACP, the United Negro College Fund, and/or the National Urban League to their donations list after 1967. Other companies which had made small contributions to one of these groups in the past increased the size of their contributions in the late 1960s. Many companies also donated resources to local community groups which they had completely ignored before 1967, and others actively sought out groups to make contributions to. However, only three of the 27 companies approached by "more militant minority-group organizations such as CORE, SNCC, and the National Welfare Rights Organization" (73) were willing to make cash donations to these groups.

Cohn's basic point about increased corporate donations to black moderate organizations is borne out by Urban League data; indeed the NUL is the only major organization to have retained information on corporate contributions (Table 13). Corporate contributions continued to climb through the 1960s, then began to fall off somewhat during the early years of the 1970s. But as a percentage of the Urban League's exogenous income, corporate gifts declined in importance after 1965. Curiously enough, the Legal Defense and Educational Fund seems to have received little in the way of corporate contributions until the 1970s. That organization's financial reports indicate no such contributions until 1968. Corporate gifts amounted to only $7,014 in 1968, $7,250 in 1969, and $3,360 in 1970, and during none of those years did they comprise more than 0.3

percent of the Fund's income. The 1980 report, however, reports corporate donations totalling $583,793, or 13.7 percent of total outside income. Although Cohn's analysis reveals that the NAACP received considerable amounts from corporate sources after 1967, I can provide no detailed verification because such information is lacking in its Annual Reports.

The established civil rights organizations were not the only beneficiaries of increased corporate involvement in urban and minority affairs. At least three new organizations were created by the nation's corporate leaders to address the same sorts of problems. The first was the *Metropolitan Applied Research Center* (MARC), formed in May 1967 and largely funded by a Ford Foundation grant for its first year. (Because of its link with foundations, MARC will be discussed in the next section.) The second was the *National Urban Coalition*, established on July 31, 1967, by a group of business, labor, religious, civil rights, and local government leaders. The Coalition's goals included emergency jobs programs, promotion of private-sector initiatives in the employment field, and a long-range program for the physical and social reconstruction of the large cities (Adams and Burke 1970: 98–99). The Urban Coalition represents another case in which black moderates obtained greater access to decisionmakers because of racial crises. The civil rights movement was represented by several moderate leaders, including Martin Luther King, Arnold Aronson (Leadership Conference on Civil Rights), John Wheeler (Southern Regional Council), Roy Wilkins (NAACP), Whitney Young (NUL), and A. Philip Randolph; numerous powerful labor and corporate leaders were also involved (Muse 1968: 312–13).

The third of the new organizations was the *National Alliance of Businessmen* (NAB), formed in 1968 to serve as a mechanism for promoting the creation of jobs for the unemployed. Launched in cooperation with the Department of Labor, it provided more than 100,000 jobs during its first year of operation (Adams and Burke 1970: 75; Sobel 1977: 62). By the early 1970s the program had fallen out of favor with the Nixon administration (Sobel 1977: 103). Along with the NAACP, the NUL, and the United Negro College Fund, the three corporate-initiated organizations received most of the benefits of increased allocations from corporations and foundations during the late 1960s.

It is apparent, then, that business involvement in civil rights and ghetto issues increased greatly during the 1960s. Sometimes this involvement included responding to certain preexisting demands by

TABLE 13   Corporate Contributions to the
National Urban League, 1961–1972, 1980

Year	Amount (dollars)	Rate of growth (percent)	Percent of income
1961	70,000		
1962	153,000	118.6	26.7
1963	527,000	244.4	43.2
1964	657,000	24.7	42.7
1965	848,000	29.1	46.5
1966	888,000	4.7	40.3
1967	1,056,000	18.9	37.6
1968	1,197,000	13.4	30.5
1969	1,521,000	27.1	17.6
1970	1,973,000	29.7	13.6
1971	1,796,000	−9.0	12.5
1972	1,782,000	−0.8	10.2
.	.	.	.
.	.	.	.
.	.	.	.
1980	2,867,000		12.5

creating jobs or by using influence to advance pro-black changes. At other times, especially after the advent of the urban riots, business involvement included donating large amounts of money to existing *moderate* black groups or creating new organizations with pro-black aims and funding them at high levels. Corporate participation in these activities seems to have been shaped by businessmen's perceptions of their own interests, and the evidence points clearly in the direction of a positive radical flank effect.

Foundations

During the late 1960s vastly increased levels of foundation support for civil rights and related organizations were responsible for much of the exogenous income gains of that decade. But like corporations, foundations as a rule entered the civil rights arena very cautiously and very late in the game. But the reluctance of foundations to involve themselves with black struggles is not surprising, given their historical pattern of conservatism. Observers of American philanthropy generally have commented upon its tendency to avoid controversy at nearly all costs and to direct charity toward the maintenance of the status quo (Reeves 1970: 13–14). Thus, until the 1960s, foundation contributions to black causes were minimal and limited to the "safest" of available black institutions and organizations. The earliest "safe" target for philanthropy was black education. During the late nineteenth century, a handful of white foundations channelled money into this area, primarily to black colleges. Then, in 1902, John D. Rockefeller created the General Education Board, which until World War I was the largest source of philanthropic support for black education in the South (Henry 1979: 176–77; Nielsen 1972: 334–37; Rhind and Bingham 1967: 429). The focus in those days was clearly on separate-but-equal institutions, educational or otherwise. For this reason, Rockefeller was able to join a small number of other philanthropists in supporting the National Urban League. The NAACP, however, he considered to be far too controversial (Henry 1979: 178).

Limited amounts of money from primarily white foundations were thus made available for certain noncontroversial efforts to improve black life. It was not until the 1950s, however, that black *collective action* was deemed a fit target for philanthropy. Certain progressive foundations—small to medium-sized ones for the most part, such as the Stern Family Fund and the Field Foundation—began to make occasional grants to civil rights organizations with integrationist leanings (Joseph 1969: 56–57). With the exception of the Ford Foundation and the Rockefeller Brothers Fund, the larger foundations remained aloof. In general, the big foundations were at the trailing edge, not the cutting edge, of change. Congressional attacks upon them in the 1950s, particularly in the case of the Ford Foundation, tended to discourage what little initiative they had been inclined to take in regard to social and racial issues (Nielsen 1972: 344).

Until recently, almost no research on foundation assistance to black collective action has been conducted (Henry 1979: 175), largely because of the secrecy—intentional and unintentional—which surrounds these institutions.[10] The information which I have been able to obtain on foundation contributions to civil rights and other black collective action units is largely limited to the 1960s and is taken from two sources. In the cases of the Urban League, the Southern Regional Council, and the Legal Defense and Educational Fund, it comes from the financial data provided by the organizations themselves. For all the other groups, the data has been extracted from *Foundation News*. As was noted earlier, the latter source is plagued by problems of reliability, and the information contained in it must therefore be interpreted with extreme caution. This information will not be combined with primary NUL, SRC, or LDEF data, for example, because it would tend to exaggerate the shares of foundations funds received by those groups. Nor will any great significance be attached to year-to-year changes. Announcements of foundation grants do not always appear in print during the same year in which they are awarded. Accordingly, I shall focus only upon the interpretation of long-term shifts in foundation involvement in the movement.

Overall, the trends in foundation contributions to the Urban League, the Southern Regional Council, and the Legal Defense Fund are much in line with the positive radical flank pattern: as the black struggles progressed and as the radicalism of the black population grew, foundation contributions became major sources of income for the Urban League, the SRC, and the LDEF (Table 14).[11] Of the three, the SRC was the most dependent upon foundations for support. By 1969 it received nearly all of its resources from this source. Since 1961 the Urban League has never relied upon foundations for more than 43.2 percent of its total income, and the organization's dependency upon foundations fell off even more during the 1970s. The LDEF pattern was quite similar; its dependency on foundations increased through the 1960s, then fell during the next decade.

Although the figures obtained from *Foundation News* are not directly comparable to those presented here, the basic trends they show are quite consistent. In categorizing the grants reported in FN, several types of information were sought, including the yearly number and amounts of foundation grants to the major organizations in the black movement, the yearly number and amounts of foundation grants made to *other* recipients for purposes consistent with major black concerns, the number of foundations which gave grants in relevant issue areas and/or to major movement organizations each year, and the degree to which changes in foundation contributions for black organizations and concerns differed from overall patterns of grants activity.

Each of these sets of data reveals that foundations were increasingly involved in the areas of minority affairs, race relations, and poverty and that this new interest in black collective action was not limited to the Urban League, the SRC, and the LDEF (Table 15). Although the figures themselves are imprecise and probably deflated to a considerable extent, they nevertheless indicate the pattern and direction of foundation activity. *FN* reported no grants

TABLE 14 Foundation Grants to Selected Black Organizations, by Year, 1952–1970, 1980

Year	NUL Amount (dollars)	NUL Percent of year's income	LDEF Amount (dollars)	LDEF Percent of year's income	SRC Amount (dollars)	SRC Percent of year's income
1952					13,000[a]	47.3
1953					23,600[a]	66.0
1954					48,460[a]	81.6
1955					65,200[a]	82.2
1956					19,500[a]	62.2
1957					85,867[a]	78.7
1958					124,281[a]	89.9
1959					107,000[a]	84.7
1960					98,400[a]	70.7
1961	62,000	24.1				
1962	239,000	41.8			149,924[a]	89.1
1963	513,000	42.0			141,500[a]	87.7
1964	665,000	43.2	179,914	12.6	616,350	92.9
1965	701,000	38.4	220,347	13.3	630,300	97.1
1966	707,000	32.1	337,350	19.9		
1967	905,000	32.2	487,155	23.8	659,934	98.5
1968	1,573,000	40.1	596,789	23.5	1,170,050	98.5
1969	2,898,000	33.6	884,733	31.5	1,354,385	98.6
1970	5,054,000	24.8	1,275,142	42.8	814,392	98.4
.	.	.	.	.	.	.
.	.	.	.	.	.	.
.	.	.	.	.	.	.
1980	1,487,000	6.5	1,257,806	29.6		

to the NAACP, CORE, or their respective tax-exempt funds until 1966.[12] After that point, foundation grants built toward a peak in 1969. CORE's ability to attract grants after it adopted a black power perspective, however, is surprising. Even more surprising is the rather high level of foundation grants it received in 1969—over half a million dollars. Why was a self-avowed black nationalist organization able to receive such high levels of support from foundations?

Part of the answer to this puzzle has to do with the source of

TABLE 15   Foundation Grants to Selected Black
Organizations, Reported in *Foundation News*,
1960–1970 (in dollars)

Year	Organization		
	NAACP[a]	SCLC[b]	CORE[c]
1960	0	0	0
1961	0	0	0
1962	0	0	0
1963	0	0	0
1964	0	0	0
1965	0	0	0
1966	60,000	0	10,000
1967	440,000	93,750	81,500
1968	200,000	245,000	45,500
1969	1,115,000	275,000	521,000
1970	314,289	125,000	60,000

Source: Foundation News, vols. 1–11 (1960–1970).
[a] Includes the NAACP Special Contribution Fund.
[b] Includes the American Foundation on Nonviolence and the Southern Christian Leadership Foundation.
[c] Includes the CORE Special Purpose Fund, the CORE Scholarship, Educational and Defense Fund, and the Scholarship, Education, and Defense Fund for Racial Equality (SEDFRE). Due to the inclusion of SEDFRE grants, CORE foundation totals may be somewhat misleading for the years following 1966. CORE and SEDFRE underwent a schism during that year and became, in effect, two separate groups (Craig Jenkins, letter to the author, June 12, 1987).

the CORE grants. For instance, $450,000 of the $521,000 that CORE received in 1969 came from the Ford Foundation, of philanthropic organizations the most active in the fields of race relations and poverty through the latter half of the 1960s. According to Allen (1969), the Ford Foundation's intentions in funding black groups generally and CORE specifically were largely manipulative. In the latter instance,

> CORE's militant rhetoric but ambiguous and reformist definition of black power as simply black control of black communities appealed to Foundation officials who were seeking just those qualities in a black organization which hopefully could tame the ghettos. From the Foundation's point of view, old-style moderate leaders

TABLE 16 Foundation Grants for Black-Related Issues, Reported in *Foundation News*, 1960–1970

Year	Movement Organizations		Others	
	Number of grants	Amount (dollars)	Number of grants	Amount (dollars)
1960	3	30,000	0	0
1961	11	346,000	14	883,000
1962	8	433,000	5	124,050
1963	16	529,864	19	605,446
1964	33	6,161,073	26	1,554,000
1965	57	5,630,027	18	24,582,550
1966	59	4,504,608	39	19,784,569
1967	70	8,472,375	76	10,927,980
1968	70	7,935,406	86	10,556,020
1969	123	13,773,376	145	17,880,240
1970	135	15,662,068	153	20,121,515

no longer exercised any real control, while genuine black radicals were too dangerous. CORE fit the bill because its talk about black revolution was believed to appeal to discontented blacks, while its program of achieving black power through massive injections of governmental, business, and Foundation aid seemingly opened the way for continued corporate domination of black communities by means of a new black elite (146–47).

But the Ford Foundation did *not* cut back its support for the "old-style" organizations such as the NAACP. Rather, according to Allen's interpretation, they simply saw CORE as potentially useful for a single purpose: the pacification of the ghetto. Although it is not clear why CORE's foundation income apparently declined in 1970, it is conceivable that it fell because Ford officials felt the task had been accomplished for the time being.

To be sure, the expansion of foundation involvement in racial issues was not limited in its effect to the seven major black organizations on which this book focuses. Dozens of other national, state, and local groups experienced vastly increased levels of philanthropic investment, especially during the late 1960s. Even the most traditional of the organizations, the United Negro College Fund, did so. *Foundation News*, reporting no grants to the UNCF in 1960, lists eight grants totalling nearly $5.25 million for 1964. During the second half of the decade, *FN* reports the UNCF's grant income to be in the range of $1 million annually. But corporation-created organizations were especially favored during the last five years of the 1960s. The Metropolitan Applied Research Center (MARC) received over half a million dollars a year from foundations after its formation in 1967, including a reported $1,058,125 in 1968. The National Urban Coalition and its local affiliates received just under $2 million in 1969 and nearly $5 million in 1970.

The trend in foundation contributions to deal with issues of concern to blacks is summed up in Table 16, which summarizes all such grants reported in *Foundation News*. The column entitled "movement organizations" includes all the grants awarded to groups focusing primarily on racial issues; these include not just the seven major organizations but a wide variety of other groups and associations concerned primarily with interracial issues or civil rights.[13] The column entitled "others" includes all grants which were coded as having been for civil rights or black-oriented antipoverty purposes but which were made to recipients not primarily in civil rights or antipoverty "businesses"—e.g., churches and religious associations, schools, universities.

Even if we keep in mind that *Foundation News* tends to *under-report* grants, their data make it obvious that awards to civil rights and antipoverty organizations of all sorts grew tremendously in the 1960s. The large increase in grants to movement organizations in 1964 is somewhat misleading, however, as it owes its existence almost exclusively to a United Negro College Fund windfall of a reported $5,252,000. If we eliminate the UNCF from consideration, the watershed occurred not between 1963 and 1964 but rather between 1964 and 1965. The amounts of grants that *FN* placed in its rather narrowly defined "Interracial Relations" category increased from $2.3 million in 1964 to $26.7 million in 1965 (*Foundation News*, January 1966: 4–5). The drastic increase in the category "Others" in 1965 is largely due to several very large Ford Foundation grants.

Although much of the expansion in foundation grants to black collective action was due to large increases in donations by such giants as the Ford and Rockefeller Foundations, this is not the whole story. During the 1960s there also occurred a vast increase in the *number* of foundations making grants in the civil rights and antipoverty areas (Figure 5). More and more individual foundations were becoming involved in funding black collective action and various pro-black reforms. Among these were some, such as the

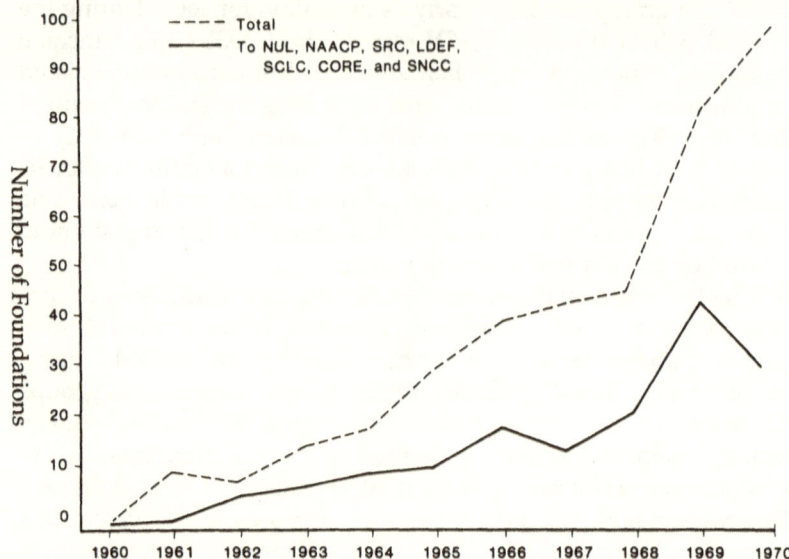

FIGURE 5. Number of foundations contributing to racial and antipoverty activities, 1960–1970.

Lilly Endowment, that had tended in the past to support strictly conservative causes and groups.

In analyzing grants reported in *Foundation News*, a special effort was made to record the intended purpose of individual grants when possible. It is difficult to reach precise conclusions as to changes in the intended uses of foundation resources because the categories are numerous and frequently overlapping. Nevertheless, a few generalizations are possible. Grants specifically directed toward more or less traditional civil rights issues—such as integration, voting rights, school desegregation, equal employment, and open housing—reached a peak by about mid-decade and remained more or less constant through 1970. Two other categories of foundation grants rose dramatically during the riot years, however. The first of these included grants targeted toward *ghetto conditions, poverty, hard-core unemployment, and inner-city economic development*. The other included grant money aimed at the development of *black community leadership and black-owned and -operated business*. It does not appear that civil rights issues of major concern to a black middle class lost prominence during the 1960s. It does appear, however, that during the years of riots and black power, foundations paid greater attention to the *class* issues of major concern to poorer inner-city residents.

One final point must be made with respect to foundation contributions to black collective action: the increasing levels of foundation support were not merely a function of overall increases in charitable contributions. As McCarthy and Zald have noted, foundation grants as a whole did, in fact, increase during the 1960s by more than 100 percent, and the increases "were especially large in the areas of race relations, urban problems, and poverty problems" (1973: 12). According to *Foundation News*, 18 percent of the foundation money granted in 1968 was *targeted* in one way or another toward poverty or race relations (*Foundation News*, March 1969: 49). My calculations, however, yield a figure considerably lower, because in analyzing grants aimed at poverty or the disadvantaged, I have included only those which were focused specifically upon *black or inner-city poverty*. Although this is a very restrictive approach—perhaps too restrictive—it is tailored to the subject of this research, and it still provides evidence of an overall increase in the priority of racial issues during the 1960s.

When the rates of growth of foundation grants as a whole, grants to "movement organizations" (see n. 12), and grants for other black-related purposes not involving primarily black-related organizations are compared, it can be clearly seen that grants for black-related issues and movement organizations grew rapidly during the decade, and especially before 1965 (Table 17). In fact, as was noted earlier, the largest increases occurred during 1964 and 1965. The rates of growth for movement organizations are significantly higher than those for grants as a whole for both five-year periods and for the decade as a whole. The rate of growth for grants to miscellaneous black activities is extraordinarily high for 1961 through 1965, but such grants actually *dropped* between 1965 and 1970 (also see Jenkins and Eckert 1986: 819–20). Combining grants to organizations in the movement and to other black-related activities, which would actually produce a rate of growth for the second five-year period *lower* than that for foundation grants as a whole, would appear to undermine the proposition that a positive radical flank effect shaped foundation funding. Such a conclusion, however, would be misleading. Grants in the non-movement category, while relevant within this framework, were often targeted toward universities and other non-movement institutions for purposes only indirectly related to civil rights—scholarships for black students, for example. From the standpoint of radical flank effects, the *movement organization* category is more crucial. It contains groups which were strictly in the business of improving conditions of life for blacks rather than only marginally or occasionally involved. I would suggest that the most significant aspect of the data on foundation grants (Tables 16 and 17) is that foundations began to target their grants more specifically toward *black movement organizations* as the decade progressed. Some of these, like the elite-spawned Metropolitan Applied Research Center, were not black-controlled collective action groups. But others were—the vastly increased levels of funding for the major moderate organizations has already been documented. Thus the data are best interpreted as evidence that the priority of black groups and issues, relative to other concerns, did in fact increase greatly during the 1960s—more so, perhaps, during the first half of the decade, but not inconsiderably during the second.

During the 1960s the involvement of foundations in racial affairs increased by leaps and bounds. Black organizations such as the Urban League and the United Negro College Fund, which had received foundation support in the past, saw that support multiply. Other organizations, such as the NAACP and CORE, which had never received substantial support from foundations, did so for the first time. Dozens of national, state, and local organizations involved in race relations and antipoverty activities also became the beneficiaries of increased foundation interest, as did hundreds of churches, schools, and associations venturing into these areas for the first time. The increased prominence of these issues is reflected in greater amounts of donated money, in greater numbers of individual grants, and in greater numbers of foundations willing to contribute money to black causes. Although total foundation grants for all purposes increased significantly during the 1960s, the increase of grants to black or black-focused groups far outstripped the general trend.

The trend in foundation contributions to black collective action and related areas is consistent with the positive radical flank effect model. To be sure, the correspondence in time of increasing numbers and amounts of grants and the radicalization of portions of the civil rights constituency does not prove that nonviolent protest, black nationalism, or riots were *causes* or even major influences upon foundation priorities. But the targets for which many grants

TABLE 17 Total Foundation Grant Funds, Grants to Movement Organizations, and Other Black-Related Grants[a]

	1961 grants	1965 grants	1970 grants	Rate of growth 1961–65 (percent)	Rate of growth 1965–70	Rate of growth 1960–70
Total foundation grants, all purposes	351,000,000	649,000,000	793,000,000	84.9	22.2	125.9
Foundation grants to movement organizations[b]	346,000	5,630,000	15,622,068	1,527.2	177.5	4,415.0
Non-movement, black-related foundation grants	833,000	24,582,550	17,880,240	2,684.0	−27.3	1,924.9

[a] Source: *Foundation News*, vol. 1–11 (1960–1970)
[b] See n. 13, p. 201.

were earmarked, the magnitude of the increases, and the similarity of the foundation and corporation trends strongly suggest a link between the two. So does a recent finding (Jenkins and Eckert 1986: 825) that foundation support for moderate black organizations *dropped* by more than half during the relatively tranquil period between 1973 and 1980.

Government

Governmental units can support the activities of social movement in several ways (McCarthy and Zald 1973: 12). One is by means of direct funding, as the case of the Community Action Programs underwritten by the Office of Economic Opportunity. Title II of the Economic Opportunity Act of 1964 called for the establishment of local antipoverty programs which would be partly designed and controlled by poor people themselves. This was a comparatively radical concept, since it put a measure of power directly into the hands of the poor and circumvented local political structures. By mandating the "maximum feasible participation" of the poor, the War on Poverty mobilized them to make demands upon municipal governments (Cloward and Piven 1975: 267–83; Piven and Cloward 1971: 261–82).

A second way in which government can support social movement activity is through indirect funding. That is, funds can be provided to organizations for use in something other than social movement activity *per se*. For instance, federal grants for manpower training programs and adult education were made to groups like the National Welfare Rights Organization. Although such grants were not intended to fund claimsmaking *per se*, they did so by providing sustenance for a social movement cadre (McCarthy and Zald 1973: 12). Undoubtedly a great deal of this sort of indirect support took place in the late 1960s. Of the seven groups on which this book focuses, however, specific information on this sort of indirect support is available only for the Urban League. As noted earlier in this chapter, the amounts of federal funds channelled through the League during the late 1960s were quite large.

The groundwork for a partnership between the federal government and the National Urban League was begun in 1962. Through a member of the Democratic National Committee who had been a NUL board member, a meeting was arranged with President Kennedy. At the meeting, Kennedy was reportedly convinced of the wisdom of increased federal involvement in the health, education, welfare, and job training of blacks. Later in the year, another

TABLE 18   Federal Funding of the National Urban League

Year	Amount	Percent of NUL exogenous income
1961	0	0
1962	0	0
1963	0	0
1964	0	0
1965	0	0
1966	294,000	13.4
1967	536,000	19.1
1968	650,000	16.6
1969	3,595,000	41.7
1970	6,913,000	47.5
1971	8,051,000	56.0
1972	13,011,000	74.1
.	.	.
.	.	.
.	.	.
1980	18,183,682	79.1

conference was held which brought League board members together with officials of the Departments of Health, Education, and Welfare and of Labor (National Urban League 1980: 46). By 1966 the NUL was receiving federal money to carry out programs for the disadvantaged; federal funding was growing rapidly, and the NUL increasingly relied upon these funds for its overall budget (Table 18). By the early 1970s the organization had become practically a branch of the federal government.

So far as I have been able to determine, no major black organization except the NUL received funds directly from the federal government. But there were subtle ways in which the government supported those groups with which political elites felt a commonality of interests. In 1963, for example, officials of the Kennedy administration arranged for the Taconic Foundation to make voter registration grants to a consortium of major civil rights groups. As the next chapter will show, these efforts were intended to encourage civil rights forces to shift to safe and politically profitable forms of activism. In addition, the government encouraged much of the increasing involvement of the corporate sector in the urban crisis during the late 1960s (Cohn 1970: 69, 80).

CONCLUSION

This chapter has been concerned with trends in resource mobilization by major black social movement organizations and trends in the contributions to these organizations by various categories of exogenous supporters. Its purpose has been to examine evidence which bears on the notion of radical flank effects.

Because it has not been possible to do a fully controlled study, the conclusions must be treated as preliminary. Bearing in mind this limitation, we are led by the radical flank effect model to look for certain patterns in the data on organizational resource mobilization. Increases or decreases in levels of outside support have been taken as rough indicators of the acceptability or unacceptability of those organizations to funding sources. If negative radical flank effects were taking place through the 1950s and the 1960s, either a decline in exogenous incomes of groups defined as moderate at a given time or a leveling of prior patterns of increasing incomes would be expected. If, however, positive radical flank effects were at work, a pattern of rising exogenous incomes among moderate groups would be expected—a pattern sufficiently strong to be inexplicable in terms of other known factors.

During the period in question, there were indeed notable changes in the income of organizations in the civil rights movement. The most significant of these are summarized below.

1. The total amounts of funds contributed to the seven organizations, taken as a whole, increased dramatically during the late 1950s and the 1960s. Given the concurrent and rapid escalation in black goals and tactics, this pattern is quite consistent with the *positive* radical flank effect model. Overall movement income derived from non-movement sources climbed very slowly during the last half of the 1950s, years during which blacks began to turn to nonviolent protest as a means of securing integrationist goals. During the early 1960s, when the scale of nonviolent protest pushed racial issues to the forefront of the nation's attention, total income increased more rapidly. Then, during the tumultuous years of the mid- and late-1960s, which saw the emergence of black nationalism and urban violence on an unprecedented scale, total movement income dipped for a year in 1966 and then shot rapidly upward.

2. The increases in total movement income, especially during the final period, were primarily a function of vast increases in income for groups perceived as moderate. Those groups which were most radical (CORE and SNCC) or which had until recently been among the most radical (the SCLC) saw their incomes peak in the mid-1960s and then decline precipitously. Those organizations which had come to play the role of moderates (NUL, NAACP, LDEF, and the SRC) were the beneficiaries of most of the new resources which poured into the movement. Again, this is precisely the pattern we would expect a positive radical flank effect to produce.

3. *The increase in the exogenous incomes of moderate groups of the 1960s did not result from a mere reallocation of a fixed sum of resources within the community of black organizations.* That is, the windfall for moderates was not produced by a shift in the loyalties of existing supporters. Such shifts undoubtedly did occur, and they certainly accounted for some part of the moderates' successes in fundraising. But they were largely the product of the injection of staggering amounts of *"new"* resources into moderate groups as the racial crisis deepened.

4. *Although the trends in mobilization of organizational resources fit the model in a general way, my attempts to predict the precise timing of major income changes were unsuccessful.* On the basis of my earlier identification of ideological and strategic watersheds in the history of black claims-making and assuming a lag of approximately one year, I predicted that the largest proportional changes in moderate incomes would occur in 1955, 1958, 1961, 1964–65, and 1967–68. This, however, proved to be inaccurate, although eliminating the lag period improved the fit of the data to the model somewhat. Moreover, it is difficult to interpret this inaccuracy: on the one hand, it might be the result of important factors which have not been incorporated into the model, such as changes in the executive personnel or fund-raising tactics of large organizations, or the impact of outside events; on the other hand, it might be the result of the internal procedures and logic of major corporate or philanthropic funding agencies. Overall, the model is insufficiently elaborate to account for short-term funding changes.

5. *Most of the new resources that went to moderate organizations as radicalism escalated came from "big money" sources: corporations, foundations, and the federal government.* The more militant, protest-oriented groups were dependent during their heydays upon "small money" sources: individuals, churches, labor unions, and other smaller organizations. With the escalation of radicalism in the mid-1960s and the increasing competition from such issues as Vietnam and student issues, many such supporters defected. As a result, these organizations saw their funding base diminish. Nevertheless, both the SCLC and CORE have managed to survive, if in less flamboyant forms.

6. *The contribution patterns among corporations and charitable foundations during the later riot years suggest that a portion of the nation's*

corporate elite recognized that it had a crucial interest in pacifying the black population, particularly in the cities, and in accommodating many black demands. Allen (1969) has described part of this process, particularly in the efforts of the Ford Foundation to co-opt what he describes as bourgeois black nationalists—i.e., groups which appealed to disaffected young blacks but which did not call for major alterations in the institution of private property. Ford's attempt to penetrate the radical flank was somewhat unusual; corporate and foundation resources were more commonly directed toward the moderate organizations (also see Cleghorn 1963; Cohn 1970). But all of the corporate and foundation approaches to increased involvement in racial and ghetto issues had in common the recognition that economic elites shared an interest responding to legitimate black demands. Just as southern businessmen had agreed to cooperate in the process of change when they realized the economic costs of racial turmoil, northern economic elites saw that "blacks must be brought into the mainstream of the economy if they would no longer remain docile while confined outside of it" (Allen 1969: 212). In other words, radicals helped moderates make their case. Only in the glow of burning cities did many powerful elites find "enlightenment"—an enlightenment that had eluded them through years of cajoling by the Urban League and the NAACP. Only then did they come to realize that the integration of black people into American society was an issue so vital that their vast resources should be marshaled on its behalf.

3   Radicals, Moderates, and the Federal Government

In the years following the Second World War, the official stance of the federal government toward the civil rights and economic welfare of American blacks underwent a sweeping transformation, the extent of which can be gauged by a comparison of the activity of the postwar era with that during the first half of the twentieth century. For example, Congress passed no civil rights legislation through the period from the end of Reconstruction to the late 1950s; then, between 1957 and 1968, five such laws were enacted. A similar pattern occurred in the executive and judicial branches, both of which had been only slightly more responsive to black claims than the Congress until the postwar years. After that, and especially during the 1960s, favorable court decisions, executive orders, and federal programs became much more numerous. More important than the number of federal responses, however, was their *content*: the laws and public policies enacted during the 1960s, though controversial, would have been unthinkable in past decades.

Viewed from the perspective of social justice rather than practical politics, these governmental responses took far too long to arrive and accomplished far too little. Despite the real benefits achieved, blacks still rank far below whites in various measures of socioeconomic status.[1] But recognition of these realities should not divert attention from one centrally important fact: *Most of the civil rights policy of this century emerged during a remarkably short time.* That is, pro–civil rights actions did not evolve gradually but rather burst forth in little more than one tumultuous decade (Table 19).

Just *why* and *how* did this transformation of civil rights policy take place? For answers to these questions, we must examine the

TABLE 19 The Achievement of Major Black Claims

Claim	Approximate date of origin	First congressional consideration	Achievement
EDUCATION			
Prohibition of *de jure* school segregation	late 1930s	1946	1954 (Supreme Court)
Withholding of federal aid to enforce school desegregation	1955		1964 (HEW)
Federal aid for school desegregation		1959	1964 (Civil Rights Act)
Authorization of Justice Department to file suit		1956	1964 (Civil Rights Act)
Attack on northern school segregation	early 1960s		1968 (HEW)
Attack on de facto school segregation	mid-1960s		1971 (Supreme Court)
Concentration of resources on black education	1963		1965 (Elementary and Secondary Educ. Act)
Black control of black community schools	mid-1960s		
VOTING RIGHTS			
Elimination of poll tax in federal elections	pre–WWII	1945	1962 (Congressional approval of amendment) 1964 (ratification)
Elimination of poll tax in all elections	pre–WWII		1966 (Supreme Court)
Full Justice Department enforcement powers	1956	1956	
Prohibition of discriminatory literacy tests			1965 (Voting Rights Act)
Use of federal marshals to enforce voting rights	early 1960s		

TABLE 19 Continued

Claim	Approximate date of origin	First congressional consideration	Achievement
EMPLOYMENT			
Prohibition of employment discrimination	post–WWII	1949	1964 (Civil Rights Act)
Permanent Employment Commission with enforcement powers	1943	1945	
Prohibition of discrimination by labor unions	late 1940s	1949	1964 (Civil Rights Act)
Federal jobs programs for the unemployed	early 1960s		1964 (Economic Opportunity Act)
Compensatory hiring of black workers	1961		(Early-1970s Affirmative Action Policies)
PUBLIC ACCOMMODATIONS			
Prohibition of discrimination in transportation	1942	1954	1946 (Supreme Court) 1950 (Supreme Court) 1955 (ICC) 1960 (Civil Rights Act)
Prohibition of discrimination in hotels, services, recreation, etc.	1942	1963	1961 (ICC) 1964 (Civil Rights Act)
HOUSING			
Nondiscrimination in public and federally assisted housing	pre–WWII	1949	1962 (Executive Order)
Prohibition of restrictive covenants	post–WWII		1948 (Supreme Court)
General open housing legislation	1950s	1966	1968 (Civil Rights Act)

TABLE 19   Continued

Claim	Approximate date of origin	First congressional consideration	Achievement
Improved ghetto housing	early 1960s		
OTHER			
Antilynching law	pre–WWII	1948	(Civil Rights Act of 1960 and Voting Rights Act of 1965 contained antiterrorism provisions
Denial of tax-exempt status to institutions practicing discrimination	post–WWII	1950	
Senate rule to limit filibusters	post–WWII		
General federal enforcement powers	1956	1956	

timing and nature of federal responses to black claims. The study of radical flank effects would lead us to expect that significant changes in societal and governmental reactions to the claims of moderates in a social movement would take place during periods in which socially-defined radicalism is increasing and/or periods in which new or more militant organizations are emerging in the movement. If *negative* radical flank effects occurred, there would be a trend away from favorable civil rights policy at the federal level. If *positive* radical flank effects occurred, the trends would be toward favorable civil rights policy. In short, we would expect to see changes in the federal government's responsiveness to the goals of *moderates* during those years when new forms of militancy were appearing.

But what are the specific times when such changes should appear? As was the case with the analysis of funding patterns (Chapter 2), the rapidity with which the ideological and tactical nature of black collective action changed makes it difficult to pinpoint specific years. On the most general level we are left with the expectation of considerable policy change through at least 1968. Assuredly, such constant change did occur, and we shall explore it further in this chapter. Still, certain years do stand out as likely springboards for radical flank effects. Nineteen sixty is such a year: the student sit-ins of that spring made up the first wave of *mass* direct action. The years 1963 and 1964 are even more likely to show government actions related to the radical flank, since this period was the high tide of direct action, the March on Washington, and the first northern urban riots. With 1965 came the Selma spectacle and, in Watts, the first truly devastating urban riot; 1966 was the point at which black power began to be articulated publicly. In 1967 and 1968 urban rioting continued and there emerged revolutionary black nationalist groups which received publicity disproportionate to their size and influence. Nevertheless, in the public mind, urban riots, armed nationalists, and black power rhetoric often appeared to be parts of the same growing crisis. The decline in urban violence after 1968, however, reduced this sense of urgency somewhat.

This chapter begins with a discussion of the structure of civil rights politics in the postwar era—that is, it describes the major actors in the continuing drama, their interrelationships, and their competing interests. The chapter continues with a summary of the timing of federal policy actions in those areas that have been of major concern to movement groups—such areas as education, voting rights and their enforcement, employment practices, discrimination in public accommodations and facilities, housing—and discusses their correspondence to goals of the movement and the degree to which these state actions appear to have been responses to escalating black militancy. As we shall see, the timing and nature of federal actions was generally consistent with the pattern of a positive radical flank effect.

Mere correspondence in time and content, of course, is not entirely conclusive. That is, it does not prove that governmental decisionmakers were motivated by the deepening racial crisis to accommodate the demands of moderates. The third section of the chapter will go further, providing an inside look at political decisionmaking through a case study of the administration of John F. Kennedy and its response to major racial crises in 1961 and 1963. Archival material will be used to show that the fear of escalating black militancy and the threat of black violence were indeed among the primary considerations in the administration's key civil rights decisions, at least during those years.

THE STRUCTURE OF FEDERAL CIVIL RIGHTS POLITICS

Federal policymaking is a complex game involving many players. This has been particularly true of civil rights policy-making during the postwar period. It is essential to understand that the fate of rights-expanding policies and laws has not been determined solely by the degree of good will or "enlightenment" among powerholders. Rather, it has emerged within a *structure of political interests* surrounding the governmental apparatus. In the context of this structure, radical flank effects must be seen as patterns of events which condition the ways in which major players define their interests.

Within the federal government, the development of civil rights and social welfare policy has been shaped by the conflict, compromise, and behind-the-scenes machinations of several key players, including Presidents and their administrations, the national political party organizations, the southern wing of the Democratic party, the federal bureaucracy, business, and other special interest groups with regular access to political decision-making. Outside the centers of power, other players by their actions and interests, have created the contexts of policy decisions. Most notable among these have been the civil rights movement and the anti–civil rights countermovement (first in the South and later in the urban centers of the North), each with its own moderate and radical flanks. Although the goal of this book is to assess the significance of certain processes emanating from black collective action, it would be a gross oversimplification to view policy as a two-way process involving only two monolithic entities, the movement and the government. Like the civil rights movement, the anti–civil rights countermovement and the government itself were divided into numerous camps with diverse perspectives and interests. And though these divisions, outside the scope of the present research, must of necessity be given less than their share of attention, they form a significant backdrop.

Undeniably, a number of politicians and government functionaries of the 1950s and 1960s were idealists driven by a sense of morality. But it would be naive to view such idealism as the central moving force in the formation of policy. For instance, it was becoming apparent by as early as the late 1940s that Supreme Court decisions and registration campaigns had made the black vote increasingly important in American politics (Newman et al. 1978: 13–14). Both major parties attempted to stress the "progressive" nature of their civil rights positions in the campaigns of 1952 and 1956, and most political observers credit John F. Kennedy's narrow victory in the 1960 general election to his virtual monopolization of the black vote (Lawson 1976: 256–57, Newman et al. 1978: 14–19). Still, black voting power is not enough to explain the "revolution" in federal policy. If it were, then the transition toward pro–civil rights policy would have appeared in the late 1940s or the early 1950s.

One of the factors complicating the balance between black voting power and political response has been the internal structure of the Democratic party. Since the shift of black allegiance from the Republicans to the Democrats and the concentration of the black electorate in northern cities, Democratic administrations have been forced to walk a tightrope: overzealousness in appealing to black voters threatened to produce a politically disastrous alienation of the southern wing of the party. The southern and northern branches had been ideologically divided for many years, but a complete breakdown in the fragile detente between the two could render any Democratic administration impotent—not only because the southerners' congressional votes were necessary but also because they controlled strategic committee seats (see Lytle 1966: 276–77). Had it not been for this strangely schizoid character of the party, a remnant of the Reconstruction, there is good reason to believe that certain pro–civil rights policy items would have emerged at least a few years sooner and much less painfully than they actually did. The deterioration in the relations between civil rights activists and the federal government during the early and mid-sixties was largely a result of the Democrats' inability to reach an internal agreement.

The tendency for bureaucratic structures to become self-perpetuating and to serve their own organizational ends has long been recognized (Clark 1948: 425–29; Merton 1962: 253–55; Michels 1959: 365–92; Perrow 1968: 309; Selznick, 1943: 49). During the 1960s, the federal service bureaucracy became a policy force in its own right. The programs of the War on Poverty were formulated and administered mostly by people not directly dependent upon the whims of the voters. As such, upper-level civil servants and political appointees came to be key actors in the policymaking process, and perhaps more importantly, in the process of policy implementation. In playing their role, they changed the character of federal-local relations and often came into conflict with local officials (Donovan 1967: 39–48; Pressman and Wildavsky 1973: 52, 94–101).

Special interests, especially corporate groups, also played a role in the formulation and implementation of federal civil rights policy. As the focus of black collective action moved northward and into the cities, the interests of the business sector in racial matters became well defined. Corporations had much to gain or lose as federal policy reached into employment practices and as the large cities from which they drew both a work force and a customer base began to explode in violence. Before the 1960s drew to a close, corporate involvement in policy toward minorities and corporate "investment" in black organizations and projects expanded. Both the Labor Department's "Philadelphia Plan" and the "Big Business Program" announced by the Johnson administration in October 1967, for example, sought to solve the urban crisis through economic development.

Other important parties in the structure of civil rights politics were the civil rights movement itself and the largely southern countermovement. Although it is the interplay between *black* militants and moderates that is the subject of this book, we should remember that the anti–civil rights countermovement also had its moderate and radical wings. Students of the civil rights movement agree that the vicious treatment of peaceful demonstrators in the South by racist white citizens and police played an important part in galvanizing northern support for black aims. Not only were such brutal reactions widely publicized by the print and electronic media, but they sometimes occurred immediately prior to key decisions in federal policy. For example, the passage of the 1965 Voting Rights Act may have been facilitated by the particularly ugly confrontation in Selma, Alabama, although it is difficult to gauge the incident's importance precisely. Similarly, the Civil Rights Act of 1968 was passed only seven days after the assassination of Martin Luther King.

There is also some evidence that the actions of antiblack extremists served to soften the stance of more moderate segregationists. Powledge contends that many southern elites saw violent repression of demonstrators, like the demonstrations themselves, as bad for business (1967: 27–32). Such persons, with a vested interest in the creation of a "New South," eventually learned to prevent trouble by anticipating it and taking the initiative in preparing their cities for inevitable changes and by seeking out black leaders with whom they could negotiate. Thus, it may well be that radical flank effects occurred in the countermovement as well as in the civil rights movement itself.

In sum, the political processes behind the enactment of various items of civil rights policy are complex and no single item, including radical flank effects, can be treated as the only factor. But we shall see that the timing of pro-black federal policy, like the patterns observed in the financial support of black organizations, supports the hypothesis that radical flank effects were important influences on many of the events of the 1960s.

FEDERAL RESPONSIVENESS ACROSS THREE ERAS OF PROTEST

In an important sense, the origins of American federal civil rights policy were in the years immediately following the Civil War. The Thirteenth Amendment to the Constitution, ratified in 1865, outlawed slavery in the United States, and the ratification of the Fourteenth Amendment three years later gave federal and state citizenship to blacks and prohibited states from passing laws which would deprive any persons of their basic rights. The Fifteenth Amendment, ratified in 1870, prohibited the denial of the right to vote to anyone on the basis of race. Moreover, five major civil rights laws were passed by Congress between 1866 and 1875 (Congressional Quarterly Service 1968: 2; Wolk 1971: 30–31). But by 1910, nearly all of the protections put in place during the Reconstruction years had been effectively neutralized through judicial modification (Congressional Quarterly Service 1968: 2; Woodward 1966: 70–71). The Reconstruction era had been the first golden age of civil rights, but it was followed by a period of neglect and retrogression which lasted through the Second World War.

The Era of Legalism: 1945–1954

During the late 1940s and the early 1950s, the civil rights movement was dominated by the NAACP. The National Urban League was timidly apolitical, giving most of its attention to providing services for blacks and appealing on a case-by-case basis to the profit motives of businessmen. CORE was small and increasingly ineffectual. Numerous local groups, especially leagues of black voters in certain southern cities, directed their efforts toward small improvements in the lives of blacks. But it was the NAACP that was building the foundation for the massive collective action that was to come.

The NAACP's dogged pursuit of racial integration and nondiscrimination through legal and legislative routes made it, for all practical purposes, the radical vanguard of black collective action. In the years between the end of the war and 1954, the NAACP achieved the very sort of record that one might expect from a group widely designated as radical. In the courts, where decisions are based more upon technical legal grounds than upon purely political considerations, it made great strides. The Congress and the Executive branch, however, were quite unresponsive.

In the field of education, for instance, success came solely through the courts. The Supreme Court's 1949 decision in *Sweatt v. Painter* held that the denial of admission of a black student to a southern law school was a violation of the principle of separate-but-equal education. In 1950, moreover, the court stated in *McLaurin v. Oklahoma State Regents* that the mere admission of black students was not sufficient to satisfy their constitutional rights; rather, they must be treated equally and given access to the same facilities as whites. These two cases removed major legal obstacles preventing federally-mandated school integration (Kluger 1976: 284). On May 17, 1954, the Supreme Court reached the logical conclusion of the NAACP/LDEF education cases with its decision in *Brown v. Board of Education*. The notion of separate-but-equal was declared to be a fiction and legally segregated education a denial of equal protection under the law. During the same period, however, Congress twice failed to act on amendments which would have denied federal funds to states or schools which maintained segregated educational arrangements.

A similar pattern appeared in the area of voting rights, where a major issue was the use of poll taxes to disenfranchise blacks (Meier 1963: 438). Such fees were a transparent means of depriving citizens of the right to vote, and between 1942 and 1949, the House of Representatives passed no fewer than five bills which would have invalidated the tax in federal elections. On each occasion, though, the bill died in the Senate. Thus, even mild civil rights reforms were difficult to achieve through legislative means during the legalistic period, and blatant denials of citizenship rights were allowed to persist.

During the postwar period the single organizational goal most actively pursued by civil rights forces was the creation of a strong Fair Employment Practices Commission (FEPC) to fight job discrimination. Although both the NUL and CORE favored this goal, it was again the NAACP which pursued it most energetically in

Washington. Two FEPC bills died in the House, which nevertheless consented to an extraordinarily weak *voluntary* commission; four were killed by the Senate. In addition, legislation aimed against discrimination in the armed services and in labor unions failed to gain Congressional support.

While fair employment efforts were being battered in Congress, some very limited gains were made through Executive Orders (Morgan 1970: 29, 44–45). These presidential measures were better than nothing, but they fell far short of the strong and permanent FEPC which the NAACP had called the "No. 1 objective" in the civil rights program (Morgan 1970: 32).

Yet another major policy area of interest to civil rights groups was public accommodations. The NUL, the NAACP, the LDEF, and CORE all fought against formal and informal barriers to the use of hotels, restaurants, recreational facilities, and the like by blacks on an equal basis. The NAACP, focusing much of its effort during the period on discriminatory accommodations in transportation, sought both judicial and executive remedies. Again the courts yielded, while the more politically-oriented legislative and executive branches gave no ground. The 1946 decision in *Morgan v. Virginia* invalidated segregation on interstate motor carriers, and a 1950 ruling in *Henderson v. U.S.* extended to interstate rail travel (Congressional Quarterly Service 1968: 7). In Congress, however, a bill which would have prohibited segregation in *all* interstate transportation died in committee.

Although it was not so salient an issue as it would become during the sixties, segregated housing was opposed in principle by all the active national civil rights organizations. The NAACP scored a significant victory in 1948 when the Supreme Court, in *Shelly v. Kraemer*, ruled that restrictive covenants forbidding the sale of property to blacks could not be enforced by the courts. But legislative amendments which would have prohibited bias in the rental of public housing units were defeated three times in the House of Representatives and twice in the Senate between 1949 and 1954. The House also failed to append a nondiscrimination clause to the Military Housing Act in 1949.

The Era of Direct Action Integrationism: 1955–1963

The NAACP and the Legal Defense Fund had been overwhelmingly successful in pursuing desegregation through the courts, in spite of their utter failure to move the Congress. But the South was quick to demonstrate that it would not allow court decisions to change the status quo without exhausting every means of resistance at its disposal. In reaction, civil rights activists took to the streets. The tide of demonstrations became a torrent after the Greensboro student sit-ins of 1960, increasing the sense of crisis and changing the character of black radicalism. The "radicals" of the pre-*Brown* era, most notably the NAACP, became the "moderates" of the direct action period. And with this shift came a gradual concurrent shift in the responsiveness of the federal government toward longstanding integrationist goals.

Through most of the direct action period, the record of civil rights victories was unspectacular. In education, for instance, civil rights advocates were unable to persuade the federal government to set firm deadlines for school desegregation or to force southern compliance through the withholding of funds. Moreover, Congress failed to approve proposals for technical assistance to districts undergoing integration and twice denied legislation that would have authorized the Attorney General to initiate lawsuits in school desegregation, voting rights, and other cases.[2]

Other efforts of the movement also met with frustration. Attempts to deny jury trials in civil contempt proceedings against those charged with violating civil rights failed, thus virtually insuring that southern whites would be acquitted of such charges by their peers. Provisions which would have empowered the President to appoint registrars to oversee voting practices in the South were weakened during debate over the Civil Rights Act of 1960. The discriminatory use of literacy tests as impediments to black voting was attacked by the NAACP but remained untouched by federal action. All of the organizations that were active in the South—the NAACP, the SCLC, SNCC, and CORE—remained dissatisfied with the federal government's actions on voting rights and its failure to use marshals and troops to insure the safety of southern protesters.

In the area of employment discrimination, civil rights groups continued to meet with frustration in their efforts to secure a strong and permanent Fair Employment Practices Commission. Antidiscrimination amendments to an armed forces bill were defeated in 1955. In addition, attempts to deny federal assistance for racially restricted housing and to ban segregation in public housing failed repeatedly (Hughes 1962: 200; Parris and Brooks 1971: 407). And although President Kennedy had promised to eliminate discrimination in federally-assisted housing by executive order (Brauer 1977:

43; Morgan, 1970: 69), he failed to do so until 1962—and his long-awaited fulfillment of the campaign pledge was far more limited than activists had hoped (Harvey 1971: 29–30; Morgan 1970: 72–75; Sundquist 1968: 258).

But in spite of these disappointments, there were more successes than during any other period since Reconstruction. The University of Alabama was ordered to admit a black student in 1956. Federal troops were used to enforce desegregation at Little Rock's Central High School in 1957 and at the University of Mississippi in 1962. Moreover, civil rights laws, though weak and dealing mostly with voting procedures, were passed by Congress in 1957 and 1960. Significantly, most of the major victories came between 1961 and 1963, when nonviolent tactics were building toward their peak. Under President Kennedy the Department of Justice and the Department of Health, Education, and Welfare began to take a far more active role in bringing about southern compliance with the law than they had under the Eisenhower administration. Congress finally approved an anti–poll tax provision in 1962, though in the form of a proposed constitutional amendment rather than as a law. In 1961 Kennedy's Executive Order 10925 created a President's Committee on Equal Employment Opportunity, the strongest such committee yet formed. In a significant public accommodations case decided in 1960, *Boynton v. Virginia*, the Supreme Court ruled that segregation in bus terminal restaurants was unconstitutional. Kennedy, believing that segregated facilities were the major cause of black unrest, directed the cabinet departments to take a more active role in combatting these abuses. In response to a 1961 request by Attorney General Robert Kennedy, the Interstate Commerce Commission extended its nondiscrimination guidelines to bus terminals. In addition, the Justice Department brought suits against a number of airports on the grounds that the Federal Airport Act prohibited racial discrimination in such facilities.

The most significant governmental response to demands by the civil rights movement during its direct action phase came during 1963 when President Kennedy, feeling the intense pressure of a deepening and ever more dangerous racial crisis, transformed a meager package of legislative requests into what was to become the Civil Rights Act of 1964. When finally submitted to Congress, the administration's bill sought authorization for the government to file suit to desegregate schools and to cut off federal aid to *any* program that was discriminatory in character; strengthened the enforcement of nondiscrimination clauses in government contracts; prohibited segregation in a wide range of public facilities, such as hotels, restaurants, and retail stores; and created a permanent Commission on Civil Rights to oversee federal civil rights activities and policies and to make recommendations. Later in this chapter the expansion of Kennedy's civil rights bill will be analyzed in greater depth.

This general pattern of governmental action on civil rights fits the positive radical flank effect model. Again, this is not to say that radical flank effects were the only factors at work. The ideological balance in Congress, for instance, was an especially important determinant of the fate of civil rights legislation. After briefly losing control of both houses in the elections of 1952 and reestablishing only slim majorities in 1954 and 1956, the Democratic party scored an astounding victory in the congressional elections of 1958. That election also moved Congress toward the liberal end of the spectrum, but not very far. For one thing, party affiliation and ideology are entirely different matters; southern Democrats remained the staunchest foes of civil rights legislation and they used their influential committee posts to fight it. Moreover, even after 1960, Congress was "formally Democratic but actually narrowly balanced between activists and conservatives" (Sundquist 1968: 478). Changes in the ideological makeup of Congress thus do not appear to have been the primary factors in civil rights politics in the era of direct action integrationism (also see Burstein 1985: 122).

Another reason for increased governmental responsiveness was the inauguration of a new administration. Eisenhower's commitment to civil rights was less than either Truman's or Kennedy's. He was willing to use his executive power to fight discrimination only in a manner consistent with the states' rights doctrine. The Kennedy administration did not share Eisenhower's views on the necessity of a limited central government. Thus, it was free to act more decisively from the start. But the simple fact of a change in the occupant of the White House is not enough by itself to explain the trend toward greater federal action under Kennedy. The new President was not known as a champion of minority interests and did little during the first two years of his tenure to gain such a reputation. As will be seen in a case study of the Kennedy administration later in this chapter, his change of heart owed much to the increasing fervor of black protest and the increasingly harsh southern reaction it provoked.

The Era of the New Radicalism: 1964–1970

The mid-1960s ushered in new forms of black radicalism, all sharing the common themes of black self-determination and self-defense. Thus, the expected victims or beneficiaries of radical flank effects during this period include the SCLC as well as the NAACP, the LDEF, and the Urban League. We would expect radical flank effects to be relatively limited through 1966—i.e., before the severe disorders and the mass media's sensationalizing of black power—and to taper off and decline after 1968, the year of the last major riots and perhaps the zenith of the new radicalism.

But in fact, an examination of federal policy patterns between 1964 and 1970 produces mixed results. For the first part of this period, the effect of the escalating crisis seems to have been positive: as the new forms of black militancy were emerging in the mid-1960s, the responsiveness of the government increased. More civil rights policy was enacted during the years from 1964 through 1968 than ever before.

The Civil Rights Act of 1964. If one federal action deserves to be singled out as a truly enormous victory for moderate organizations in the movement, it would be the Civil Rights Act of 1964. Although the law hardly pleased everyone, it included long-awaited responses to the demands of moderates in four major areas. Title I added significantly to existing laws on voting rights by barring the unequal application of requirements and the use of minor omissions and errors on application forms to invalidate registrations, and by restricting the use of literacy tests. The remaining weaknesses in enforcement provisions were partially remedied in 1965 through the Voting Rights Act. Title II satisfied a long-standing demand for a broad legal prohibition of restricted public accommodations. To CORE and SNCC, both of which had become disillusioned with the capacity of legislation to effect change, this title was no landmark. But in satisfying a central goal of the NAACP and the SCLC dating back to the 1940s, Title II alone approached the *Brown* decision in importance. The Attorney General was authorized to bring a civil action in cases in which a *pattern* of violation was evident, and Title III authorized the Justice Department to file suits to desegregate state or locally owned public facilities against which a complaint had been filed. Title I prohibited federal assistance to institutions and programs which practiced racial discrimination. Finally, Title VI of the 1964 law made most forms of job discrimination unlawful, thus answering demands dating back to at least 1949, and created a new Equal Employment Opportunity Commission empowered to investigate and mediate, but not enforce (Burstein 1985: 2–9). The bill easily passed the House; the real test came in the Senate, which for the first time in history voted to shut off a southern-led filibuster and vote on the bill. Success was the result of a complex confluence of historical and strategic forces (see Lytle 1966). But one of the most important of these was the perception, stated by Senator Everett Dirksen—never before a supporter of civil rights laws—that civil rights was "an idea whose time has come."

Voting rights. The time had also come for further insurances of equal voting rights. The Twenty-fourth Amendment to the Constitution, ratified in 1964, finally prohibited the requirement of poll taxes. That same year, in *Anderson v. Martin*, the Supreme Court banned the listing of candidates by race on local ballots. The Voting Rights Act of 1965 contained most of the remaining provisions that civil rights organizations had been seeking. It went beyond earlier legislation's reliance on individual complaints and litigation by instituting a "triggering formula" to identify chronic violators among southern states (Lawson 1976: 312). For those states it empowered federal examiners to determine voting qualifications, suspended the use of literacy tests under certain specific conditions, required Justice Department approval of any new voting regulations, and restricted the use of poll taxes in state and local elections. It also empowered voting examiners to impound ballots and to supervise voting and vote-counting in affected areas, and it established criminal penalties for voting rights infringements and voting fraud. But a provision that would have authorized intervention by federal registrars whenever it was determined that *any form* of illicit barrier to voting existed failed to make it into the final bill, thus preserving several means of disenfranchising blacks (Lawson 1976: 313–14).

Poverty. Up until 1961 or 1962, civil rights and black economic welfare were two more or less distinct sets of issues so far as movement groups were concerned. With the exception of the National Urban League, the civil rights organizations did not directly address welfare issues. But in the early 1960s, this began to change. CORE and SNCC were the first to direct attention to economic issues other than fair employment. Both stressed the need to provide meaningful jobs for the unemployed, to feed the hungry, and to bring about decent housing and health care. Martin Luther King also moved into the economic sphere, especially after the Selma campaign of 1965 (Brooks 1974: 275-77).

The period from 1964 through 1970 saw a vast expansion of federal welfare efforts, much of which was aimed at the urban black poor. The most significant aspect of this expansion was the declaration of a War on Poverty and the creation of the Office of Economic Opportunity. Although these programs bore the signature of President Lyndon Johnson and were constructed after he took office, their foundation was laid late in the Kennedy administration (Donovan 1967: 23-24). Unlike much other civil rights policy, the War on Poverty cannot be seen as a *direct* response to *specific* claims of the movement. When the antipoverty programs were being conceived, existing movement organizations had not yet formulated coherent agendas for action against poverty. In fact, the immediate impetus for the programs seems to have come exclusively from within the administration. It is fairly clear, however, that the administration's new programs were conditioned by the general goals of the movement.

Although the War on Poverty consisted of a wide range of programs, its beginning was signified by the passage of the Economic Opportunity Act on July 23, 1964. The major provisions of the Act included: (a) a federal job program (the Job Corps), a work-training program (later named the Neighborhood Youth Corps), and a work-study program for students; (b) a Community Action Program, providing for the development of antipoverty efforts financed up to 90 percent by the federal government and to be "developed, conducted, and administered with the maximum feasible participation of the residents of the areas and members of the groups served," an Adult Basic Education Program, and a preschool program for deprived children (later named Project Head Start); (c) rural poverty programs; (d) a program of small business loans, and (e) the Office of Economic Opportunity to coordinate the various aspects of the War on Poverty and related programs, Volunteers in Service to America (VISTA), and advisory mechanisms related to the OEO.

Surprisingly, the Economic Opportunity Act passed through Congress with few difficulties. But the period of calm was short. The Community Action Program became particularly controversial, as did the Job Corps. By 1966 Congress began earmarking appropriations so as to limit such items and to channel more money into popular programs like Project Head Start. Although appropriations climbed through 1971, the Eighty-ninth and Ninetieth Congresses refused to expand the funding of the antipoverty programs to the degree the administration desired. By the middle of the more tranquil and fiscally conservative 1970s, OEO had ceased to exist.

Though it would be incorrect to ascribe the War on Poverty solely to political decision-makers' fears of social turmoil, it is clear that the Economic Opportunity Act of 1964 might have been seen as an effective insurance policy. As originally passed, it *restructured* conventional politics on the local level by giving to the urban poor both tangible services and a mechanism by which to act in their own behalf through approved channels. As Piven and Cloward have noted, many of the framers of the Great Society hoped that the allegiance of the urban black vote to the national Democratic party could be secured by bypassing unresponsive local powerholders. (1971: 261–63; Cloward and Piven 1975: 268–70). This was a very big gamble, of course, as those very local elites were also important to the party's fate. But the schism between the northern and southern wings made the concentrated black vote increasingly crucial, and the gamble appeared to be worth it. Thus, the War on Poverty was a response to political turmoil, which included political realignments as well as increasing black volatility. While not intended solely as a means to "moderate disorder in the ghettos" (Cloward and Piven 1975: 265), it was meant to channel disorder in ways favorable to the interests of those in power.

Needless to say, the federal government's antipoverty efforts were not confined to the Office of Economic Opportunity. Other government actions of the late 1960s involved expansions of the Aid to Families with Dependent Children (AFDC), food stamps, and federal employment programs. Overall, both welfare eligibility policies and food stamp exchange levels during the final years of the decade were liberalized (Sobel 1977: 42, 46–47). In fact, caseloads and costs of such "traditional" welfare programs skyrocketed. Total national welfare expenditures rose from about $4 billion to nearly $15 billion between 1960 and 1970, with the greatest increases occurring in large cities after 1964. According to Piven and Cloward, the expansion of the AFDC program was in large part a result of the War on Poverty itself: as Title II programs bypassed local power structures and forged a direct relationship between the urban poor and the federal government, the poor were mobilized on the grass-roots level to make greater demands on county and city governments (1971: 196–98, 285–90, 329–30).

But Piven and Cloward maintain that the expansion of welfare, like the War on Poverty, was also facilitated in part by the urban violence of 1964 through 1968 (Piven and Cloward, 1977: 272–273).[3] This thesis has proved controversial. Some researchers, such as Albritton (1979), have found that the expansion of AFDC caseloads and benefit levels were related to policy changes occurring *before* the riots. Berkowitz (1974) concluded that whatever changes in relief policies may have occurred, they had negligible effects on income, employment and housing in riot areas. Feagin and Hahn (1973) and Welch (1975) have presented evidence indicating that the primary lasting effect of riots was to increase expenditures for law enforcement rather than for welfare. On the other hand, several studies have yielded results that are generally consistent with the Piven and Cloward position (Betz 1974; Button 1978; Hicks and Swank 1983; Isaac and Kelly 1981; Schram and Turbett 1983).

The Civil Rights Act of 1968. Like the trend toward higher rates of external income for moderate black organizations, the winning streak in civil rights policy was temporarily halted in 1966. The primary setback came with the failure of the Senate to shut off a filibuster on the 1966 Civil Rights Act, which had been passed by the House. Had it passed the Senate as well, the bill would have banned racial discrimination in the sale and rental of most private housing and added to the Attorney General's existing enforcement powers in the field of school desegregation. The setback of 1966 proved to be temporary, however, and the housing provisions of the bill were reintroduced by the administration the next year. No final action was taken in 1967, but in the midst of the 1968 rioting Congress unexpectedly passed it. The Civil Rights Act of 1968 (PL90-284) banned racial restrictions in the financing, sale, and rental of approximately 80 percent of all housing by 1970. The primary weakness of the law was that it conveyed no direct enforcement powers to a federal agency. Nevertheless, the bill had to weather strong opposition from real estate interests, and most moderate civil rights leaders were jubilant when it passed.

Besides the legislation of 1964, 1965, and 1968, other civil rights accomplishments occurred during the era of the new militancy. A few of these addressed new demands by the movement which were first voiced during the 1960s. For instance, a federal judge ordered Washington, D.C. to end *de facto* segregation in its schools—i.e. segregation based on residential patterns rather than overt restric-

148 tions. This was the first of a series of favorable court rulings on this issue; by the 1970s busing would become widespread and demands would be heard that *de facto* desegregation efforts be launched on a metropolitan basis. Attempts to address the problem through legislation had failed in 1964 and 1965. Several of the War on Poverty programs addressed new demands for special attention to minority children's needs, as did Title I of the Elementary and Secondary Education Act of 1965 (James 1972: 81). New HEW rules issued in 1968 applied, for the first time, to northern as well as southern schools. Although they did not require the correction of school segregation resulting strictly from housing patterns, they did prohibit the denial of education "generally obtained" by other students strictly on the basis of race, religion, or origin. Demands by black power advocates for black control of schools in their communities met with failure. Although new black demands for *preferential* hiring of blacks to remedy past discrimination were not completely embraced by the federal government, efforts were launched to attract business investment to black communities and to encourage employment of minorities in the private sector (Adams and Burke 1970: 156).

Most of the remaining federal actions, however, addressed "old" movement goals—that is, goals which were consistent with moderate integrationism and had been pursued for many years—rather than newly emerged demands. Such federal actions included Supreme Court rulings for bidding poll taxes in states known to be chronic violators of voting rights (*Harper v. Virginia State Board of Education, Butts v. Harrison*), a 1969 decision stipulating that school desegregation must begin "at once" rather than "with all deliberate speed" as specified in the 1954 decision (Adams and Burke 1970: 159), and President Johnson's executive orders strengthening fair federal employment procedures (Morgan 1970: 88). Perhaps most importantly, the 1964–1970 period saw the executive and judicial branches take more initiative and become much more aggressively involved in pursuing racial equality in education, voting, employment, and public accommodations.

All in all, the federal government was more receptive to movement claims during 1964–1970 than ever before. It responded far less to the demands of black nationalists and black power advocates, however, than to the goals of those who had preceded them. The new laws and policies were overwhelmingly integrationist—based, albeit imperfectly, on movement claims dating back years and even decades. The antipoverty program of the Johnson administration and other policy items addressed the grievances of the ghettos, to be sure, but in ways quite consistent with demands, such as for jobs and housing, that the SCLC, the NAACP, CORE, and the Urban League had voiced between 1961 and 1963. These federal responses generally support the pattern of *positive radical flank effects*. However, the analysis of the 1964–1970 period does not suggest that federal responsiveness was markedly enhanced during 1967 and 1968. Although no devastating backlash took place, the trend toward major civil rights policy seems to have reached its peak in 1964 and 1965 rather than during the high points of nationalism and civil disorder. For the first two years of the period, civil rights moderates established momentum in all three branches of the government. After 1966 the *consistency* of pro-black federal actions declined. This discontinuity suggests that there is no linear relationship between increasing radicalism and government response, but rather that escalations may reach thresholds or points of diminishing returns beyond which government responses reverse themselves.

THE KENNEDY ADMINISTRATION AND RACIAL CRISIS, 1961–1963

Thus far, we have seen that the temporal pattern of federal actions on civil rights and racial issues, when examined throughout the legalistic, direct action, and "new radicalism" eras of black protest, are consistent with a positive radical flank effect explanation. That is, the government's responsiveness to the demands of *moderates* has tended to vary in proportion to tactical and/or ideological escalations by more militant groups. But though the patterns described in the first part of this chapter support such an interpretation, they are not conclusive. We can only infer that concern over a deepening racial crisis was a prime motivation for the decisions of policy-makers. Without more solid evidence from specific decision-making episodes, then, radical flank effects are stalled at the point of *plausibility*.

A close and detailed examination of each important accomplishment by the movement—i.e., each law, presidential order, or Supreme Court ruling—is far beyond the limits of this study. In this section, however, I shall examine a particularly illuminating case:

the civil rights record of the administration of President John F. Kennedy. The focus will be upon selected administration actions, each of which represents a hesitant response to a crisis generated by escalating black activism. This general theme is not new: previous writers such as Miroff (1976), Navasky (1971), Piven and Cloward (1977), and Zinn (1965) have also characterized the Kennedy administration as a reluctant ally of the black movement. My hypothesis, however, is that the administration's response to the escalating racial crisis developed through two phases. The first of these phases is seen most clearly in the *Voter Education Project*, a foundation-sponsored voter registration drive begun in early 1962, which represented for the most part an attempt to divert activists in the movement from one form of collective action to another. It represented a radical flank effect in that the activists gained something, funds and assistance, though not precisely what they were after. The second phase—which took shape in 1963, especially in the aftermath of the Birmingham, Alabama, crisis—involved *direct and positive responses to demands by the movement* rather than mere attempts to divert or channel its tactics. Central among these concessions were behind-the-scenes meetings to stimulate private sector compliance with black claims, a vast and significant expansion of the President's civil rights bill (passed as the Civil Rights Act of 1964 after his assassination), and the decision to cooperate with the planned March on Washington in 1963.

The Stakes in the Civil Rights Arena

Scholars and insiders alike (Brauer 1977; Miroff 1976; Sorensen 1965; Wofford 1980) generally concede that during his pre-presidential years, John F. Kennedy evidenced no great commitment to the issue of civil rights for black Americans. His social background led him toward interests in foreign affairs and the art of politics, not domestic moral issues. During his term in the Senate, he maintained cordial relations with Southern Democrats in that chamber, thus arousing the suspicions of black leaders. Perhaps the greatest sin of Kennedy's senatorial tenure, however, was committed during consideration of the Civil Rights Act of 1957, when he voted against civil rights advocates on both a key procedural vote and the jury trials amendment. This amendment, which extended the right to a trial by jury to defendants in civil rights cases, was objectionable to movement groups because it allowed charges of discrimination or brutality to be decided by white southerners, thus severely limiting the effectiveness of the new law.

The Electoral Stake. When Kennedy won the Democratic nomination for the presidency, he immediately realized the importance of his image among blacks. For the first time since the Roosevelt administration, the black vote could not be taken for granted by the Democrats, especially as Richard Nixon still had a reasonably good reputation among black voters. Given the misgivings many black leaders shared about Kennedy's voting record and lack of apparent commitment to their cause, and given the closeness of the race, the Democratic nominee saw the necessity of courting the black vote. His first step was to recruit as an advisor Harris Wofford, a white attorney with strong connections to the civil rights movement. He also issued statements endorsing the student sit-ins of 1960 and made other symbolic gestures intended to further his image as the civil rights candidate. Perhaps most significantly, he had a strong civil rights plank in the party platform to run on, and he promised during the campaign to eliminate racially segregated housing "with the stroke of a pen"—i.e., by executive order.

And once he was in office, the black vote remained important to the success of Kennedy's administration. Nowhere was this truer than in the South, where the President and his advisors hoped that increasing numbers of black voters would lead white politicians to adopt more moderate positions on race and thus enhance southern support for the administration on other issues. This is one of the reasons the administration later supported voter registration by civil rights groups, a topic to be discussed at length in this chapter.

The Partisan Tightrope. At the same time that President Kennedy needed to increase the numbers and the loyalty of black voters, he faced a delicate situation with the southern wing of his own party. In the South, the Democratic Party was the party of white supremacy. Its allegiance to the national party organization was precarious, and any presidential action which seriously alienated the southern Democrats could, at worst, destroy national party unity and sabotage his administration. According to Miroff, "Kennedy hoped that he could walk a tightrope between these southern Democrats and his civil rights supporters" by keeping a low profile on civil rights and weighing every comment on the issue for its likely impact on southern opinion (1976: 231). Ultimately, however, this strategy proved to be untenable.

America's Image Abroad. The civil rights situation also increasingly affected Kennedy's foreign policy agenda. The President and his advisors discerned that the international attention drawn to the second-class citizenship of blacks cost the United States moral capital around the world and indirectly strengthened the hand of communist enemies. Such a concern was first expressed in public by Attorney General Robert Kennedy in a May 1961 speech at the University of Georgia. It was also evidenced in periodic reports compiled for the President by the United States Information Agency, summarizing the coverage of racial incidents by the foreign press (USIA 1963). Also of concern were episodes of discrimination against African diplomats in the Washington, D.C., area (Brauer 1977: 77–78), which embarrassed the administration and damaged its efforts to forge friendly relations with newly emerged African nations.

The Problem of White Brutality. Especially damaging to America's image abroad, white brutality against blacks occurred with increasing frequency as blacks turned to techniques of direct action—sit-ins, freedom rides, and mass marches, for example. Moreover, since white attacks on blacks in the South were more blatant and visible during the Kennedy years than ever before, such incidents were more thoroughly covered by the news media.

Not only did these occurrences of violent reprisal embarrass President Kennedy and his administration, but they forced difficult decisions about protection and law enforcement. Southern police were usually either directly or indirectly involved in such incidents of violence against blacks. This situation led to demands that the federal government provide protection—marshals or even troops—to protect activists. Kennedy, however, wanted to avoid this step at nearly any cost. Thus, it was in the interest of the administration to prevent situations which led to white violence or open defiance of federal authority.

The Implications of Direct Action. The discussion up to this point highlights a central challenge facing President Kennedy, Attorney General Robert Kennedy, and their respective advisors: the increasing stridency of black demands and their expression through confrontational direct action tactics such as demonstrations threatened administration interests on several levels. Demonstrations, marches, and other protests forced the administration's hand. They increased the likelihood of police brutality and vigilante terror, precipitated high-stakes decisions about the use of federal personnel to protect constitutional rights in the South, and made the administration have to choose sides between civil rights supporters and southern Democrats. And the direct action tactics themselves added to the problem of maintaining the image of the United States as the moral leader of the free world. According to Miroff, the young militants who were on the rise during 1960 and 1961 represented a side of the civil rights movement which, although it wasn't clear at first, "would eventually come to perplex the President just as deeply as the white South" (1976: 232).

The first incident in which the implications of confrontational black protest became apparent was the Freedom Rides campaign. The Supreme Court's decision in the case of *Boynton v. Virginia* in 1960 had prohibited segregated terminal facilities in interstate bus travel. To test compliance with this ruling, small interracial groups organized largely by the Congress of Racial Equality (CORE) set out on bus journeys through the South beginning in May 1961. They were beaten by white mobs and, in one case, their bus was burned. In a pattern that was to be repeated in coming years, the bloody reception met by the demonstrators became a national and international media event. And, for the first time, the Kennedy administration was asked to intervene on the side of civil rights protesters.

The White House and the Justice Department responded to the crisis by expressing concern over the attacks and, in one case, dispatching almost 400 marshals to protect one group of Freedom Riders who had been attacked as they were released from an Alabama jail. Moreover, Robert Kennedy stayed in contact with southern state officials to try to insure safe passage for the protesters. But at the same time, administration officials also sought to curtail the protests. Presidential advisor Harris Wofford, who had connections within the movement, writes that President Kennedy called him in the midst of the crisis to say

> without any of his characteristic humor, "Stop them! Get your friends off those buses!" He felt that Martin Luther King, James Farmer [of CORE], Bill Coffin, and company were embarrassing him and the country on the eve of the meeting in Vienna with Khrushchev. He supported every American's right to stand up or sit down for his rights—but not to ride for them in the spring of 1961 (Wofford 1980: 125).

On May 24 the Attorney General made a public plea for a "cooling off period," which amounted to a call for an end to the Freedom Rides. As the rationale for such a moratorium, he cited the President's impending meeting with Nikita Khrushchev of the Soviet Union (Brauer 1977: 106–7). And on the evening of the same day, he made the same request by phone to Martin Luther King, who was serving as a spokesman for the Freedom Rides.[4]

Freedom Rides of one sort or another continued through the end of 1961, but the deepest part of the crisis came in the summer. All in all, the Kennedy administration handled the episode successfully. But it had been a close call, and a lesson had been learned: direct action tactics, no matter how morally justifiable, could lead to catastrophic outcomes. Therefore, it was important for the administration to discourage a repetition of such incidents while at the same time avoiding the appearance of being unsympathetic. The energies of civil rights protesters needed to be redirected into areas which were less threatening and, in the opinion of administration insiders, more fruitful in the long run. The most desirable of these areas was voter registration.

The Voter Education Project

The mechanism through which President Kennedy, his brother, and their staffs sought to encourage the civil rights movement to shift from demonstrations to voter registration was the Voter Education Project (VEP), which was announced in early 1962. Superficially, the VEP was a purely private operation, administered by the Southern Regional Council in Atlanta and funded by grants from several philanthropic foundations, principally the Taconic Foundation, the Field Foundation, and the Stern Family Fund (Brauer 1977: 115; Cleghorn 1963). These funds were distributed to other organizations, including CORE and the Student Nonviolent Coordinating Committee (SNCC), to pay the expenses of registration drives in the Deep South. The VEP dispensed $870,000 (Blumberg 1984: 87) and registered nearly 580,000 by the spring of 1964 (Brauer 1977: 320).

The sequence of events that led to the formation of the Voter Education Project is not entirely clear. Brauer suggests that the idea of funding a large-scale voter registration project came not from the administration itself but rather from "several philanthropic foundations interested in social change" (1977: 114). Identifying Stephen Currier of the Taconic Foundation as their "leader," Brauer notes that Currier was not a "Kennedy man" at the time. Most accounts, however, suggest that the idea of a voter registration project came from within the administration itself (Blumberg 1984: 87; McAdam, 1982: 170; Piven and Cloward 1977: 231–35). Harris

Wofford, President Kennedy's civil rights advisor, maintains that the idea emerged at a June 1961 meeting of the Subcabinet Group on Civil Rights, an informal group of administration officials formed to coordinate and monitor racial progress within the executive branch of the federal government. "It was agreed," he wrote, "that if federal agencies took the initiative and used their full power to protect and promote equal rights, *the necessity for popular pressure could be removed or at least reduced*" (emphasis mine). He went on to say that "[Assistant Attorney General for Civil Rights] Burke Marshall said that he and the A.G. were encouraging vigorous voting registration efforts and thought 'it would be valuable if some of the present energy were channeled into this vital work'" (1980: 158).

In a previous interview Wofford suggests an even earlier origin for the concept of the VEP, maintaining that the original idea of such a tax-exempt, nonpartisan, foundation-funded drive first emerged during the 1960 election campaign (Wofford 1968: 82–83). There are also other indications that these ideas were being considered within the administration at an earlier date than is sometimes supposed: during a 1964 interview, Martin Luther King stated, for example, that Robert Kennedy was pushing voter registration to him *before the Freedom Rides* of 1961 (King 1964: 22). In any case, Attorney General Robert Kennedy, Assistant Attorney General Burke Marshall, and Presidential Assistant Harris Wofford met with civil rights groups during the early summer of 1961 and offered their cooperation with registration work (Brauer 1977: 116). And after the VEP was underway, the Justice Department began a campaign of voting rights suits aimed at areas of abuse in the South.

Whatever the precise timing, it appears fairly certain that the idea of encouraging voter registration as a project for civil rights activists was the brainchild of Kennedy advisors. It is also fairly clear that the desire to divert those activists away from direct action tactics was among—perhaps paramount among—their intentions. James Farmer of the Congress of Racial Equality viewed the offer of money for registration drives as a "deal" in which tax-exemption was being offered to CORE and SNCC in exchange for an end to demonstrations.[5] After his brother's assassination, Robert Kennedy asserted to Anthony Lewis that there were in fact four reasons for supporting voter registration over demonstrations.[6] First, he contended that the Justice Department had more authority to enforce voting rights than to protect demonstrators. Second, he argued that the right to vote would be the key that would unlock the door to all other rights for blacks. Third, he felt that voting campaigns would lead to "less internal struggle and strife within the country as a whole." Fourth, and somewhat redundantly, he stated that there would be less opposition to registration work than to Freedom Rides, Sit-Ins, and marches among white southerners: "I mean, how can anybody really get very mad because you're making an effort to make sure that everybody votes?" The last of these arguments, though, turned out to be quite naive, as events of the Mississippi Freedom Summer of 1964 demonstrated.

Harris Wofford concedes that the effort to maintain control of civil rights activities was among the motivations for raising foundation money and offering it to the activist groups, but he balks at the suggestion that this represented a "devious stratagem to divert the civil rights movement into a less embarrassing area and to destroy the direct action movement" (Wofford 1980: 158). The question of deviousness, however, merely clouds the issue. Wofford, Marshall, and their colleagues may well have felt that a shift from demonstrations to registration was in the best interests of the movement itself. But this does not contradict the basic point: the administration felt that the escalation of direct action tactics was divisive and dangerous and hoped it could be avoided. The Voter Education Project was not a trick. Rather, it was an inducement, seen by Kennedy people as an offer of something better for both activists and the administration.

The Voter Education Project had both positive and negative results. On the positive side, some 287,000 new voters were registered, although many of them came from areas where there was little official resistance. And it appears that they had an immediate impact: "As early as the 1962 elections, racial moderates saw signs that the new registrants were having a salutary effect on the South's politics" (Brauer 1977: 115). On the other hand, Robert Kennedy's assumption that the voting issue would arouse little hostility among white southerners proved to be tragically incorrect. Attacks on registration workers in the Deep South were vicious and sometimes lethal, and the federal government failed to provide protection. This led many participants to feel betrayed and, by 1963, to include the federal government among the enemies of black Americans.

Regardless of the net results, the Voter Education Project may be seen as the exemplar of the first Kennedy strategy for managing a crisis. Largely a reaction to the political crisis surrounding the Freedom Rides, it was in part an attempt to steer the rising tide of civil rights activism in a particular direction—not to *diminish* it, as some have suggested, but to *channel* it into areas that were viewed as potentially the most fruitful. What distinguishes this strategy from the administration's course in 1963 was the fact that officials were in effect bargaining with activists and trying to exert a direct influence on the movement's selection of tactics and goals.

The Specter of Escalating Violence

Direct action tactics such as demonstrations were not all that President Kennedy had to fear. Although during the early 1960s the civil rights movement was still dominated by the paradigm of nonviolent resistance and protest, some blacks were beginning to turn away from peaceful means. In mid-July 1961 groups of blacks in Chicago attacked whites in apparent retaliation for the killing of a young black man days earlier. Sixty-five arrests occurred in connection with these incidents (Sobel 1967: 106). In April 1962, a white youth was shot and killed in Augusta, Georgia. He was apparently "nightriding" through a black part of town during a period of tension surrounding a supermarket boycott (Sobel 1967: 148). And in July, Martin Luther King declared a "day of penance" after black protesters in Albany, Georgia, pelted police with bricks and rocks (Sobel 1967: 155).

Although violence had marked race relations in the South for decades, in 1962 the perpetrators were not exclusively white, and this seemed to mark an ominous turn. The Kennedy administration was not taken totally by surprise. Even before the inauguration, Harris Wofford mentioned in a memo that the President-elect should plan measures to enhance equality of job opportunity and integrated housing because "the northern vicious circle of Negro slums taking over the central cities, with white suburban nooses tightening around an expanding, demoralized Negro population, is as explosive as any southern school crisis. The present rising tensions can lead to serious race riots" (Wofford 1980: 5).[7] Not until 1963, however, did the trend toward more frequent black violence and greater white repression of black demonstrations reach a critical stage. The first clear signs emerged in Birmingham, Alabama.

The Turning Point: Birmingham

During the winter of 1962 and 1963, Martin Luther King's Southern Christian Leadership Conference had begun planning a large-scale assault on discrimination in Birmingham, Alabama, perhaps the most segregated city in America. The group's demands included the desegregation of public accommodations, the improvement of hiring practices in the business community, and the creation of a biracial committee to work toward the desegregation of other areas of life in the city. Demonstrations began in early April, leading to the jailing of King and many of his followers. Shortly after King's arrest, the first incidents of rock- and bottle-throwing by young blacks occurred. When King was released on bail after a week in prison, secret negotiations between blacks and leaders of Birmingham's business community were held. These sessions bore no fruit, and the demonstrations in the streets were intensified. In one of the most infamous episodes in the history of the civil rights movement, police brutalized the demonstrators—using nightsticks, police dogs, and high-pressure hoses—and Governor George Wallace sent state troopers to assist them in "preserving order."

On May 4, Burke Marshall and Assistant Deputy Attorney General Joseph Dolan were sent to Birmingham to attempt to mediate the dispute. Within three days, black leaders and moderate white businesspeople were again meeting secretly. An agreement was worked out whereby public facilities in the city would be desegregated, blacks would be hired by certain private businesses, and regular biracial communications would be established. This agreement, if it had held up, would have represented a substantial victory for the SCLC.

Matters were complicated, however, by a controversial runoff election in the city. In early April, T. Eugene "Bull" Connor, the police commissioner, had been narrowly defeated in the mayoral race by a more racially moderate opponent but challenged the results in court. As the suit was still unsettled by the time the interracial agreement had been hammered out, the outgoing city commission—composed largely of extreme white supremacists—refused to step down. So Birmingham had two city commissions. The old commission and the more resistant whites in the community refused to accept the agreement. Stores that had acquiesced to SCLC demands became the targets of a white boycott, and a wave of terrorism swept the black community.

On May 11, both a black-owned motel and the home of Martin Luther King's brother were bombed. Late that night, young blacks took to the streets. A serious riot continued until the next morning —blacks attacking Birmingham police and Alabama state troopers with rocks and bottles. Rumors spread that some had guns and planned, on the evening of May 12, to engage in "headhunting"[8] for white law enforcement officers.

During June 1963, violence was not limited to Birmingham. Although it received less worldwide publicity, a serious situation also existed in Cambridge, Maryland. Fighting between blacks and whites broke out on June 11 following civil rights demonstrations. Two whites were injured by shotgun blasts during these confrontations. On June 14 nearly five hundred National Guardsmen began to enforce a limited martial law, which remained in effect through the first week of July. When the National Guard left on July 8, however, demonstrations, shootings, and other violence resumed. Only on July 23, after intense federal mediation, was the situation at last resolved (Sobel 1967: 188–89).

The significance of violence by blacks was not lost on President Kennedy and his advisors. Days earlier, in his "Letter from Birmingham Jail," Martin Luther King had warned that nationalist groups like the Black Muslims were "nourished by the Negro's frustration over the continued existence of racial discrimination."[9] If the nonviolent movement met with failure, he wrote, then "millions of Negroes will, out of frustration and despair, seek solace and security in black-nationalist ideologies—a development that would inevitably lead to a frightening racial nightmare" (King 1963; 90–91). Just such a future was very much on the minds of the President, the Attorney General, and several of their advisors in the Oval Office on June 12 as they struggled to plan their response. On the difficult issue of restoring order, Robert Kennedy told those present:

> The argument for sending troops in, for taking a forceful action, is . . . "what's going to happen in the future?" You're going to have these kinds of incidents. The Governor's virtually taken over the city . . . you're gonna have his people around sticking bayonets in people, hitting people with clubs and guns, etc. You're gonna have rallies all over the country calling upon the President to take some forceful action. . . . [The] reports that we get from other cities, not just in the South, is that this could trigger off a good deal of violence around the country, with the Negroes saying that they've been abused for all these years and that they're gonna have to start following the ideas of the Black Muslims and not go along with the white people. If they feel, on the other hand, that the federal government is their friend . . . then we can take some of that off.[10]

As this meeting proceeded, it was decided to send Burke Marshall back to Alabama to resume his mediating role, to put federal troops on alert and make known that they were ready to move into

Birmingham if necessary, and to announce that the President had begun preparations for federalizing the Alabama National Guard. These steps were aired publicly by the President in an emotional national broadcast that evening.

Within days of the President's televised speech on May 12, the situation in Birmingham had been temporarily resolved, although violence was to flare up again in September. In spite of the truce, however, the demonstrations and violence had a deep impact on blacks nationwide and on the administration. And the fears about future events that were expressed at the meeting on June 12 in the Oval Office were not limited to those present. From mid-May through early July, numerous persons within the administration or with indirect links to it communicated their concern about the direction race relations were taking and recommended various actions to maintain control over events. For example, Louis Martin of the Democratic National Committee reported to Robert Kennedy on May 13 that the "accelerated tempo of Negro restiveness" that had galvanized around Birmingham "and the rivalry of some leaders for top billing coupled with the resistance of segregationists may soon create the most critical state of race relations since the Civil War" (quoted in Brauer 1977: 238). Two days later, Assistant Attorney General Berl Bernhard warned Assistant Special Counsel Lee White that unless the administration was able to devise "alternatives to mass demonstrations for securing constitutional rights, explosive situations such as Birmingham may be repeated elsewhere"[11] A memorandum from Solicitor General Archibald Cox to President Kennedy also referred to the necessity of acting in advance to avoid similar situations and recommended the creation by Executive Order of an independent mediation commission to intervene when they arose.[12]

G. Mennen Williams, Assistant Secretary of State for African Affairs and a former Michigan governor, urged Kennedy on June 15 to send a full Civil Rights package to Congress as an insurance policy against further escalation and to plan "a series of hard hitting administrative actions to be instituted every 10 days or so":

> In this way the President would not only retain the initiative but he might be able to take off the sharp edge of dissatisfaction that results in impassioned demonstrations. While I recognize the importance of demonstrations to keep on the pressure for action, there is the possibility that the inter-action of fervent demonstration and brutal repression would reach such a pitch that public peace and safety would be endangered beyond reasonable control.[13]

In placing these recommendations before the President, Williams stressed the danger not only of violence and counterviolence but of a major shift in the spectrum of black collective action:

> Unless there is a satisfaction of legitimate Negro aspirations the situation will be fraught with danger.
>
> In this situation the Negro masses tend no longer to look to traditional white liberal or even progressive Negro leadership. The prestige of the progressive Negro leader among the masses is endangered. *Unless results are achieved soon, Negroes unquestionably will look to untried and perhaps less responsible leaders.*[14]

In closing this memo, Williams recommended several policy actions, including a Fair Employment Practices Commission long sought by civil rights activists, and stressed: "Temporizing will only lose the confidence and support of the responsible Negro and give the extremists on both sides a chance to seize the initiative."[15]

Concerns about the fate of moderate black leaders were also expressed by a black Foreign Service officer, who wrote to Robert Kennedy of his worry that the nonviolent black leaders such as King "might not be able to contain the hostile feelings on the part of many Negroes much longer."[16] Upon receiving this letter, aides recommended that the Attorney General meet personally with the individual to discuss such concerns.

A memo from John Kenneth Galbraith, Ambassador to India and trusted Kennedy advisor, provides a final example of the sort of message the administration was receiving during the summer. Writing to the Attorney General on June 11, Galbraith began by noting:

> In past months, as we all know, the Negroes have been abandoning their erstwhile dependence on legal process and moving massively to direct social pressure. This is working and there is no chance of it being reversed. The Government, sensing in part the pressure of demand and partly the danger of things going to extremes is moving to match the new development by new legislation. This is appropriate, but, in my judgement, insufficient. We must, I think, match the Negroes [sic] discovery of social pressure by social pressure from the Federal Government. *This is the one chance to remain in command of matters, not to be visibly laggard in our pressure for civil rights and of avoiding the most serious eventuality which is the possible need to use force to restrain Negro violence.*[17]

Galbraith's specific recommendation in this memo was a "Civil Equality Drive" in which communities, interstate corporations, and labor unions would be rallied behind a federally-guided and highly visible campaign for greater black opportunity. Although his plan was not adopted in its entirety, it did include elements which found a place in the administration's efforts to bring about voluntary progress through behind-the-scenes work.

The events in Birmingham and elsewhere during the early summer of 1963 produced a subtle but extremely important shift in the Kennedy administration's approach to the civil rights movement. In reaction both to black violence and to the appearance that a shift in allegiance from moderate leaders to the Muslims might be imminent, the President and his advisors entered a second phase of crisis management. Attempting to forestall further tactical escalation by blacks, they did not try to divert activists into "safe" tactics and goals as they had done through the Voter Education Project but rather responded strategically—within the boundaries of political feasibility—to the stated demands of the civil rights leaders themselves. In other words, they began trying to strengthen black moderates by responding visibly to several of their long-standing pleas. These responses took several forms.

The Beefed-up Civil Rights Bill. The most historic aspect of Kennedy's reaction to the growing racial crisis was the decision to submit to Congress the wide-ranging bill that eventually became the Civil Rights Act of 1964. Since taking office, Kennedy had been very reluctant to send Congress any civil rights legislation at all, and for good political reasons. Key advisors, including longtime civil rights sympathizer Harris Wofford, had been counseling against such a move. It would cost the President precious political support in the 1964 election, they argued, and would jeopardize other vitally important legislative initiatives, such as his tax-cut bill. The administration's failure to propose civil rights legislation, along with the President's refusal to keep a campaign promise by issuing a housing order, was a major disappointment to the civil rights movement.

Kennedy finally did ask Congress for legislation on February 28, 1963, but his requests were limited to relatively minor voting and educational changes. Apparently, the belated decision to propose a mild legislative package was based upon the President's need to shield himself from both Republican and black criticism (Brauer 1977: 221–22). This package, however, was far from satisfactory to civil rights forces.

Then came the crisis in Birmingham, which changed the stakes of the game. Two issues were particularly conspicuous: first, the specter of increasing violence by blacks as well as by whites, and second, the virtual helplessness of the federal government to protect civil rights activists in the South. The rights that demonstrators were seeking were, of course, not yet legally recognized. The failure of individual states to grant those rights—and even the brutality of southern police—often violated no existing federal law. Thus, when called upon to intervene on behalf of demonstrators, the federal government often lacked the legal means by which to do so. This predicament would recur until those legal means were established by Congress.

By early May, President Kennedy was looking at an array of possible means by which to forestall the growing racial crisis. One of these was an expansion of his legislative requests: the Justice Department was considering the feasibility of laws dealing with public accommodations, voting rights, federal protection, school desegregation, and fair employment.

During a televised news conference on May 22, the President announced that a new civil rights law would be proposed. And on June 19, in the midst of intensified direct action protests around the country, the administration's bill was introduced. In addition to the weak measures that were part of the February legislative request, the new bill included a powerful section which outlawed discrimination in public accommodations, authorized cutting off federal funding to government contractors who discriminated, and established a Community Relations Service to help solve racial disputes before they became violent. Though strengthened, the bill by no means included everything that even the more moderate civil rights leaders like Roy Wilkins wanted. In particular, it failed to call for a Fair Employment Practices Commission to end job bias, the most widely sought antidiscrimination action of the twentieth century. Nevertheless, the administration's bill was the most far-reaching legislation ever proposed by a President, and it represented a favorable response to numerous black demands that were decades old. With this new proposal, the administration was no longer attempting to determine the movement's goals and tactics. Rather, it was trying to manage a deepening crisis by acceding to the "reasonable" demands of moderates in the movement. It must be noted, however, that these demands came to be seen as "reasonable" only in the context of the crisis of the early 1960s.

Behind-the-scenes Meetings. Another means by which Kennedy sought to prevent future trouble was through quietly encouraging interracial dialogue and voluntary resolution of racial problems. Beginning less than two weeks after the Birmingham crisis reached its most serious point, a series of meetings was held with groups of leaders thought to be instrumental to racial progress.[18] These included businessmen (June 4 and July 11), a conference of mayors in Honolulu (June 9), religious leaders and lawyers (June 21), civil rights leaders (June 22), and prominent women (July 9). The meetings were intended to persuade those in attendance to do what they could to work quietly for civil rights and to remove the causes of racial strife. The businessmen who came to the White House on July 11, for instance, were to step up their training and hiring of unemployed blacks and to change the racial policies and practices in their southern branches and subsidiaries.[19] Within weeks, administration people were able to demonstrate concrete gains as a result of these actions. Each meeting also involved a call for active support for the administration's civil rights legislation. Civil rights leaders who visited the White House on June 22 were asked to refrain from any actions, such as large demonstrations, which might antagonize congressmen and threaten the passage of the bill.[20] One such demonstration that was in the planning stages was the March on Washington, which will be discussed below.

In each of the meetings in this series,[21] a familiar theme was given voice: *Those in attendance were told that the racial crisis in the South and elsewhere was reaching a danger point and that concrete progress in meeting responsible civil rights demands must occur lest violent consequences follow.* As a businessman who attended the July 11 meeting reported, "The President pointed out that the problem had become critical and must be dealt with directly if the situation is to be kept within bounds,"[22] and the Attorney General "felt that the key to the demonstrations, the riots and other serious situations" was the existence of segregated public establishments; "this one single thing . . . more than any other is behind the emotion and elements of radicalism that get support from both Negro and white people for demonstrations and sit-ins".[23] Thus, anything that businesspeople could do to lessen this daily reminder of subordinate status was a step in the direction of social tranquility.

In a 1964 interview with Anthony Lewis, Robert Kennedy was very clear about the underlying intentions of both the civil rights bill and the behind-the-scenes meetings in the White House. His remarks are important enough to warrant quoting at length:

Lewis: Did you ever think or talk to the President or among yourselves about the tremendous question of what kind of leadership the Negroes in Mississippi would eventually have? Whether it would be a revolutionary leadership or whether it was still possible to provide a middle-class political leadership of the more traditional kind. It wasn't a danger of . . .

Kennedy: Yes. We talked about that problem, not just for Mississippi, but for the country. And going back to the earlier question of my basis for sponsoring legislation, my basis for having the meetings, the basis for that whole effort in 1963 and 1964 was really *not only the passage of legislation, but what, in my judgement, was even more important, to re-obtain the confidence of the Negro population in their government and in the white majority. I thought that there was a great danger of losing that unless we took a very significant step, such as the passage of legislation.* So, to answer that question, I don't think that it was just confined to what was going to happen to the Negro leadership in Mississippi. It was far broader than that. Although the legislation itself wouldn't affect the Negro in the North, I think that it was important to pass the legislation just to show the Negro in the North that the white population was going to do something about this problem.[24]

The Administration and the March on Washington. The original focus of the March on Washington was to have been *jobs*. Both CORE and SNCC became involved immediately, seeing great possibilities for a mass demonstration and sit-in. The nature of the proposed demonstration began to change, however, when Martin Luther King was brought into the planning process to help legitimize the march (set for August) and to draw the other major civil rights organizations and white liberals into the project (Hodgson 1976: 194).

At the June 22 meeting in the White House, mentioned above, President Kennedy was advised of the plans. Outspoken in his opposition to the idea, he tried to persuade the black leaders that it was not in their interest to stage a mass march in the capital just prior to congressional action on the civil rights bill. During the discussion of the issue, however, Kennedy was forced to acknowledge that demonstrations had brought successful results in the recent past and that indeed they had caused him to move faster in accommodating black demands. Moreover, the President recognized that as the March was already planned, it would probably occur even if the leaders attempted to call it off at the last moment; accordingly, the best way to insure that it remain peaceful was to proceed with careful and disciplined preparations (Brauer 1977: 272–73). Somewhat reluctantly, Kennedy thus agreed to cooperate with the organizers. He directed federal agencies in Washington to cooperate and, through the actions of his advisors and the moderates involved with the project, set about to insure that it would be a "safe" event.[25]

Through these processes of negotiation, compromise, and unity-building, the shape of the planned March on Washington changed dramatically. The job issue lost its top priority, much to the chagrin of CORE. The NAACP and the Urban League, the most moderate of the organizations involved in the march, balked at using direct action tactics such as a sit-in, so these plans were dropped. And SNCC leader John Lewis, who was intending to deliver remarks highly critical of the administration and to employ the word "revolution" in his speech, was persuaded to change the text in order to prevent the moderate groups from pulling out. Although SNCC activists were hardly pleased at these developments, such was the price to be paid for the involvement of the bigger organizations and for the blessings of the administration. From the administration's perspective, the March on Washington was a tremendous success: the appearance of over 200,000 peaceful marchers of both races had a positive effect—if indeed it had any affect at all—on the fortunes of the civil rights bill.

It is clear, then, that the reality of growing black militancy and the threat of *black* violence were among the variables which Kennedy officials weighed when shaping their stance on racial issues. Such considerations led them first to attempt to direct the insurgents toward less perilous strategies. When the futility of this approach became clear, they made a conscious effort to preserve the moderates' reputations among restive blacks by providing them with victories—on the moderates' *own* terms. Thus, the oft-heard charge that the Kennedy administration "manipulated" the civil rights movement had much validity through 1962. But by 1963 the line between "manipulation" and "accommodation" had become indistinct. The administration's actions cannot be thought of as mere co-optation and window-dressing. The responses of the administration yielded real gains—not just illusory ones—for civil rights forces and the black people for whom they spoke.

CONCLUSION

One of the initial hypotheses of this book was that the ability of a movement organization to achieve its goals may be related to the goals and actions of other organizations that make up the larger social movement. Groups defined as moderate may be caught up in backlashes caused by more radical organizations or collectivities. I have labeled such patterns *negative radical flank effects*. On the other hand, radical groups may bring about a greater level of responsiveness to the claims of moderates, either by making the latter appear more "reasonable" or by creating crises which can be resolved by the lesser concessions required by moderates. I have termed these patterns *positive radical flank effects*.

Although neither the design of the research nor the nature of the variables allows precise, quantitative tests, the preceding analysis of government actions has yielded results generally consistent with the positive radical flank pattern. The responsiveness of the federal government to black claims followed a pattern which corresponded generally to the increase of black radicalism. As newer forms of tactical and ideological militancy emerged, the government tended to react more favorably to the claims of the "neo-moderates," i.e., those organizations which had previously made up the militant vanguard but whose militancy had since been eclipsed by others. This pattern is most evident in the period from 1960 through 1965, during which a number of major federal actions recognized black demands dating back to as early as the 1940s. Decades of activity by the NAACP had produced results prior to the 1960s—results which were dramatic for the times—but these had been achieved almost exclusively through the courts. Congress had yielded almost nothing, and the executive branch had been the source of largely limited and symbolic victories. During the later 1950s, however, when southern blacks began to apply some of the tactics of the labor movement, the pattern began to shift toward greater congressional responsiveness. Even so, the Civil Rights Acts of 1957 and 1960 were weak and limited mostly to the issue of voting rights.

The pace of federal recognition of civil rights accelerated dramatically during the very period when direct action tactics had reached a massive scale. The most important pieces of legislation affecting the rights of black Americans—the Civil Rights Act of 1964, the Economic Opportunity Act, the Elementary and Secondary Education Act, and the Voting Rights Act of 1965—were all enacted in the midst of an unprecedented racial crisis which seemed to reflect a widespread rejection by blacks of gradualist, legalistic means. Yet for the most part, these laws did not reflect new demands but rather put the stamp of governmental approval on goals which the NAACP and the NUL had sought for years: increased federal protection of the black franchise; integration of schools; nondiscrimination in transportation, public facilities, and other aspects of everyday life; a decent standard of living for the poor; equal access to employment and job training; and decent schooling for the disadvantaged.

Why did these achievements have to wait until the mid-1960s?[26] Part of the answer lies in the vagaries of electoral politics, the changing makeup of Congress, and legislative strategies employed to pursue individual bills. World events and the desire of the United States to present itself to the world as the champion of freedom and equality were also involved. But the close relationship between levels of black radicalism and the success of moderate groups in achieving their policy objectives suggests that the changing character of black insurgency was also crucial. And more compelling than mere correspondence in time are the statements of President Kennedy and those surrounding him, some of which were described in this chapter. These statements show conclusively that at least during the JFK years, the frustration and radicalization of blacks in the deepening racial crisis became a major concern of those at the center of state power, and that acquiescence to the pleas of moderates was selected as a means of calming the troubled waters. Militant agitators appear to have gained importance not so much from their ability to make more moderate demands seem "reasonable" as from their capacity to raise the costs of inaction. Militants created political dilemmas for those in power by disrupting their routines for reacting to threats. Given such pitfalls, it is little wonder that Kennedy and Johnson went to great lengths to discourage protest and encourage conventional political participation. Nor is it any wonder that they came to see the NAACP and the NUL as groups with whom they could deal.

If the years of 1964 and 1965 represented a peak of federal responsiveness to integrationist civil rights demands, did the late 1960s represent a retreat? The evidence does not entirely support such a view. Financial support, the subject of the preceding chapter, is a continuing necessity; increasing one's contribution to a movement organization *this* year does not mean that the organization has no need for one's money *next* year. But policy responses are different: once a law is passed which recognizes a particular movement claim, it becomes unnecessary to pass an identical law again. Barring actual reversals, the passage of a civil rights law or the issuing of an executive order closes the books on an issue for the time being. Attention is then turned to enforcement of the new policy and to calls for policy in other areas. Thus, given the winning streak of 1964 and 1965, the fact that only one civil rights law was passed between 1966 and 1969 cannot in itself be seen as a reflection of a retreat.

It must also be kept in mind that the role of the federal government in *enforcing* civil rights increased considerably during the late 1960s. The Departments of HEW, Justice, and Labor became activists of sorts, acting on their own initiative to bring about compliance with the law. But at the same time, it is clear that the surge in *northern* protests and the wave of urban violence were associated with a leveling off of favorable actions by the government. It is also clear that the replacement of the demand for equality of *opportunity* with the demand for equality of *condition*—a demand which was embodied not only in the post-1965 ideology of the black movement but in President Johnson's Howard University speech as well—alienated a small but influential group of liberals. Metamorphosed as "neoconservatives," they began to oppose openly many of the newer goals of black collective action, including compensatory treatment of all sorts. The greater resistance to civil rights and social welfare policy which occurred after 1966 underscores a central flaw in my tentative view of radical flank effects in the introduction to this book: by default, I implied that there would be a *linear* correspondence (direct or inverse) between radicalism in the movement and the success of moderates. The partial reversals of the late 1960s suggest instead that radical flank effects may be positive up to a certain point on the scale of perceived radicalism, after which a degree of backlash may set in.

One of the concerns aroused by the massive direct action protests of the early and middle 1960s was that they would lead to violence among members of both races. When widespread black violence occurred, however, did it lead to a radical flank effect? The evidence for a negative effect on federal action is weak. It is true that antiriot measures of various sorts (Button 1978: 107–52; Feagin and Hahn 1973: 226–39) were instituted and that federal law-enforcement agencies harassed groups believed to be responsible for fomenting violence. But there is little evidence that the fortunes of black *moderates* were damaged in any significant way. Although the urban rioting may have contributed to the defeat of the 1966 civil rights bill, it appears that the bill would have failed on its own. In any case, even five consecutive summers of rioting were not enough to prevent an open housing bill in 1968.

Neither is there evidence—especially after 1966—for any overwhelming *positive* radical flank effect based on the new militancy or the rioting. As Button (1978) has shown, the departments of the executive branch directed considerable money toward the northern ghettos between 1964 and 1966 in an apparent attempt to remedy the grievances that were believed to have caused the outbreaks. But beginning in 1967, these expenditures began to level off, and though appropriations for the antipoverty programs continued to rise, they rose at a slower rate and were more specifically designated by Congress. This reaction was partly a consequence of the increasing cost of the Vietnam War, but it also apparently reflected a growing belief that expenditures were at best no cure for riots and at worst a reinforcement of lawlessness.

From the analysis of federal action on black demands, the following conclusions emerge:

> 1. *Federal policy toward black claims has not followed a unified pattern over the years.* Rather, different segments of the government have responded to the escalation of black collective action in different ways. Throughout the period, the judicial branch has proved the most favorably inclined, followed by the executive and, finally, by the legislative branch. During the 1960s, however, especially the latter half, the executive departments became increasingly active in enforcing legally-recognized civil rights on their own initiative.
> 2. *Governmental responses favorable to integrationist claims have tended to occur during periods of crisis.* It was immediately after the high tide of direct action protest and during the years of the early urban riots that the White House, the Cabinet departments, and the Congress were the most active in responding to long-standing demands for racial progress.
> 3. *Federal policy continued to reflect basically integrationist principles even after the hegemony of integrationism in the movement broke down,* although attempts were made to address ghetto grievances to a relatively limited degree.
> 4. *Urban violence and revolutionary black radicalism did not lead to policies markedly less favorable toward the claims and goals of moderates*—i.e., to a negative radical flank effect. In fact, during the first two or three summers of urban violence, radicalism appears to have reinforced the pro–civil rights stand of those already supportive of such claims.
> 5. *The threat of violence appears to have been more productive of pro-black federal actions than the actual occurrence of violence.* The peak of positive response from the government corresponded to the peak in nonviolent direct action, which stimulated a negative radical flank effect among southern anti–civil rights forces and created apprehension among powerful government officials of impending

violence. The most favorable government responses came during 1964 and 1965, *when the potential for racial violence was becoming clear but before black violence had become commonplace.*

During the period in question, black radicalization interacted with the changing political climate to produce the pattern of federal law and policy which characterized the 1960s. Direct action radicalism was especially effective, in that it produced certain social and political effects which at last led powerholders to respond favorably to old integrationist claims. Initially black violence and separatism had similar effects, but continued unrest in the ghettos over several consecutive years demonstrated the futility of employing more liberal, integrationist measures for the purpose of bringing peace to the inner cities.

Thus, it appears that changes in federal responses to black claims were shaped not so much by radicalism *per se* as by the impact of particular forms of radicalism on existing political interests at specific times.

4 Radicals, Crises, and Concessions

Black protest in America has been examined by more scholars and in more ways than any other social movement. This book is yet another such study, but one that is unique in its perspective. The focus of the preceding chapters has been upon the shifting ideological and tactical spectrum of the movement and the impacts of "radical" groups on the fate of other segments of the movement, their capacity to mobilize resources, and their success in achieving their goals. I have used the term *radical flank effect* to designate these impacts, be they harmful or helpful. And in contrast to most observers, I have suggested that the net effect of the rising black rage of the postwar years has been to pave the way for unprecedented yet gradual change. In this concluding chapter, I shall summarize the major empirical findings of the investigation and briefly discuss some of the issues they raise.

SUMMARY OF FINDINGS

Though public opinion was not a major focus of this study, Chapter 1 nevertheless included an examination of opinion poll data from the 1940s through the 1960s. These data trace an overall trend of increasingly favorable white opinion toward civil rights goals and a stubborn disapproval of the movement's tactics. These trends are somewhat puzzling when taken as indicators of radical flank effects among the white public. It appears that black radicalization and urban violence turned some whites against even the moderate civil rights groups, although others reacted by increasing their support.

Overall, however, it seems that neither a clear positive effect nor a clear backlash occurred. Rather, aggregate white approval of racial integration continued to increase, albeit more slowly, until the early 1970s.

Chapter 2 analyzed trends in exogenous financial support—i.e., the amounts and sources of funding for black collective action originating *outside* black organizations. The findings strongly support the notion that increasing black radicalism and its emergence in new, more threatening forms led to a greater willingness among certain funding sources—notably those with the greatest stake in the restoration of racial peace—to underwrite forms of black collective action which were more consistent with their interests.

The analysis of the emergence of federal policy on black claims in Chapter 3 also yielded results which are generally consistent with a positive radical flank effect model. Victories for black moderates tended to coincide with periods of crisis, particularly during the direct action phase of the black revolt. The threat of violence seems to have been a major ingredient in this pattern, although actual outbreaks of black rioting were somewhat less productive of concessions.

It is clear, then, that by the end of the period I have been describing: (a) the white public had grown far more aware of black claims, but not necessarily more supportive; (b) wealthy and powerful elites had become "sponsors" for moderate black organizations and causes, sometimes by underwriting existing organizations and sometimes by creating new ones; and (c) the federal government had adopted policies that were supportive of claims of moderate (and occasionally militant) black organizations to a degree that would have been unimaginable in the mid-1950s.

OTHER FACTORS

The research design employed in this study has focused largely upon one variable: the existence and activity of radical groups in the civil rights movement. But no single factor is sufficient for explaining broad historical episodes. Although I have concluded that radical flank effects were quite important in producing long-awaited victories for the movement, I have not asserted that they were the only dynamics at work. Such a claim would be absurd. Rather, I have merely attempted to examine the role of radical flank effects in the civil rights movement and to give them their rightful place amidst the plethora of other processes that operated during those years. A number of these other factors deserve to be mentioned briefly.

One such factor is the role of *southern white repression* in both the resource mobilization activities and the political achievements of the movement. The increased visibility of nonviolent protest brought in its wake increased visibility for the violent reaction of southern segregationists. Needless to say, there was nothing new about violence against blacks in the South. Lynchings, for example, were most frequent in the 1880s and 1890s.[1] What was different about the late 1950s and especially the early 1960s was that the outrages committed by white supremacists and by southern law enforcement officers were given widespread publicity. Many northerners were shocked by such events as the savage beatings of the Freedom Riders in 1961, the use of dogs and high-pressure hoses against peaceful demonstrators in Birmingham and the assassination of NAACP leader Medgar Evers in 1963, the killing of three civil rights workers by Mississippi Klansmen in 1964, and "Bloody Sunday" in Selma in 1965.[2] Indeed, some of them responded with financial contributions to civil rights groups; these early 1960s contributions, however, seem to have gone to the nonviolent "radicals" of the SCLC, CORE, and SNCC more often than to the NAACP and LDEF moderates. Although it is difficult to assess the importance of repression in facilitating resource mobilization among civil rights groups, I would argue that reactions against white repression were mostly of benefit to direct action groups (i.e., the radicals of the early 1960s), that these reactions were most significant among individual contributors and churches, and that they were not important causes of the massive increases in the resources of moderates during the *late* 1960s (the resistance was less vicious by that time and received less publicity as public attention shifted to the riots).

It has also been suggested that the brutal southern reaction to the movement was instrumental in bringing about changes in federal policy which were favorable to the civil rights cause. Scholars disagree, however, as to the role of confrontations, such as those in Birmingham and Selma, in the passage of major civil rights legislation. My research provides no systematic means for determining how much moral outrage such events produced among policymakers throughout the period of study or how that moral outrage affected their deliberations. The case of the Kennedy administration suggests that the brutality of white supremacists during the early 1960s did exert a strong influence on emerging civil rights policy, but that it did not do so simply because of moral indignation. Civil rights was too volatile an issue to be decided on moral considerations alone. Rather, the repressive measures employed in the South were important primarily because they forced policymakers to take actions that they would have preferred avoiding, such as proposing stronger civil rights legislation or becoming allied to voter registration efforts—actions which were politically costly but seemed the only option available under the circumstances.

Another alternative explanation of patterns in resource mobilization and policy during the 1960s is the *fluctuation in white participation*. Until the mid-sixties, the organized civil rights movement had been fundamentally interracial. The March on Washington of August 1963 probably represented the high tide of the civil rights/white liberal coalition. Significant numbers of white college students also participated in the Freedom Summer of 1964, often putting their lives on the line and, in three cases, dying in the process. It might be suggested that, other things being equal, the more whites that actively participated in the movement, the greater would be the federal government's responsiveness to movement claims. If this were true, we would expect federal responsiveness to decline after about 1966 both because the advocates of black power had rejected coalitions with whites and because white supporters had been siphoned off into the antiwar and other movements. Both processes indeed did occur, and both probably did have deleterious effects. These effects, however, should not be exaggerated. For one thing, legislation is not the only measure of federal responsiveness: many of the legislative goals of the moderates had been achieved by the late 1960s, and the government began to take a more active role in enforcing newly recognized civil rights.

Similarly, the analysis of the funding structure of the movement suggests that the decline of white participation was not overwhelmingly damaging to the movement as a whole. This decline in participation *was* financially damaging to CORE and SNCC, but such lessened support seems to have been a price these organizations were willing to pay for ideological purity. But whatever losses of white dollars the *moderate* organizations may have suffered were more than counteracted by the growing support of institutional elites, especially those in the corporate sector and in foundations. In a sense, civil rights was becoming a big business. As such, it was increasingly immune to the whims of individual white contributors. Nearly everyone who has looked at black collective action during the mid-1960s recognizes that certain backlash-like phenomena did in fact occur. My point is not to argue otherwise. Rather, I suggest that *behind* the superficial backlashes of those years, different sorts of processes—radical flank effects—were occurring. The overall withdrawals of white liberal cash from moderate civil rights groups—to whatever extent such withdrawals may have occurred—were made up for by vastly increased sums from large institutions. Similarly, the increasing reluctance of Congress to pass pro–civil rights and social welfare legislation during the 1960s was at least counterbalanced by greater activism among federal bureaucrats and judges. Regardless of trends in mass support, elite support was growing. The best theoretical conclusion may actually be that *both positive and negative radical flank effects happen simultaneously in all complex social movements*. The important question concerns the *net effect*, the sum total of differential reactions to "extremism," and whether this total is pro- or anti-moderate. Central to this question, in turn, is the social, economic, and political *power* of those groups which are the agents of positive radical flank effects. From a standpoint limited to cost-effectiveness, it is undoubtedly more important that corporations and foundations became more active in pro-black issues than that mass white financial support failed to grow. The net payoff was greater, and moderate groups were able to survive the decade as viable entities in spite of the lower priorities that were placed on their basic claims in the 1970s.

Yet another important consideration is the *social and political climate*, i.e., the "times."[3] Without question, the 1960s were not just another decade. At least three aspects of the social climate were undoubtedly important in shaping reactions to black collective action: Democratic party dominance of the White House through 1968, a relatively high level of general political liberalism, and a favorable economy.

With such circumstances, it might be expected that federal responsiveness to the civil rights movement would take a turn for the better during the 1960s, even in the absence of radicalization. The general elections of 1960 ended eight years of Republican domination of the Presidency, the Congress was more liberal from 1958 through 1966, and it was during this period that most of the fundamental civil rights legislation was passed. But although the ideological makeup of the federal government provided a suitable environment for the emergence of governmental action on civil rights, it is doubtful that this factor alone would have accounted for such a torrent of civil rights progress. Rather, the favorable political environment should be viewed as the context which helped to shape the political response. A radical flank effect would most likely have occurred regardless of the ideological leanings of the government. Had conservatives controlled the White House and Congress, the increase of black radicalism would have been interpreted as either evidence of the futility of governmental action in moral issues such as racial equality or the undesirable result of overweening expectations from attempts at social engineering. But, in fact, the radicalization occurred during a time when majorities or near-majorities of federal decision-makers were already favorably inclined toward *some* sort of racial equalization. Accordingly, large numbers of these decision-makers came to see the crisis as the result of insufficient progress in racial and welfare issues and, more importantly, came to view various degrees of acquiescence to moderate demands as appropriate.

In terms of increased financial support for the civil rights organizations, much the same role might be attributed to the liberal climate of the decade (Taylor, Sheatsley, and Greeley 1978: 45–46). In and of itself, such liberalism is of little use to activists; rather, it has to be mobilized and turned to the movement's advantage. So far as the white public in the North was concerned, this was accomplished during the first few years of the 1960s. Among the important financial supporters of the civil rights organizations—not only the moderate legalists but the nonviolent militants as well—were white liberals. Many of these had been transformed into supporters by the widely-publicized protest campaigns in the South and by the reaction that these drew. But once again it would be a mistake to label liberalism the "cause" of increased resource mobilization. Instead, it should be viewed as part of the context most likely to produce a positive radical flank effect.

Finally, a *favorable economic situation* has been cited as a factor conducive to pro–civil rights reactions in America (Blackwell 1982: 329–31). A favorable economy undoubtedly had an effect on both policy enactment and financial support. During periods of affluence, it might be expected that those in positions of power would be less inclined to guard jealously the privileges of dominant groups. In other words, it is easier to talk about equal access to jobs, decent education, income security, and the like, and to make policies which ensure such access, during times when the goods can be delivered without seriously depriving dominant groups. Such a situation generally prevailed during the 1960s. Between 1960 and 1970, the Gross National Product increased 64 percent, from just under $600 billion to $982.4 billion. But the 1950s were also a prosperous decade, during which the GNP rose by 76.8 percent. Thus, it is clear that economic abundance, like liberal ideology, must serve as context rather than cause. Similarly, economic prosperity facilitates resource mobilization by social movement organizations. It does so first and foremost by increasing the supply of discretionary wealth from which individuals and organizations draw contributions (McCarthy and Zald 1973). It may also have an effect on this level by reducing the sense of threat posed by challenges from members of subordinate groups and thereby breaking down the hesitancy of members of dominant groups to help.

RADICAL FLANKS AND SOCIAL INTERESTS

Thus far, I have said very little of an explicit nature about variations in the responses of various groups to black radicalization. Consider, for example, the differences between the findings of Chapter 2 and Chapter 3. Chapter 2 demonstrates that increases in corporate and foundation contributions were greatest near the end of the decade, especially after 1967. But Chapter 3 shows that the greatest expansion in federal government responsiveness to black claims occurred earlier, between 1963 and 1965. What accounts for the differences? Why did the threat of increasing nonviolent protest prod the federal government into action but fail to stimulate unified, large-scale corporate and philanthropic response? The answer may lie in the different circumstances which faced the public and private sectors. Nonviolent protest was threatening to the Democratic administration of John F. Kennedy because it forced the President and his advisors into difficult political situations. Many instances of nonviolent protest, such as the Freedom Rides, virtually demanded that the federal government take some action or issue some statement in support of the protesters and in opposition to their tormentors. The success of many of the protests was a result of their artistry in making the protesters appear morally superior to the segregationists and southern police: this air of moral superiority, in turn, often caused white northerners to demand federal action. Moreover, the refusal of several southern state governments to comply with federal law also forced the administration's hand; school desegregation crises in Arkansas and Mississippi were the two most serious examples. Waves of nonviolent protest also tended to make some southern politicians even more adamant in their refusal to yield, even when it meant openly defying federal authority, and this in turn forced the federal government to assert itself.

In short, mass nonviolent protest contributed in several ways to a North-South political schism. The dangers of this schism were especially acute for the Democrats. Acting affirmatively against southern resistance involved a high price: it threatened to destroy Democratic unity in Congress and thereby the administration's ability to get its bills enacted into law. In addition, nonviolent protest on a mass scale threatened to escalate into *inter*racial violence. Sooner or later, southern blacks would refuse to turn the other cheek, to listen to King's admonitions about the power of love, to heed *CORE Rules for Action*. Sooner or later, they would respond in kind when attacked. Kennedy and his advisors knew this, and their prescience was confirmed by the events in Birmingham. Thus, nonviolent direct action struck at the heart of powerful political interests because it could so easily turn to violence. The result was federal action designed to make further protest unnecessary.

Nonviolent direct action did not threaten the interests of the corporate class in the same way it threatened those of the Kennedy administration. To be sure, the specter of a demonstration in front of one's factory or a boycott of one's store might be enough to prompt a given businessman to yield to protesters' demands. But in the North, direct action was not enough to force large concessions or to prompt corporate powerholders on a national level to become either official or unofficial sponsors of change. Riots, however, were another matter. If the cities burned, as McGeorge Bundy of the Ford Foundation noted in an address to the National Urban League convention in 1966, "the white man's companies will have to take the losses" (quoted in Allen 1969: 72). Urban violence and the black power ideologies which seemed to fuel it hit American business leaders in a spot where nonviolent direct action had not: their *collective* economic interests. Consequently, an unprecedented collective response emerged from the top of the economic structure during the late 1960s. The largest corporations and charitable foundations in the United States began to "invest" in racial reform and civil rights. In many cases the beneficiaries of this investment were such moderate organizations as the Urban League, the NAACP, and the Legal Defense Fund. In other cases, corporate efforts were directed not at established organizations but at issues and programs which had been espoused for some time: jobs, better housing, development of urban black leadership, educational upgrading, and aid to an emerging black bourgeoisie. In either case black moderates, as they had come to be defined by the latter half of the 1960s, were the winners. They emerged from the decade not merely intact but strong, with levels of influence they had not known before. Had it not been for the radicalism they so frequently deplored, such would not have been the case.

The differences between the timing of corporate/foundation responses and governmental responses suggests a vitally important conclusion: It is not radicalism *per se* that is the operative mechanism in radical flank effects but rather the intersection of particular forms of radicalism with particular group interests.

TOWARD A THEORY OF RADICAL FLANK EFFECTS

In order to move toward an adequate understanding of radical flank effects in social movements, future research must accomplish three objectives. First, it must demonstrate convincingly that such processes actually occur. Secondly, it must show that they are not limited to a single movement but instead are relatively recurrent features of multiorganizational collective action. Third and finally, research must specify the conditions under which radical flank effects occur and the conditions under which they are differentiated as positive or negative. The goal of this book, strictly speaking, has been to contribute to the first of these objectives. Accomplishment of the second must await investigations of other social movements. So too must the third, although it is possible even at this early stage to speculate about the conditions which might shape positive or negative effects:

1. *Relative threat*. When the goals and tactics of moderate groups are perceived by relevant third parties as representing far less of a threat to their interests than those of radical groups, other things being equal, support of moderates is more likely. When the goals and tactics of moderate groups are perceived as representing as great or nearly as great a threat to those interests, support for moderates will not be interpreted as a beneficial strategy. In fact, attempts may be made to undermine the movement as a whole.

It might also be suggested that a positive radical flank effect is a more likely outgrowth of a crisis when the responding group stands to gain through an accommodative response rather than merely to minimize losses. Such federal agencies as the Department of Health, Education, and Welfare, for example, had a vested bureaucratic interest in adopting what Turner (1969) called a "protest interpretation" of urban rioting. Such an interpretation contributed to an effective argument for increased budgets and power.

2. *Relative correspondence of group goals and societal values.* Other things being equal, a positive radical flank effect is much more likely when goals of moderate groups are perceived as more consistent with cherished societal values than the goals of radical groups. Civil rights moderates during the legalistic and direct action phases of the movement, for instance, enjoyed a distinct advantage in that their goals—e.g., the right to vote—were perceived as being quintessentially "American." Conversely, a negative radical flank effect is more likely when the goals of both moderates and radicals appear to contradict such values. It should be noted, however, that the emergence of *new* radicals may lead to changes in such perceptions; i.e., one group's goals may appear to challenge cherished values until more "outlandish" agendas emerge. At that point, there may be attempts to integrate or normalize the older claims and to deal with them more sympathetically.

3. *Perceived appeal of radical groups.* The case of black collective action suggests that supportive responses by elites are much more likely to occur when radical groups are perceived by elites as appealing to substantial numbers of potential constituents. Repressive responses are more likely when the appeal of radicals appears unlikely to grow. In the former instance, elites may conclude that the influence of militants will grow unless something is done to limit it. To do so, they may attempt to repress the radicals—a procedure which may carry considerable political risks—or they may try to "strengthen the middle."[4] As an illustration of the latter pattern, we have only to recall the frequent references to the growing appeal of Black Muslims during the Kennedy administration and the perceived importance of providing more responsible black leaders with visible successes.

4. *Power of the constituent pool.* A related factor has to do with the perceived power of the movement's constituent pool—i.e., the population from which moderate and/or radical organizations attempt to draw supporters. Other things being equal, elite support of moderates seems more likely when the power of the movement's constituent pool is perceived to be on the rise. For instance, politi-

cal leaders recognized that urbanization was increasing the power of the black vote after World War II. Although this development hardly insured that powerful elites would align themselves with civil rights forces, it contributed to a climate in which support for "reasonable" black organizations could be acceptable. No such incentive exists, however, when the power of the constituent pool is perceived to be weak or waning. Under such circumstances an elite which prefers to neutralize even moderate challenges may be able to use the radical threat to do so.

5. *Perceived links between moderates and radicals.* An especially important factor in shaping the reaction of elites is their perception of the relationship between militants and moderates. Supportive involvement by elites depends upon the perception that the two flanks of a movement are separate and distinct—i.e., that moderates are neither linked to nor responsible for the actions and statements of the radicals. It is for this reason that black moderate leaders were so careful to condemn the urban riots and the harsher versions of black power. Had they allowed themselves to be charged with complicity in the riots or the trend toward black nationalism, their white support would have dissolved.[5]

6. *Political climate.* The openness of the political process is variable. There occur periods during which, for a number of possible reasons, collective claimsmaking stands a relatively good chance of success. Conversely, there occur periods during which the political center is relatively closed (McAdam 1982: 40–43; McAdam 1983; also see Goldstone 1980: 1037–40). For social movements support by elites is more likely during periods like the 1960s, when elites are relatively receptive to group claims *in general*. On the other hand, elites are more likely to ignore demands of a movement or to support the repression of challenges during periods like the early 1980s, when overall receptivity is diminished.

7. *Perceived efficacy of accommodation and support.* Accommodating or co-opting the moderate segment of a given social movement may or may not be seen by powerful elites as a fruitful neutralizing strategy. Support by elites is most likely when an accommodative response seems to stand a good chance of weakening the radical threat. During the 1950s and the 1960s, elites were divided over the appropriate response to racial turmoil. Some doubted that old-line moderate organizations still had a hold over young urban blacks, while others increased their support of those organizations.

THE CONSEQUENCES OF REACTIVE SUPPORT BY ELITES

As we have seen, both financial and political support for civil rights by elite groups was largely reactive in nature: elites appear to have been motivated to align themselves with proponents of change largely because of the threat of deepening black insurgency. But for the black movement itself, what of the *consequences* of support by elites? Are alliances with powerful outsiders necessarily of benefit to social movements and their constituents? Two contradictory points of view on this issue have emerged in recent years.

Resource mobilization theory suggests that external support is a virtual necessity under contemporary circumstances. According to this perspective, most aggrieved populations will lack the indigenous resources necessary to carry on a sustained challenge. Without benefactors, therefore, they will be doomed to failure. Elites are not the only sources of external support, to be sure, but their power and wealth make them very attractive. The dependence upon external resources, of course, constrains the tactical choices of insurgents. If the premise that external benefactors are necessary is accepted, it follows that disruptive or socially-disapproved tactics are unwise, as they will most likely lead to frustration and failure, undermining the external resource base and "starving" the collective challenge. It is far better, from this point of view, for protest leaders to concentrate on building stable mass organizations or professionalized reform groups with alliances to influential and/or rich third parties.

Much recent social movement analysis, however, seems to contradict this school of thought. The involvement of elites, it is claimed, can be a trap. This view is based upon the premise that social movements are not so dependent upon external support as resource mobilization theory has suggested (McAdam 1982; Morris 1984). If this premise is true, organizers need not worry so much about rocking the boat; indeed, the classic statement of this perspective by Piven and Cloward (1977) maintains that the movements of the powerless have a chance to succeed precisely because of their disruptive potential. Doing outside fund-raising or trying to build bureaucratic, professionalized organizations only distracts such movements from what they do best: forcing change through creating crises. Similarly, McAdam (1982) concludes that elite involvement in social movements threatens to lead to co-optation and to channel insurgents toward ineffective strategies. Insofar as this is true, movement leaders are well advised either to forgo elite support or to accept it very selectively so as to maintain a high level of militancy.

Generally, the investigation described in this book has yielded results consistent with the position of McAdam and of Piven and Cloward. It has suggested that elite involvement was indeed reactive and motivated at least partly by the need to manipulate insurgency and manage crises. In at least two ways, however, the analysis of radical flank effects in the black revolt leads in somewhat different directions.

First, the debate over the desirability of elite support and its tactical implications has thus far assumed a two-way interaction—i.e., an exchange relationship involving only two groups, "elites" and "insurgents." But social movements tend to be more complicated than this. Elites are typically confronted with several movement groups with whom they must deal simultaneously, and their reactions to one challenger will be conditioned by the problems and opportunities that other challengers in the movement present.[6] The analysis of positive radical flank effects suggests that an unintentional "division of labor" may develop within movements—a division of labor in which moderates and radicals perform very different roles. Each of these roles has its advantages and disadvantages. Moderates typically enjoy greater levels of contact and influence with elites and decisionmakers but because of their more favored position are prohibited from rocking the boat. To create crises is to imperil the ability to cajole, bargain, or beg for limited concessions. Radicals, on the other hand, have no reputation or influence to protect, as they are outsiders from the beginning. Accordingly, their chances of receiving concessions from decision-makers or resources from well-heeled supporters are minimal, but so are the constraints upon their actions.

My examination of the black protest movement suggests that a strategic balance can be struck, a symbiosis between radicals and moderates. In this relationship radicals specialize in generating crises which elites must deal with, while moderates specialize in offering relatively unthreatening avenues of escape. Radicals, themselves difficult to deal with, come to be seen as boisterous, rude, and disorganized. In contrast, moderates—with their identifiable leaders who are adept at the arts of negotiation and compromise—appear polite, "realistic," and businesslike. Such features make moderates more attractive to responding groups, but all the more so when more militant activists are applying pressure. Thus, when positive radical flank effects are at work, moderates may be able to maintain good relations with outside supporters by distancing themselves from radicals while at the same time profiting from the crises the radicals create.

MOVEMENT SUCCESS AS STEPWISE CHANGE

The second sense in which I differ from the conclusions of McAdam and of Piven and Cloward has to do with their assumption of the undesirability of the involvement of elites in social movements. Admittedly, support by elites is unlikely to benefit the relatively militant vanguard of a social movement because it will rarely be either directed toward them or consistent with their goals. It will be directed instead toward safer targets—groups with whom elites can do business. But it cannot be assumed in an *a priori* fashion that such a selection of targets will normally produce only minimal benefits *for a movement's constituents*. To adopt that position would be to fall victim to a sort of "immediatist bias" (as opposed to a "gradualist bias"), to an unrealistic sense of what is possible in most socio-political climates.

In place of this pessimistic assessment of the consequences of involving elites, I would argue that the unfolding of the black revolt supports a "stepwise" view of movement success. From this perspective, all that social movements can realistically expect to accomplish in most periods is relatively gradual motion in the direction of their goals. The likelihood of even gradual progress, however, is not necessarily enhanced by activists moderating their demands and being "realistic." Collective action is much like bargaining: skilled negotiators will ask for more than they really expect to receive and seek to press the other side into giving up as much as possible. Herein lies the utility of radical flanks—they force the opponent's hand and may also stretch the terms of the negotiations.

If at least a portion of the elites choose to recognize "reasonable" claims of moderates and/or to accommodate moderate groups rather than ignoring or repressing them, a positive radical flank effect has taken place. This may temporarily resolve the crisis, but it is quite unlikely that it will do so for long. Rather, the resolution of the crisis merely establishes a new line of scrimmage from which further insurgency will spring. New collective challenges may be a long time coming. But in the meantime, real gains will probably have accrued.

Black insurgency is a case in point. As we have seen, elites became involved in supporting moderate civil rights groups because of the sense of crisis and threat. By all appearances, their strategy worked. That is, militant black insurgency waned during the 1970s—although elite involvement was hardly the only reason for the decline. What might have happened had the militant momentum of the late 1960s been sustained is open to speculation. But the achievements that had come as part of the bargain were quite considerable: legal recognition of a wide range of civil rights, affirmative action programs in both the public and private sectors, and social services intended largely for minority targets, to name only the most visible. These were late in coming and not altogether satisfactory, but to deny that they constituted victories is absurd. Even more important was the completely new sense of efficacy that was felt by segments of the black population, a confidence which led to new initiatives within the political and economic structure. Setbacks occurred during the inactive 1970s, but these losses were not so great as to take blacks back where they started before the movement began. Many of the accomplishments of the 1960s came to be virtually taken for granted in subsequent years. I would argue further—but this is of course speculative—that another round of militant black insurgency is almost inevitable. Although no one can predict precisely what form it will take or how much success it will meet with, it will likely center around new issues that would have been unimaginable—"non-negotiable"—before the round of collective action.

Appendix: Supplementary Tables

INCOME DATA: NUL, NAACP
LDEF, SRC, SCLC, CORE, AND SNCC

TABLE A-1 National Urban League (NUL): Sources of Funding (dollars)

Year	Type of source							Total exogenous income
	Government funds	Corporate funds	Foundation grants	Labor funds	Church funds	Misc. org. funds	Individual donations	
1961	0	70,000	62,000	16,000		39,000	70,000	257,000
1962	0	153,000	153,000	18,000		56,000	106,000	572,000
1963	0	527,000	513,000	16,000		78,000	87,000	1,221,000
1964	0	657,000	665,000	27,000		86,000	104,000	1,539,000
1965	0	848,000	701,000	27,000		96,000	152,000	1,824,000
1966	294,000	888,000	707,000	31,000		117,000	164,000	2,201,000
1967	536,000	1,056,000	905,000	0		72,000	243,000	2,812,000
1968	650,000	1,197,000	1,573,000	25,000		100,000	376,000	3,921,000
1969	3,595,000	1,521,000	2,898,000	24,000		156,000	425,000	8,619,000
1970	6,913,000	1,973,000	5,054,000	30,000		193,000	379,000	14,542,000

Note: Amounts in the first seven columns do not add up to the amount in the right-hand column, since actual or estimated total exogenous income includes funds from other sources as well. See notes to Table 8 for a description of procedures used to calculate total exogenous income.

TABLE A-2 National Association for the
Advancement of Colored People (NAACP):
Sources of Funding (dollars)

Year	Type of source		
	Internally derived	Externally derived	Total
1952			
1953	309,954	16,437	326,391
1954	337,230	30,944	368,174
1955	471,727	40,606	512,333
1956			
1957	439,262	103,907	543,169
1958	489,626	90,679	580,305
1959	523,691	93,703	617,394
1960	587,676	103,838	691,514
1961	591,908	96,936	688,844
1962	580,020	81,547	661,569
1963	828,729	251,579	1,080,308
1964	698,433	292,738	991,171
1965	1,245,494	388,077	1,633,571
1966	1,266,552	597,425	1,863,977
1967	1,145,064	1,294,909	2,439,973
1968	1,242,722	1,904,513	3,147,235
1969	1,250,000	2,418,000	3,668,500
1970	1,313,002	2,665,373	3,978,375

Note: See Table 8, note *a*, for a description of the procedure used to determine internally-derived and externally-derived income for the NAACP. Empty cells: no data available.

TABLE A-3 Legal Defense and Education Fund, Inc. (LDEF): Sources of Funding (dollars)

Year	Type of source							Total exogenous income
	Government funds	Corporate funds	Foundation grants	Labor funds	Church funds	Misc. org. funds	Individual donations	
1952								210,624
1953								224,321
1954								200,021
1955								
1956								346,947
1957								319,537
1958								315,081
1959								357,988
1960								489,540
1961								560,808
1962								669,427
1963								1,197,204
1964			179,914	455		36,921	891,252	1,425,321
1965			220,347	3,355		70,729	766,746	1,661,793
1966			337,350	3,225		101,899	837,315	1,695,718
1967			487,155	1,700		77,400	933,477	2,046,356
1968		7,015	596,789	5		56,871	1,256,374	2,535,430
1969		7,250	884,733	0		11,496	1,181,701	2,811,826
1970		3,360	1,275,142	0		9,871	1,041,791	2,980,998

Note: Amounts in the first seven columns do not add up to the amount in the right-hand column, since actual or estimated total exogenous income includes funds from other sources as well. See notes to Table 8 for a description of procedures used to calculate total exogenous income. Empty cells: no data available.

APPENDIX

TABLE A-4 Southern Regional Council (SRC) General Fund: Sources of Funding (dollars)

Year	Type of source							Total exogenous income
	Government funds	Corporate funds	Foundation grants	Labor funds	Church funds	Misc. org. funds	Individual donations	
1952			13,000		4,060	3,303	6,781	27,495
1953			23,600	3,700	4,190	449	2,718	35,735
1954			48,460	4,700	3,389	148	1,620	59,043
1955			65,200	4,350	3,995		3,694	79,309
1956			19,500	4,500	4,020	233	3,116	31,369
1957			85,867		4,095	5,568	4,815	109,062
1958			124,281	4,500	4,100	1,109	1,042	138,274
1959			107,000		3,380	2,619	6,730	126,285
1960			98,400	3,425	4,050	360	28,871	139,106
1961								
1962			149,924	1,200	4,025	100	1,729	168,247
1963			141,500	600	2,043	11	3,569	161,311
1964			158,500			6,155	3,230	180,005
1965			92,800	5,000	0	105	3,200	101,105
1966								
1967			135,125	0	0	100	3,445	138,670
1968			258,900	0	5,000	100	5,112	269,112
1969			200,700			325	3,556	204,591
1970			161,500			300	12,521	174,321

Note: Amounts in the first seven columns do not add up to the amount in the right-hand column, since actual or estimated total exogenous income includes funds from other sources as well. See notes to Table 8 for a description of procedures used to calculate total exogenous income. Empty cells: no data available.

TABLE A-5 Southern Regional Council (SRC), General Fund and Special Projects: Sources of Funding (dollars)

Year	Type of source							Total exogenous income
	Government funds	Corporate funds	Foundation grants	Labor funds	Church funds	Misc. org. funds	Individual donations	
1964			616,350			31,904	14,857	663,111
1965			630,300	5,000	4,250	9,355		648,905
1966								
1967			659,934	0	3,200	1,850	4,867	669,851
1968			1,170,050	5,000	3,200	1,572	7,602	1,187,424
1969			1,354,385			500	19,431	1,373,816
1970			814,392	0	0	300	12,546	827,238

Note: Amounts in the first seven columns do not add up to the amount in the right-hand column, since actual or estimated total exogenous income includes funds from other sources as well. See notes to Table 8 for a description of procedures used to calculate total exogenous income. Empty cells: no data available.

TABLE A-6 Southern Christian Leadership Conference (SCLC): Sources of Funding (dollars)

Year	Type of source							Total exogenous income
	Government funds	Corporate funds	Foundation grants	Labor funds	Church funds	Misc. org. funds	Individual donations	
1959				120	15,255	5,239		(est.) 25,000
1960				3,157	16,114	19,024		54,726
1961				1,235	15,103	31,994		193,168
1962								197,565
1963						12,209		728,172
1964						51,228		578,787
1965				1,585	5,471	6,367		(est.) 1,643,000
1966								(est.) 932,000
1967								(est.) 932,000
1968								(est.) 1,000,000
1969								(est.) 500,000
1970								(est.) 400,000

Note: Amounts in the first seven columns do not add up to the amount in the right-hand column, since actual or estimated total exogenous income includes funds from other sources as well. See notes to Table 8 for a description of procedures used to calculate total exogenous income. Empty cells: no data available.

TABLE A-7 Congress of Racial Equality (CORE): Sources of Funding (dollars)

Year	Type of source							Total exogenous income
	Government funds	Corporate funds	Foundation grants	Labor funds	Church funds	Misc. org. funds	Individual donations	
1952						637	3,580	4,604
1953						726	5,135	5,989
1954						153	4,972	5,600
1955						181	6,724	6,911
1956								
1957						65		15,506
1958								22,936
1959				695				55,324
1960			1,000	1,347				130,609
1961				6,100				213,248
1962				13,500				244,034
1963				40,000		18,655		437,043
1964			114,000	40,000		54,908	318,722	694,558
1965			67,902	40,000		50,387	435,053	677,785
1966			10,000					(est.) 400,000
1967			81,500					(est.) 280,000
1968			45,500					(est.) 250,000
1969			521,000					(est.) 670,000
1970			60,000					(est.) 210,000

Note: Amounts in the first seven columns do not add up to the amount in the right-hand column, since actual or estimated total exogenous income includes funds from other sources as well. See notes to Table 8 for a description of procedures used to calculate total exogenous income. Empty cells: no data available.

TABLE A-8 Student Nonviolent Coordinating Committee (SNCC): Sources of Funding (dollars)

Year	Type of source							Total exogenous income
	Government funds	Corporate funds	Foundation grants	Labor funds	Church funds	Misc. org. funds	Individual donations	
1960								
1961								
1962								71,927
1963					142,595	32,674	74,429	302,894
1964						433,530	181,198	631,439
1965						506,488	96,980	637,736
1966						301,946	79,590	397,237
1967								(est.) 250,000
1968								(est.) 150,000
1969								(est.) 50,000
1970								(est.) 25,000

Note: Amounts in the first seven columns do not add up to the amount in the right-hand column, since actual or estimated total exogenous income includes funds from other sources as well. See notes to Table 8 for a description of procedures used to calculate total exogenous income. Empty cells: no data available.

Notes

INTRODUCTION

1. Throughout this study, radicalism will be defined in terms of the degree to which a group of actors, their goals, their rhetoric, and their tactics (a) are widely viewed as unconventional, inappropriate, or illegitimate; (b) are widely perceived as threatening; and (c) call for fundamental social change. A more detailed definition will be presented in Chapter 1.

2. The term is adapted from Freeman's (1975) analysis of the women's movement, in which she characterizes more extreme feminist groups as the "radical flank." Further, she argues that the feminist radical flank helped to lend legitimacy to moderate women's groups by absorbing the inevitable charges of "revolutionary" and "far out."

3. For an empirical test and critical analysis of this thesis, see McAdam (1982).

4. A recent analysis of "professional" movement organizations and the funding of the civil rights movement (Jenkins and Eckert 1986) touches upon the issue of radicalism and crisis in an indirect manner; this study will be discussed in Chapter 2.

5. Among the best general historical works on the civil rights movement are Blumberg (1984), Brisbane (1974), Brooks (1974), Killian (1968), Lawson (1976), Muse (1968), and Powledge (1967). Garrow's 1986 study is outstanding both as a biography of King and as a focused history of the movement he came to symbolize. Two excellent recent books with a more theoretical orientation are McAdam (1982) and Morris (1984). Useful editions of primary sources include Friedman (1968) and Raines (1977).

6. Some recent analyses have concluded that the indispensability of external supporters, particularly elites, has been exaggerated by some versions of resource mobilization theory (McAdam 1982; Morris 1984). Morris, for example, argues that "indigenous resources are far more likely to be

198 crucial in the early phases of movements, because outside resources tend to be sporadic and highly conditional, in most cases coming in response to pressure from indigenous movements already under way" (283). Such a conclusion is consistent with the evidence which I will present in Chapter 2, and I will consider the issue at that time.

CHAPTER 1

1. According to Morris (1984), southern harassment of the NAACP during the 1950s, though rather successful in the short run, led to a "protest vacuum" which came to be filled by newly-organized church-related groups; these new groups contributed to the organizational foundation for later direct-action protest (30–35, 37–39).

2. Scholarly discussions of civil rights activism during this period clearly support Killian's (1972) point concerning shifting definitions of militancy. As late as 1964, Marx was able to conclude that a "militant Negro is one who actively opposes discrimination and segregation . . . , encourages civil rights demonstrations," believes that "Negroes should spend more time in the secular activity of demonstrating than in the otherworldly one of praying," and would or already has taken part in demonstrations (42). By the time Marx's book was published (1967), these characteristics were being seen by many as marks of moderation.

3. These and other episodes of NAACP participation in direct action should not be interpreted as indications that the Association had become a protest organization. The relationship between the NAACP and supporters of such protest activities has been complex. Although the NAACP leadership expressly disapproved of demonstrations in earlier periods of the organization's existence, it gradually moved in the direction of selectively supporting such actions. Moreover, local branches varied in their support for and participation in protests. But through it all the NAACP as a national organization has typically treated direct action as a secondary and peripheral tactic, especially before 1960. After 1960 its role, and the role of the Legal Defense and Educational Fund, was usually as a source of bail money and legal assistance for demonstrators (Meier 1963: 439).

4. The potential impact of the black voter, especially in the South, was clear. Many southern counties had large minorities and sometimes majorities of black residents. It was clear to voter registration workers that significant political clout would accrue if formal exclusionary practices (literacy tests, etc.) and informal ones (threat and terror) could be overcome. The invalidation of the white primary in 1944 was a major step in the elimination of the former, but the violent repression of black voting power was more difficult to defeat. Nevertheless, black voter registration in the South increased from about 750,000 in 1950 to approximately 1.2 million in 1952 (Lawson 1976; Newman et al. 1978: 13–14, 19).

5. During 1963 only two SNCC staff members received salaries as large

as $3,000, thirteen got from $1,000 to $2,000, 96 got between $100 and $500, and 49 received less than $100 each. A memo written by James Forman reveals that an increase in the pay of Mississippi SNCC workers from the standard of $10 a week to $20 proved somewhat controversial. This information is taken from internal SNCC reports and memos supplied by Clayborne Carson, a former member and the most recent historian of the organization.

6. In discussing the racial violence of the 1960s, one encounters serious terminological and methodological difficulties. The words used to describe these events tend to be emotionally charged and to convey subtle interpretations. "Riot" and "disorder" evoke images of random, senseless, and purposeless rage; while this imagery may closely resemble the interpretations of many whites in 1964 and 1965, studies of the events do not support this view entirely (Fogelson 1971; National Advisory Commission 1969; Feagin and Hahn 1973; Bullock 1969). Both "revolt" (Feagin and Hahn 1973) and "rebellion" (Allen 1969 and others), imply a degree of organization and political purposefulness that may be unwarranted. In this research, I employ the term "riot" in most instances, more for its conventionality than for any analytic baggage it may carry (Sears and McConahay 1973). In discussing trends and making comparisons, major difficulties emerge from the problem of deciding what constitutes a "riot." Feagin and Hahn (1973:135) note that different analysts have required that anywhere from four to a hundred participants be involved in order for an episode of collective violence to be termed a riot, and that others have made assumptions about the nature, target, and motivation of the violence in defining it this way. Since a theoretical analysis of collective violence is not among the foci of this study, and since my immediate concern is more with group perceptions and interpretations of riots than with the events themselves, I focus mainly on official measurements. See National Advisory Commission 1968 and Muse 1968, especially chs. 14, 18, 19, and 20.

7. For example, see James Farmer's statements in *CORE-labor* 107 (July-August 1964): 1–2, and the NAACP *Annual Report for 1966*.

CHAPTER 2

1. McAdam (1980) found resource mobilization theory inadequate as an explanation of black insurgency, since changes in external support appeared to *follow* rather than precede changing levels of movement-initiated activity.

2. Each of the organizations still in existence—i.e., all except SNCC—were contacted and asked for the necessary information on outside contributions through 1970. Only the National Urban League and the Southern Regional Council provided the data directly. I subsequently examined the financial records of the NAACP and the Legal Defense and Educational Fund at their respective headquarters in New York. Partial financial data

200 on the Southern Christian Leadership Conference, the Congress of Racial Equality, and the Student Nonviolent Coordinating Committee were obtained at the Martin Luther King Library and Archives in Atlanta, Georgia. Secondary sources were used to fill in the gaps in the data set.

3. The otherwise excellent collections of original SCLC and SNCC materials maintained at the Martin Luther King Library and Archives (which also contains microfilms from the well-known University of Wisconsin collections) contain only very incomplete financial information. Surviving material of the Congress of Racial Equality are somewhat better, but post-1967 information on finances is missing. Even those still existing organizations which have maintained generally complete and detailed financial records have lost older material. The Urban League is unable to locate financial reports for the years prior to 1961. The SRC, the NAACP, and the LDEF have also lost financial records for a few years of the 1950–1970 period.

4. While I lack estimates of the incomes of the Urban League and the NAACP for 1952, I believe it is quite reasonable to estimate total movement exogenous income for that year at not more than $450,000 (Table 8). Assuming that this were true, the proportionate increase between 1952 and 1957 would have been nearly 83 percent. Such a rate of growth over six years is not inconsiderable, yet the total amounts are so small in comparison to later years that the increases seem unspectacular.

5. See notes to Table 8.

6. The financing of the SCLC during the 1960s depended heavily upon direct-mail campaigns organized in New York (Garrow 1986: 155, 168, 225, 353, 429, 710). The success of these campaigns seems to have been determined largely by King's activities.

7. Estimates of CORE's exogenous income during the late 1960s are adapted from McAdam's data (1982). My estimates are higher than his, however, due to the addition of foundation grant income as reported in *Foundation News*.

8. *Foundation News* reports only grants which exceed $10,000 and only those grants which the foundations themselves report or which are otherwise publicized. Thus, there is a tendency toward underreporting, and whatever biases are involved in this underreporting are difficult to assess. For example, many foundations have been criticized for supporting "extremist" groups of various sorts. While it is doubtful that this practice was ever widespread, it is possible that grants to more militant black groups might have been less frequently publicized. I doubt, however, that this represents a serious problem for the present research, since I am more directly concerned with trends in foundation grants to groups which were *less* controversial.

Unfortunately, there seems to be a significant amount of error in *Foundation News*'s reporting of grants to moderate organizations as well. Comparisons of the official financial reports of the Urban League and the Southern Regional Council to *FN* reveals that *FN* is often off the mark by a considerable degree. Underestimation can be understood largely as a result of the failure of foundations to report. The occasional instances of *over*estimation, which are much less frequent, are probably the results of publishing grants during the year after they were actually made.

9. In its early days, SNCC was also dependent upon donations of money and other resources by other civil rights organizations. Its first office, in fact, was a corner of the SCLC headquarters. As late as 1964, internal memos of SNCC suggest that considerable amounts were obtained from NAACP and CORE groups and other sources within the movement.

10. A notable exception is recent work by Craig Jenkins, who has investigated foundation involvement in social movements generally and with civil rights organizations in particular (Jenkins 1986 and 1987; Jenkins and Eckert 1986).

11. This has been independently confirmed recently by other researchers who used different measures of foundation support (Jenkins and Eckert 1986).

12. In order to locate foundation grants to these and a large number of other civil rights and related organizations, it is not sufficient to utilize only the "Interracial Relations" category used routinely by *Foundation News*. The following sections of each volume of *FN* from 1960 (the first volume) through 1970 were searched: Business and Labor, Community Funds, Delinquency and Crime, Economics, Educational Associations, Educational Research, Endowment, Fellowships, General Welfare, Government, Higher Education, Interracial Relations, Law, Medical Education, Relief and Social Agencies, Religious Associations, Religious Welfare, Scholarships and Loans, Social Science, Sociology, Vocational Training, and Youth Agencies. Large numbers of relevant grants were found in sections other than Interracial Relations.

13. In addition to the seven primary organizations, these include: local Urban Leagues, the National Committee Against Discrimination in Housing, Brotherhood-in-Action, the National Catholic Conference for Interracial Justice, the Lawyers' Committee for Civil Rights Under Law, the Law Students' Civil Rights Research Council, the Interracial Council for Business Opportunity, the United Negro College Fund, the National Scholarship Service and Fund for Negro Students, state Human Relations Councils, the National Urban Coalition and all local Urban Coalitions, the Metropolitan Applied Research Center, the Citizens' Crusade Against Poverty, and Urban America.

CHAPTER 3

1. For example, blacks in the 1970s still lagged behind whites in income, even after controlling for educational attainment and other variables (Farley 1977, 1984; Smyth 1976). Black unemployment rates have remained

202 consistently higher than white rates by margins of two to almost seven percent (Newman et al. 1978: 43–64). On the aggregate level, black housing remained of lower quality than white housing (Newman et al. 1978: 146), and residential segregation declined little through 1970 (Sorensen, Taeuber, and Hollingsworth 1975; Taeuber and Taeuber 1969; Van Valey, Roof, and Wilcox 1977).

2. These became known as "Part III powers," named after the section of the 1957 civil rights bill which sought to expand the Justice Department's role in the enforcement of civil rights. (Lawson 1976: 168–69, 178–82).

3. In a more recent work (1982), Piven and Cloward show that the effect of insurgency on relief turned out to be somewhat durable. Far from ending with the protests, liberalization of relief eligibility caused AFDC rolls to stay high and Medicare and food stamp rolls to continue expanding until the Reagan cuts of the 1980s.

4. Robert F. Kennedy, interview by Anthony Lewis, December 6, 1964, John F. Kennedy Library Oral History Program, pp. 575–76; Martin Luther King, interview by Berl I. Bernhard, March 9, 1964, John F. Kennedy Library Oral History Program, p. 24.

5. James Farmer, interview by Paige Mulhollan, July 20, 1972, Lyndon Baines Johnson Library, p. 19.

6. Robert F. Kennedy, Oral History Interview, 1964, pp. 586–91.

7. Wofford's concern here was clearly with *northern urban* violence. On April 24, 1963, as violence was developing in both Birmingham, Alabama, and Cambridge, Maryland, a memo from George Reedy to Vice President Lyndon Johnson mentions similar fears on the part of a black lawyer who had been close to the Kennedy campaign. Noting that she had "forgotten about the problems of the underprivileged Negroes because [she] had been practicing law for too many years on K Street," she shared with Reedy her concerns over the "explosive force" that existed in every city in America and her sense that the only solution was to be found in "some massive public works programs." George Reedy to Lyndon B. Johnson, April 24, 1963, Papers of Theodore Sorensen: Civil Rights Statements, John F. Kennedy Library.

8. White House Recording, May 12, 1963, Item no. 86.2, John F. Kennedy Library.

9. The Black Muslims were, in fact, increasingly portrayed as an unpleasant alternative to more moderate civil rights forces (Brauer 1977, 241–43, 354n.) In an article in the *London Economist*, Malcolm Baldrige stated that the "question now is whether the long-frustrated Negro can be confined to the peaceful methods preached by the leader of the Birmingham demonstrations." He described how Burke Marshall had told Birmingham businessmen that the Muslims would be their next antagonists if they rejected King (Memorandum, Baldrige to Marshall, June 13, 1963, Papers of Burke Marshall, John F. Kennedy Library).

10. White House Recording, May 12, 1963, Item No. 86.2, John F. Kennedy Library.

11. Memorandum, Berl Bernhard to Theodore Sorensen and Lee White, May 15, 1963. Burke Marshall Papers: Memoranda January 1962–May 1963. John F. Kennedy Library.

12. Memorandum, Archibald Cox to the President, June 17, 1963. Papers of Robert F. Kennedy: Attorney General's General Correspondence, Civil Rights 6/16–6/30/63. John F. Kennedy Library.

13. Memorandum, G. Mennen Williams to Theodore Sorensen, June 15, 1963, emphasis added. Papers of Robert F. Kennedy: Attorney General's General Correspondence, Civil Rights 6/16/63–6/30/63. John F. Kennedy Library.

14. Memorandum, Williams to the President, June 15, 1963. Papers of Robert F. Kennedy: Attorney General's General Correspondence, Civil Rights 6/16/63–6/30/63. John F. Kennedy Library.

15. Williams to the President, June 15, 1963.

16. Correspondence, William B. Davis to Robert F. Kennedy, June 18, 1963. Papers of Robert F. Kennedy: Attorney General's General Correspondence, Civil Rights 7/1/63–7/15/63. John F. Kennedy Library.

17. Memorandum, John Kenneth Galbraith to Robert F. Kennedy, June 11, 1963, emphasis added. Burke Marshall Papers: Community Relations Service, General, July 1963. John F. Kennedy Library.

18. In fact, the first such meeting occurred even earlier but was not part of this series of meetings. On May 15, the President and the Attorney General met with a group of newspaper editors from Alabama to try to enlist their support in resolving the civil rights crisis. In this meeting the Kennedy brothers included an argument that was becoming quite familiar: that if moderate demands were not met in a reasonable manner, then frustrated blacks would begin turning to more extreme leaders and to violent tactics (Brauer 1977: 241).

19. Correspondence, F. R. Kappel to the Business Council, July 17, 1963. Papers of Lee C. White, Business Council Meeting. John F. Kennedy Library.

20. Memorandum, Lee C. White to the President, June 22, 1963. Papers of President Kennedy, Civil Rights, General 6/14/63–6/30/63. John F. Kennedy Library.

21. Unfortunately, no transcriptions of these meetings were made, so it is impossible to reconstruct what was said except by using the recollections of those present. But the files housed at the John F. Kennedy Library do contain numerous memos and notes that the President's advisors made in advance of the meetings. These materials have been used extensively in this research.

22. Walter Reuther, labor leader and ally of the civil rights movement, was making a similar argument in his dealings with business leaders. During the June 22 civil rights meeting, he told President Kennedy:

> In Detroit, I've talked to these fellas. I went to the president of the General Motors Corporation, I talked to young Henry Ford, I talked

204   to... the president of Chrysler, I talked to all of 'em, and I said "Look, you can't escape this problem. Now there are two ways of resolving it: either by reason or by riots. The civil war that this is gonna trigger is not gonna be fought in Gettysburg, it's gonna be in your back yard, in your plants, where your kids are growing up." I got 'em all! I got the president of General Motors, Ford, Chrysler, American Motors, all to serve on a local civil rights committee. Now we've got to do that for the whole nation (White House Recording, August 28, 1963, Item 108.2, Boston: John F. Kennedy Library).

23. Kappel to Business Council, July 17, 1963.
24. Robert F. Kennedy, Oral History Interview, 1964, pp. 831–33.
25. Government preparations included the drafting of documents authorizing the use of armed forces to restore civil order in the event of a riot in Washington during the March. These documents were prepared in advance and required only the President's signature if needed. See Papers of Robert F. Kennedy, Attorney General's Correspondence, Personal, 1961–1964. John F. Kennedy Library.
26. In his recent study of Equal Employment Opportunity legislation, Burstein (1985) maintains that a favorable turn in public opinion was of key importance in ending Congressional inaction. "Title 7 [which contained the employment provision of the 1964 Civil Rights Act] passed shortly after members of Congress could say with some confidence, for the first time, that more than half the public favored EEO and felt strongly that civil rights was a major public problem" (1985: 181). In contrast with my analysis, he credits the civil rights movement only with providing reasons for congressmen to monitor public opinion on these issues, with intensifying opinion trends that were already improving, and with convincing legislators that EEO legislation would satisfy public demands. While my analysis is generally consistent with Burstein's, I believe he underestimates the degree to which political leaders were concerned over the disruptive potential of movement activities.

CHAPTER 4

1. Nor was antiblack violence limited to the South. During the early twentieth century, for example, major antiblack urban riots occurred in New York City; Springfield, Ohio; Springfield, Illinois; East St. Louis; Chicago, and Washington, D.C. (see Feagin and Hahn 1973; National Advisory Commission on Civil Disorders 1968; Rudwick 1964; Waskow 1966).
2. Some scholars have argued that nonviolent methods depended for their success upon the violent reactions they provoked. Even practitioners like Dr. King were aware of the manner in which their opponents' brutality tended to work to the benefit of the protesters (Colaiaco 1986).
3. Recent analyses have recognized the importance of historically specific forces in determining the outcomes of movements. Jenkins (1985), for

instance, has shown how the successful organization of a farm workers union had to await the arrival of the receptive political context of the 1960s. Similarly, Barkan's (1985) study of trials of civil rights and antiwar protesters highlights the broader social climate in determining activists' legal fates.

4. Recent U.S. policy toward politically unstable client states in the Third World may provide several examples of this dimension. There is some indication that the Reagan administration began inching away from the traditional tendency of the U.S. to support unpopular client regimes as completely and as long as possible. In the case of Chile, for example, some administration officials have argued with some success that American support of a moderate opposition might help to limit the popularity of the far left. This point of view seems to have developed in recognition of events which led to the overthrow of Anastasio Somoza in Nicaragua and to the perception that the Chilean left appeals to a significant portion of that nation's population. A similar sequence of events seems to have been involved in the belated withdrawal of support for Ferdinand Marcos of the Philippines and may yet play a role in the resolution of the South African situation.

5. The discrediting effect of perceived links with radicals is illustrated in the recurrent difficulties over "communists" in the SCLC. The involvement of Stanley Levison and Jack O'Dell, both of whom had past links with the radical left, was a crucial element in the FBI's surveillance and harassment of the organization (Garrow 1986: 200–2, 235–36, 303–4, 322, 361–62, 468).

6. The interactions of elites and movements is made even more complicated, of course, by the fact that elites themselves may not be unified. This is an additional source of complexity which exceeds the scope of this book.

Bibliography

Aberbach, Joel D., and Jack L. Walker. 1970. "The Meanings of Black Power: A Comparison of White and Black Interpretations of a Political Slogan." *American Political Science Review* 64: 367–88.

Adams, A. John, and Joan M. Burke. 1970. *Civil Rights: A Current Guide to the People, Organizations, and Events*. New York: R. R. Bowker.

Albritton, Robert B. 1979. "Social Amelioration through Mass Insurgency? A Reexamination of the Piven and Cloward Thesis." *American Political Science Review* 73 (Dec.): 1003–11.

Allen, Robert L. 1969. *Black Awakening in Capitalist America: An Analytic History*. Garden City, N.Y.: Anchor.

Barkan, Steven E. 1979. "Strategic, Tactical, and Organizational Dilemmas of the Protest Movement Against Nuclear Power." *Social Problems* 27 (1): 19–37.

———. 1985. *Protesters on Trial: Criminal Justice in the Southern Civil Rights and Vietnam Antiwar Movements*. New Brunswick, N.J.: Rutgers Univ. Press.

Bell, Inge P. 1968. *CORE and the Strategy of Nonviolence*. New York: Random House.

———. 1970. "CORE and the Strategy of Nonviolence." In *Minority Responses*, ed. Minako Kurokawa, 249–58. New York: Random House.

Benson, J. Kenneth. 1976. "Militant Ideologies and Organizational Contexts: The War on Poverty and the Ideology of 'Black Power'." In *Social Movements and Social Change*, ed. R. J. Lauer, 107–20. Carbondale, Ill.: Southern Illinois Univ. Press.

Berkowitz, William R. 1974. "Socioeconomic Indicator Changes in Ghetto Riot Tracts." *Urban Affairs Quarterly* 10 (1): 69–94.

Betz, Michael. 1974. "Riots and Welfare: Are They Related?" *Social Problems* 21(3): 345–55.

Blackwell, James E. 1982. "Persistence and Change in Intergroup Relations: The Crisis Upon Us." *Social Problems* 29 (4): 325–45.

Blumberg, Rhoda L. 1984. *Civil Rights: The 1960s Freedom Struggle*. Boston: Twayne.

Bowles, Samuel, and Herbert Gintis. 1982. "The Crisis of Liberal Democratic Capitalism: The Case of the United States." *Politics and Society* 11: 51–93.

Bowles, Samuel, David M. Gordon, and Thomas E. Weisskopf. 1983. *Beyond the Wasteland: A Democratic Alternative to Economic Decline*. Garden City, N.Y.: Anchor.

Brauer, Carl M. 1977. *John F. Kennedy and the Second Reconstruction*. New York: Columbia Univ. Press.

Brisbane, R. J. 1974. *Black Activism: Racial Revolution in the United States, 1954–1970*. Valley Forge: Judson.

Brooks, Thomas R. 1974. *Walls Come Tumbling Down: A History of the Civil Rights Movement, 1940–1970*. Englewood Cliffs, N.J.: Prentice-Hall.

Bullock, Paul. 1969. *Watts: The Aftermath—An Inside View of the Ghetto by the People of Watts*. New York: Grove.

Burstein, Paul. 1979. "Public Opinion, Demonstrations, and the Passage of Anti-Discrimination Legislation." *Public Opinion Quarterly* 43: 157–72.

———. 1985. *Discrimination, Jobs, and Politics: The Struggle for Equal Employment Opportunity in the United States since the New Deal*. Chicago: Univ. of Chicago Press.

Button, James W. 1978. *Black Violence: Political Impact of the 1960s Riots*. Princeton: Princeton Univ. Press.

Carmichael, Stokely, and Charles V. Hamilton. 1967. *Black Power: The Politics of Liberation in America*. New York: Vintage.

Carson, Clayborne. 1981. *In Struggle: SNCC and the Black Awakening of the 1960s*. Cambridge, Mass.: Harvard Univ. Press.

Chafe, William H. 1980. *Civilities and Civil Rights: Greensboro, North Carolina, and the Black Struggle for Freedom*. New York: Oxford Univ. Press.

Clark, S. D. 1948. *Church and Sect in Canada*. Toronto: Univ. of Toronto Press.

Cleghorn, Reece. 1963. "The Angels are White: Who Pays the Bills for Civil Rights?" *New Republic* 149 (Aug.): 12–14.

Cloward, Richard A., and Frances F. Piven. 1975. *The Politics of Turmoil: Poverty, Race, and the Urban Crisis*. New York: Vintage.

Cohn, Jules. 1970. "Is Business Meeting the Challenge of Urban Affairs?" *Harvard Business Review* 48 (2): 68–82.

Colaiaco, James A. 1986. "Martin Luther King, Jr. and the Paradox of Nonviolent Direct Action." *Phylon* 47 (Spring): 16–28.

Congressional Quarterly Service. 1968. *Revolution in Civil Rights*, 4th ed. Washington, D.C.: Congressional Quarterly Service.

Crawford, Alan. 1980. *Thunder on the Right: The "New Right" and the Politics of Resentment*. New York: Pantheon.

Demerath, Nicholas J., III, Gerald Marwell, and Michael T. Aiken. 1971. *Dynamics of Idealism: White Activists in a Black Movement*. San Francisco: Jossey-Bass.

Dick, William M. 1972. *Labor and Socialism in America: The Gompers Era*. Port Washington, N.Y.: Kennikat.
Donovan, John C. 1967. *The Politics of Poverty*. New York: Pegasus.
Drake, St. Clair. 1968. "Urban Violence and American Social Movements." In *Urban Riots: Violence and Social Change*, ed. Robert H. Connery, 15–26. New York: Vintage.
Elinson, Howard. 1966. "Radicalism and the Negro Movement." In *Problems and Prospects of the Negro Movement*, ed. R. J. Murphy and Howard Elinson, 355–75. Belmont, Calif.: Wadsworth.
Erskine, Hazel. 1967. "The Polls: Demonstrations and Race Riots." *Public Opinion Quarterly* 31: 655–77.
———. 1968a. "The Polls: Negro Employment." *Public Opinion Quarterly* 32: 132–53.
———. 1968b. "The Polls: Recent Opinion on Racial Problems." *Public Opinion Quarterly* 32: 696–703.
———. 1968c. "The Polls: Speed of Racial Integration." *Public Opinion Quarterly* 32: 513–24.
Ewen, Stuart. 1976. *Captains of Consciousness: Advertising and the Social Roots of the Consumer Culture*. New York: McGraw-Hill.
Fairclough, Adam. 1986. "Martin Luther King, Jr. and the Quest for Nonviolent Social Change." *Phylon* 47 (Spring): 1–15.
Farley, Reynolds. 1977. "Trends in Racial Inequalities: Have the Gains of the 1960s Disappeared in the 1970s?" *American Sociological Review* 42 (Apr.): 189–208.
———. 1984. *Blacks and Whites: Narrowing the Gap?* Cambridge, Mass.: Harvard Univ. Press.
Farmer, James. 1972. Interview by Paige Mulhollan. July 20, 1972. Tape recording and transcription, Lyndon Baines Johnson Library, Austin, Tex.
Feagin, Joseph R., and Harlan Hahn. 1973. *Ghetto Revolts: The Politics of Violence in American Cities*. New York: Macmillan.
Fogelson, Robert M. 1971. *Violence as Protest: A Study of Riots and Ghettos*. Garden City, N.Y.: Doubleday.
Foner, Philip S. 1974. *Organized Labor and the Black Worker, 1619–1973*. New York: Praeger.
Fones-Wolf, Elizabeth. 1986. "Industrial Recreation, the Second World War, and the Revival of Welfare Capitalism, 1934–1960. *Business History Review* 60 (Summer): 232–57.
Freeman, Jo. 1975. *The Politics of Women's Liberation*. New York: McKay.
Friedman, Leon, ed. 1968. *The Civil Rights Reader: Basic Documents of the Civil Rights Movement*. New York: Walker.
Gamson, William A. 1975. *The Strategy of Social Protest*. Homewood, Ill.: Dorsey.
Garraty, John A. 1968. *Labor and Capital in the Gilded Age*. Boston: Little, Brown.
Garrow, David J. 1978. *Protest at Selma: Martin Luther King, Jr. and the Voting Rights Act of 1965*. New Haven: Yale Univ. Press.

———. 1986. *Bearing the Cross: Martin Luther King, Jr., and the Southern Christian Leadership Conference.* New York: Morrow.

Geschwender, James A. 1977. *Class, Race, and Worker Insurgency: The League of Revolutionary Black Workers.* New York: Cambridge Univ. Press.

Ginger, Ray. 1949. *Eugene V. Debs: The Making of an American Radical.* New York: Macmillan.

Ginzberg, Eli, ed. 1968. *Business Leadership and the Negro Crisis.* New York: McGraw-Hill.

Golden, Harry. 1964. *Mr. Kennedy and the Negroes.* Cleveland: World.

Goldstone, Jack. A. 1980. "The Weakness of Organization: A New Look at Gamson's *The Strategy of Social Protest.*" *American Journal of Sociology* 85 (5): 1017–60.

Gregor, A. James. 1970. "Black Nationalism: A Preliminary Analysis of Negro Radicalism." In *Minority Responses,* ed. Minako Kurokawa, 317–31. New York: Random House.

Hadden, Jeffrey K. 1969. *Gathering Storm in the Churches.* Garden City, N.Y.: Doubleday.

Hare, A. Paul, and H. H. Blumberg, eds. 1968. *Nonviolent Direct Action, American Cases: Social-Psychological Analyses.* Washington, D.C.: Corpus.

Harvey, James C. 1971. *Civil Rights During the Kennedy Administration.* Hattiesburg, Miss.: The University and College Press of Mississippi.

Henry, Charles P. 1979. "Big Philanthropy and the Funding of Black Organizations." *Review of Black Political Economy* 9: 174–90.

Hicks, Alexander, and Duane H. Swank. 1983. "Civil Disorder, Relief Mobilization, and AFDC Caseloads: A Reexamination of the Piven and Cloward Thesis." *American Journal of Political Science* 27 (Nov.): 695–716.

Hodgson, Godfrey. 1976. *America in Our Time: From World War II to Nixon, What Happened and Why.* New York: Vintage.

Hough, Joseph C., Jr. 1968. *Black Power and White Protestants: A Christian Response to the New Negro Pluralism.* New York: Oxford Univ. Press.

Howard, John R. 1974. *The Cutting Edge: Social Movements and Social Change in America.* Philadelphia: Lippincott.

Hubbard, Howard. 1968. "Five Long Hot Summers and How They Grew." *Public Interest* 12: 3–24.

Hughes, Langston. 1962. *Fight for Freedom, The Story of the N.A.A.C.P.* New York: W. W. Norton.

Isaac, Larry, and William R. Kelly. 1981. "Racial Insurgency, the State, and Welfare Expansion: Local and National Level Evidence from the Postwar United States." *American Journal of Sociology* 86 (May): 1348–86.

Jackson, Maurice. 1976. "The Civil Rights Movement and Social Change." In *Social Movements and Social Change,* ed. R. L. Lauer, 174–89. Carbondale, Ill.: Southern Illinois Univ. Press.

James, D. B. 1972. *Poverty, Politics, and Change.* Englewood Cliffs, N.J.: Prentice-Hall.

Jenkins, J. Craig. 1985. *The Politics of Insurgency: The Farm Worker Movement in the 1960s.* New York: Columbia Univ. Press.

———. 1986. "Foundation Funding of Social Movements." Department of Sociology, University of Missouri at Columbia. Photocopy.

———. 1987. "Nonprofit Organizations and Policy Advocacy." In *The Nonprofit Sector: A Research Handbook,* ed. Walter W. Powell, 296–318. New Haven: Yale Univ. Press.

———, and Craig M. Eckert. 1986. "Channeling Black Insurgency: Elite Patronage and Professional Social Movement Organizations in the Development of the Black Movement." *American Sociological Review* 51 (Dec.): 812–29.

———, and Charles Perrow. 1977. "Insurgency of the Powerless: Farm Workers Movements (1946–1972)." *American Sociological Review* 42: 249–68.

Jezer, Marty. 1977. *The Power of the People: Active Nonviolence in the United States.* Culver City, Calif.: Peace.

Joseph, J. A. 1969. "New Strategies for Private Foundations." *New South* 24 (Summer): 56–61.

Kennedy, John F. Papers, Presidential Papers, Presidential Recordings, Civil Rights, 1963. John F. Kennedy Library, Boston.

———. President's Office Files. John F. Kennedy Library, Boston.

Kennedy, Robert F. Attorney General's Correspondence. John F. Kennedy Library, Boston.

———. Interview by Anthony Lewis. December 6, 1964. Tape recording and transcription, Oral History Program, John F. Kennedy Library, Boston.

Killian, Lewis M. 1968. *The Impossible Revolution?: Black Power and the American Dream.* New York: Random House.

———. 1972. "The Significance of Extremism in the Black Revolution." *Social Problems* 20: 41–48.

King, Martin Luther, Jr. 1963. "Letter from Birmingham Jail." In *Why We Can't Wait,* 77–100. New York: Harper and Row.

———. 1964. Interview by Berl I. Bernhard. March 9, 1964. Tape recording and transcription, Oral History Program, John F. Kennedy Library, Boston.

Kluger, Richard. 1976. *Simple Justice. The History of Brown v. Board of Education and Black America's Struggle for Equality.* New York: Knopf.

Laue, James H. 1970. "The Changing Character of the Negro Protest." In *Minority Responses,* ed. Minako Kurokawa, 267–75. New York: Random House.

Lawson, Steven F. 1976. *Black Ballots: Voting Rights in the South, 1944–1969.* New York: Columbia Univ. Press.

Lipsky, Michael. 1968. "Protest as a Political Resource." *American Political Science Review* 62: 1144–58.

Lomax, L. E. 1968. "The Freedom Rides." In *The Civil Rights Reader: Basic*

Documents of the Civil Rights Movement, ed. L. Friedman, 51–60. New York: Walker.
Lytle, Clifford. 1966. "The History of the Civil Rights Bill of 1964. *Journal of Negro History* 51: 275–96.
Marable, Manning. 1980. "Black Nationalism in the 1970s: Through the Prism of Race and Class." *Socialist Review* 50/51: 57–108.
Marger, Martin N. 1984. "Social Movement Organizations and Response to Environmental Change: The NAACP, 1960–1973." *Social Problems* 32 (Oct.): 16–30.
Marine, Gene. 1969. *The Black Panthers*. New York: Signet.
Marshall, Burke. White House Staff Files. John F. Kennedy Library, Boston.
Marx, Gary T. 1967. *Protest and Prejudice: A Study of Belief in the Black Community*. New York: Harper and Row.
Masotti, Louis H., et al. 1969. *A Time To Burn? An Evaluation of the Present Crisis in Race Relations*. Chicago: Rand-McNally.
McAdam, Doug. 1980. "The Generation of Insurgency and the Black Movement." Paper presented at the Annual Meetings of the American Sociological Association, New York, N.Y., August.
———. 1982. *Political Process and the Development of Black Insurgency, 1930–1970*. Chicago: Univ. of Chicago Press.
———. 1983. "The Decline of the Civil Rights Movement." In *Social Movements of the Sixties and Seventies*, ed. Jo Freeman, 279–319. New York: Longman.
McCarthy, John D., and Mayer N. Zald. 1973. "The Trend of Social Movements in America: Professionalization and Resource Mobilization." Morristown, N.J.: General Learning Press.
———. 1977. "Resource Mobilization and Social Movements: A Partial Theory." *American Journal of Sociology* 82 (6): 1212–41.
Meier, August. 1963. "Negro Protest Movements and Organizations." *Journal of Negro Education* 32 (Fall): 437–59.
———. 1965. "On the Role of Martin Luther King." *New Politics* 4 (Winter): 52–59.
———, and Elliot Rudwick. 1973. *C.O.R.E., A Study of the Civil Rights Movement, 1942–1968*. New York: Oxford Univ. Press.
———. 1976. *From Plantation to Ghetto*. 3rd ed. New York: Hill and Wang.
Merton, Robert K. 1962. *Social Theory and Social Structure*. Glencoe, Ill.: Free Press.
———. 1967. *On Theoretical Sociology*. New York: Free Press.
Michels, Robert. 1959. *Political Parties*. New York: Dover.
Miroff, Bruce. 1976. *Pragmatic Illusions: The Presidential Politics of John F. Kennedy*. New York: McKay.
Moore, Charles H. 1970. "The Politics of Urban Violence: Policy Outcomes in Winston-Salem." *Social Science Quarterly* 52 (2): 374–88.
Moore, Jesse T. 1981. *A Search for Equality: The National Urban League, 1910–1961*. University Park, Pa.: The Pennsylvania State Univ. Press.

Morgan, Ruth P. 1970. *The Presidency and Civil Rights: Policy-Making by Executive Order*. New York: St. Martin's.
Morris, Aldon D. 1984. *The Origins of the Civil Rights Movement: Black Communities Organizing for Change*. New York: Free Press.
Muse, Benjamin. 1968. *The American Negro Revolution: From Nonviolence to Black Power*. Bloomington, Ind.: Indiana Univ. Press.
NAACP. 1959. *Annual Report for 1959*. New York: National Association for the Advancement of Colored People.
———. 1963. *Annual Report for 1963*. New York: National Association for the Advancement of Colored People.
———. 1966. *Annual Report for 1966*. New York: National Association for the Advancement of Colored People.
National Advisory Commission on Civil Disorders. 1968. *Report of the National Advisory Commission on Civil Disorders*. New York: Bantam.
National Urban League, Inc. 1980. *70th Anniversary*. New York: National Urban League, Inc.
Navasky, Victor S. 1971. *Kennedy Justice*. New York: Atheneum.
Newman, Dorothy K., et al. 1978. *Protest, Politics, and Prosperity: Black Americans and White Institutions, 1940–1975*. New York: Pantheon.
Nielsen, Waldemar A. 1972. *The Big Foundations*. New York: Columbia Univ. Press.
Nye, Russel B. 1963. *Fettered Freedom: Civil Liberties and the Slavery Question, 1830–1860*. Lansing, Mich.: Michigan State Univ. Press.
Oberschall, Anthony. 1973. *Social Conflict and Social Movements*. Englewood Cliffs, N.J.: Prentice-Hall.
Parris, Guichard, and Lester Brooks. 1971. *Blacks in the City: A History of the National Urban League*. Boston: Little, Brown.
Patterson, James. 1966. "Business Response to the Negro Movement." *New South* 21 (1): 68–74.
Peck, James. 1968. "Freedom Rides—1947 and 1961." In *Nonviolent Direct Action, American Cases: Social Psychological Analyses*, ed. A. P. Hare and H. H. Blumberg, 49–75. Washington, D.C.: Corpus Books.
Perrow, Charles. 1968. "Organizational Goals." In *International Encyclopedia of the Social Sciences*, Vol. 11, ed. D. L. Sills, 305–11. New York: Macmillan.
Pinkney, Alphonso. 1968. *The Committed: White Activists in the Civil Rights Movement*. New Haven: College and University Press.
Piven, Frances F., and Richard Cloward. 1971. *Regulating the Poor: The Functions of Public Welfare*. New York: Vintage.
———. 1977. *Poor People's Movements: Why They Succeed, How They Fail*. New York: Vintage.
———. 1982. *The New Class War: Reagan's Attack on the Welfare State and Its Consequences*. New York: Pantheon.
Powledge, F. 1967. *Black Power, White Resistance: Notes on the New Civil War*. Cleveland: World.

Pressman, Jeffrey L., and Aaron B. Wildavsky. *Implementation*. Berkeley, Calif.: Univ. of California Press.

Raines, Howell. 1977. *My Soul is Rested: Movement Days in the Deep South Remembered*. New York: Putnam's.

Ramirez, G. 1978. *When Workers Fight: The Politics of Industrial Relations in the Progressive Era, 1898–1916*. Westport, Conn.: Greenwood.

Rayback, Joseph G. 1966. *A History of American Labor*. New York: Free Press.

Reeves, Thomas C., ed. 1970. *Foundations Under Fire*. Ithaca, N.Y.: Cornell Univ. Press.

Rhind, Flora M., and Barry Bingham. 1967. "Philanthropic Foundations and the Problem of Race." In *U.S. Philanthropic Foundations: Their History, Structure, Management, and Record*, ed. Warren Weaver, 428–39. New York: Harper and Row.

Rudwick, Elliot. M. 1964. *Race Riot at East St. Louis*. Carbondale, Ill.: Southern Illinois Univ. Press.

———, and August Meier. 1970. "Organizational Structure and Goal Succession: A Comparative Analysis of the NAACP and CORE, 1964–1968." *Social Science Quarterly* 51 (June): 9–24.

Schram, Sanford F., and J. Patrick Turbett. 1983. "Civil Disorder and the Welfare Explosion: A Two-Step Process." *American Sociological Review* 48 (June): 408–18.

Scott, R. L., and W. Brockriede. 1969. *The Rhetoric of Black Power*. New York: Harper and Row.

Sears, David O., and John B. McConahay. 1973. *The Politics of Violence: The New Urban Blacks and the Watts Riot*. Boston: Houghton Mifflin.

Selznick, Phillip. 1943. "An Approach to a Theory of Bureaucracy." *American Sociological Review* 8: 47–54.

Sheatsley, Paul B. 1966. "White Attitudes Toward the Negro." In *The Negro American*, ed. T. Parsons and K. B. Clark, 303–23. Boston: Beacon.

Skolnick, Jerome H. 1969. *The Politics of Protest*. New York: Ballentine.

Smythe, Mabel M. 1976. *The Black American Reference Book*. Englewood Cliffs, N.J.: Prentice-Hall.

Sobel, Lester A., ed. 1967. *Civil Rights: 1960–1967*. New York: Facts on File, Inc.

———. 1977. *Welfare and the Poor*. New York: Facts on File, Inc.

Sorensen, Theodore C. 1965. *Kennedy*. New York: Harper and Row.

———. White House Staff Files. John F. Kennedy Library, Boston.

Sorensen, Annmette, Karl E. Taeuber, and Leslie Hollingsworth, Jr. 1975. "Indexes of Racial Residential Segregation for 109 Cities in the United States, 1940–1970." *Sociological Focus* 8 (Apr.): 125–42.

Southern Regional Council. 1964. "The South of the Future: A Statement of Policy and Aims of the Southern Regional Council, December 12, 1951." *New South* 19 (1): 27–28.

Spring, Joel H. 1972. *Education and the Rise of the Corporate State*. Boston: Beacon.

St. James, Warren D. 1958. *The National Association for the Advancement of Colored People: A Case Study in Pressure Groups*. New York: Exposition.
Sundquist, James D. 1968. *Politics and Policy: The Eisenhower, Kennedy, and Johnson Years*. Washington, D.C.: The Brookings Institution.
Taeuber, Karl E., and Alma F. Taeuber. 1969. *Negroes in Cities*. New York: Atheneum.
Taylor, D. Garth, Paul B. Sheatsley, and Andrew M. Greeley. 1978. "Attitudes Toward Racial Integration." *Scientific American* 238 (June): 42–49.
Turner, Ralph J. 1969. "The Public Perception of Protest." *American Sociological Review* 34 (6): 815–31.
Tuttle, William M. 1970. *Race Riot: Chicago in the Red Summer of 1919*. New York: Atheneum.
USIA. 1963. "Recent Worldwide Comment on the U.S. Racial Problem." United States Information Agency Research and Reference Service Report R-135-63 (A). Presidential Office Files: National Security Files, Civil Rights 7/12/63–7/19/63. John F. Kennedy Library, Boston.
Van Valey, Thomas L., Wade C. Roof, and Jerome E. Wilcox. 1977. "Trends in residential segregation: 1960–1970." *American Journal of Sociology* 82 (Jan.): 826–44.
Vander Zanden, J. W. 1963. "The Non-violent Resistance Movement Against Segregation." *American Journal of Sociology* 68 (Mar.): 544–59.
Von Eschen, Donald, Jerome Kirk, and Maurice Pinard. 1976. "The Disintegration of the Negro Non-violent Movement." In *Social Movements and Social Change*, ed. R. H. Lauer, 203–26. Carbondale, Ill.: Southern Illinois Univ. Press.
Walker, Jack. 1963. "Protest and Negotiation: A Case Study of Negro Leadership in Atlanta, Georgia." *Midwest Journal of Political Science* 7 (2): 99–124.
Waskow, Arthur I. 1966. *From Race Riot to Sit-In*. Garden City, New York: Doubleday.
Welch, Susan. 1975. "The Impact of Urban Riots on Urban Expenditures." *American Journal of Political Science* 19 (4): 741–60.
White, Lee. White House Staff Files. John F. Kennedy Library, Boston.
Williams, Robert F. 1962. *Negroes with Guns*. New York: Marzani and Munsell.
Wofford, Harris. 1968. Interview by Larry Hackman. Tape recording and transcription, Oral History Program, John F. Kennedy Library, Boston.
———. 1980. *Of Kennedys and Kings: Making Sense of the Sixties*. New York: Farrar, Straus, and Giroux.
Wolff, Miles. 1970. *Lunch at the Five and Ten: The Greensboro Sit-Ins, A Contemporary History*. New York: Stein and Day.
Wolk, Allan. 1971. *The Presidency and Black Civil rights: Eisenhower to Nixon*. Rutherford, N.J.: Farleigh Dickinson Univ. Press.
Woodward, C. Vann. 1966. *The Strange Career of Jim Crow*. 2nd rev. ed. New York: Oxford Univ. Press.

Zald, Mayer, and Roberta Ash. 1966. "Social Movement Organizations: Growth, Decline and Change." *Social Forces* 44 (March): 327–41.

Zald, Mayer, and John D. McCarthy. 1979. "Social Movement Industries: Competition and Cooperation Among Movement Organizations." CRSO Working Paper No. 201. Ann Arbor, Michigan: Center for Research on Social Organization.

Zieger, Robert H. 1986. *American Workers, American Unions, 1920–1985*. Baltimore: The Johns Hopkins Univ. Press.

Zinn, Howard. 1965. *SNCC: The New Abolitionists*. Boston: Beacon.

Index

Aberbach, Joel D., 58, 64
Abernathy, Rev. Ralph, 86
abolitionist movement, 2, 3
accommodation, as organizational philosophy, 15
Adams, A. John, 112, 148
Adult Basic Education Program, 145
affirmative action, 131, 186
Aid to Families with Dependent Children (AFDC), 146, 202
Aiken, Michael T., 101
Alabama, University of, 141
Albany, Ga., 41, 157
Albritton, Robert B., 147
Alcatraz Island, Native American occupation of, 6
Allen, Robert L., 59, 61, 62, 64, 97, 117, 128, 179, 199
American Foundation on Nonviolence. *See* Southern Christian Leadership Conference
American Indian Movement, 6
Anderson v. Martin, 144
antiabortion movement, 7–8
anti–civil rights countermovement, 134, 136–37; *see also* police brutality, violence
antilynching legislation, 132

antinuclear movement, 2, 3
antipoverty program. *See* War on Poverty
armed services, discrimination in, 139
Aronson, Arnold, 112
Ash, Roberta, 96
assimilation of blacks, 22, 26, 75
Association of White Citizens' Councils of Alabama, 31
Atlanta University Archives, 85
Attorney General, civil rights enforcement powers of, 140, 143–44, 147
Augusta, Ga., 1962 racial violence, 157

backlash, 1–2, 53, 73, 90, 98, 167, 175–76; *see also* radical flank effects, negative
Baker, Ella, 35
Baldrige, Malcolm, 202
Barkan, Steven E., 2, 3, 40, 41, 205
Bell, Inge P., 23, 40, 61
Benson, J. Kenneth, 65
Berkowitz, William R., 147
Bernhard, Berl, 160, 202, 203
Betz, Michael, 147
"Big Business Program," 136

"Big money" funding sources, rise in importance of, 101, 127; *see also* corporations, elites, federal government, foundations
Bingham, Barry, 114
biracial committees, 107
Birmingham, Ala.: black violence in, 158, 179, 202; and Freedom Riders, 37; and Kennedy administration, 150, 157–63; Operation "C," 38–39, 50, 107
black capitalism: foundation grants for, 120; as organizational philosophy, 20, 62
black churches, as mobilization centers, 105
black collective action, 15–16, 74–76; character of: pre-War years, 17–20, 1945–1954, 20–29, 1955–1963, 29–46, 1964–1970, 46–74; funding of, *see* exogenous income
black consciousness, 59; *see also* black power, cultural nationalism
black education, foundation support for, 114
Black Legion, 69
Black Liberation Army, 61
Black Manifesto movement, 69–70
Black Muslims, 55, 159, 162, 181, 202
black nationalism, 16, 64, 93, 126, 159; *see also* cultural nationalism, revolutionary black nationalism, separatism
Black Panther Party, 56–57, 60–61, 63, 67–68, 72, 75; relations with SNCC, 60–61
Black Panther, The, 68
black power, 2, 16, 57–63, 175; comparison of CORE, SNCC, and Black Panther versions of, 62–63, 117; and corporate interests, 179; definition, 58–59, 60; differing interpretations of,
64–65; and federal government responsiveness to movement demands, 133, 143; and foundation grant priorities, 121, 179–80; and radical flank effects, 79, 90, 96; reaction of moderate civil rights leaders to, 65–66, 182; slogan, 58, 87
black pride, 59; *see also* black power, cultural nationalism
black vote, impact in electoral politics, 135, 146, 151, 182, 198
Blumberg, H. H., 40
Blumberg, Rhoda, 16, 154, 197
Bowles, Samuel, 4, 10
Boynton v. Virginia, 36, 141, 153
Brauer, Carl M., 140, 150, 152, 154–55, 156, 160, 162, 165, 202, 203
Brisbane, R. J., 16, 25, 30, 37, 55, 63, 68–69, 70, 80, 197
Brockriede, W., 3, 65
Brooks, Lester, 18, 21–22, 28, 41, 42, 49, 66, 80, 86, 106, 107, 140
Brooks, Thomas R., 16, 30, 31, 145, 197
Brotherhood-in-Action, 201
Brown, Hubert "Rap," 57, 61
Brown v. Board of Education, 19, 25–26, 138; and radical flank effects, 79; as turning point in civil rights movement, 29–30, 75
Bullock, Paul, 199
Bundy, McGeorge, 179
Burke, Joan M., 112, 148
Burstein, Paul, 32, 38, 142, 144, 204
Business Council, 203, 204
Busing, 148
Button, James W., 147, 169, 170
Butts v. Harrison, 148

California, University of, 56
Cambridge, Md., 1963 rioting, 159, 202
capitalism, and racial oppression, 59

INDEX

Carmichael, Stokely, 55, 57–58, 60–61, 62, 65, 87; white opinion of, 1966, 73
Carson, Clayborne, 33, 35–36, 38, 44, 48, 50, 54–55, 57–58, 61, 65, 80, 106, 199
caste issues, 19
Chafe, William H., 34
Chicago, Ill., 24; 1961 interracial violence, 157
Chile, 205
christianity, and civil rights, 104–5
churches: as financial supporters for black organizations, 13, 80, 93, 104–5, 174; race-related foundation grants to, 119, 122; *see also* black churches
Citizens' Crusade Against Poverty, 201
civil disobedience, as organizational tactic, 15; *see also* direct action, nonviolence.
Civil Rights Act of 1957, 141, 150, 167, 202
Civil Rights Act of 1960, 131–32, 140, 141, 167
Civil Rights Act of 1964, 39, 130–31, 141–42, 143–44, 150, 167, 204
Civil Rights Act of 1966, 147, 169
Civil Rights Act of 1968, 131, 136, 147–48
Civil Rights Commission, 142
Clark, S. D., 135
class issues, 19, 121
Cleaver, Eldridge, 68
Cleghorn, Reece, 128, 154
Cloward, Richard A., 5, 9, 13, 124, 146–47, 150, 154, 183–85, 202
Coalitions, 12
Coffin, Bill, 153
COFO. *See* Council of Federated Organizations
Cohn, Jules, 110–11, 125, 128
Colaiaco, James A., 40, 44, 204
colonialism, 59

Commission on Interracial Cooperation. *See* Southern Regional Council
Community Action Programs, 124, 145–46
community organizing, 35, 61
Community Relations Service, 163
Congress of Racial Equality (CORE), 11, 137–149 *passim*; activities of: 1945–1954, 24–25, 27, 29, 137, 1955–1963, 32, 43, 44; and black power, 61–63, 97, 116–18; church contributions to, 105; and COFO, 48; conflict with labor unions, 106; contrasted to NAACP, 96; CORE Scholarship, Educational and Defense Fund, 117; corporate support for, 111; criticism of white participation in, 49–50, 62; decline of commitment to nonviolence, 54, 61; exogenous income, 83–89, 96–97, 98, 101, 126–27, 175, 194; financial data on, 80, 100, 200; financial support for SNCC, 201; foundation support for, 97, 116–18, 122, 194; and Freedom Rides, 36–37, 153; individual contributors to, 102–4, 194; labor contributions to, 194; and March on Washington, 165–66; radicalization of, 57, 70, 71, 75; Scholarship, Education, and Defense Fund for Racial Equality (SEDFRE), 117; and sit-ins, 34–35; Special Purpose Fund, 117; viewed as radical, 1966, 76; and Voter Education Project, 154–55
Congressional Quarterly Service, 137, 139
Connor, Eugene "Bull," 37, 158
conservatism, resurgence in 1970s, 2
CORE. *See* Congress of Racial Equality

CORE Rules for Action, 32
corporations: and black movement goals, 106–7, 136; as financial supporters, 13, 80, 81, 100–1, 105–6, 107–13, 127–28, 175–76; and National Urban League, 107
Council of Federated Organizations (COFO), 48
Cox, Archibald, 160, 203
Crawford, Alan, 2
Crises, role in movement outcomes, 9, 98, 170, 173
Cultural nationalism, 63–64
Currier, Stephen, 154

Davis, William B., 203
De facto segregation, 25, 130, 147–48
De jure segregation, 25, 29, 130
Deacons for Defense and Justice, 54
Demerath, Nicholas, J., III, 101
Democratic party, 62, 176; and black voters, 146, 151; National Committee, 124, 160; and 1958 congressional elections, 142; 1964 National Convention, 48–49; North-South division, 49, 135, 142, 151, 178–79
Demonstrations, (1940s) 24, (1950s) 32, (1960s) 38, 140; Kennedy administration efforts to forestall, 160, 164; 1964 call for moratorium on, 53; white participation in, 101; *see also* direct action, nonviolence
Department of Health, Education, and Welfare, 125, 141, 148, 168
Department of Justice, 48, 130, 141, 144, 153, 155, 163, 168
Department of Labor, 112, 125, 136, 168
Detroit, Mich., 1967 rioting, 67, 110
Dick, William M., 2
direct action integrationism, 29–46, 101; federal government responsiveness during era of, 140–43
direct action tactics, 23–26, (1950s) 34, (early 1960s) 33–46, 167; and corporate interests, 179; definition, 30; and exogenous incomes of moderate organizations, 95; and federal government responsiveness to movement demands, 133, 170–71; as moderate, 50; and political pressures on Kennedy administration, 152–54, 155; as radical, 37, 75, 95; reasons for effectiveness of, 40–41; white opinion of, 46–47, 50, 53, 72–73; *see also* demonstrations, nonviolence
direct-mail fundraising. *See* Southern Christian Leadership Conference
Dirksen, Everett, 144
disruption, role in movement outcomes. *See* crises
Dodge Revolutionary Union Movement (DRUM), 70
Dolan, Joseph, 158
Donovan, John C., 106, 135, 145
Drake, St. Clair, 3
DuBois, W. E. B., 19

Ebenezer Baptist Church, 105
Eckert, Craig M., 121, 124, 197, 201
economic climate, as factor in movement successes, 177–78
economic development of black communities, 65, 66, 97, 110, 120, 136
economic issues and black collective action, 51, 144–45
Economic Opportunity Act of 1964, 124, 131, 145–46, 167; *see also* War on Poverty
education: federal policy, 124, 138, 140, 147–48, 163; foundation

grants for, 179; as a movement issue, 29, 107, 120, 130; *see also* black education
Eisenhower, Dwight D., 141, 142
Elementary and Secondary Education Act of 1965, 130, 148, 167
Elinson, Howard, 3
elites, 8–9; black, 27, 118; consequences of reactive support by, 183–85; and co-optation of movements, 183, 185–86; divisions among, 205; financial support of black collective action, 81, 101, 128, 173, 175–76, 197; reaction to cultural nationalism, 64; role in movement outcome, 9–10, 40, 125; southern, 136–37
employment: compensatory/preferential hiring programs, 131, 148; corporate programs, 110, 112, 120, 164; federal, 148; federal programs, 131, 146; foundation grants for, 179; as movement issue, 22, 24, 38, 131, 138–39, 140, 163; provisions of Civil Rights Act of 1964, 144; public opinion on equal opportunity in, 204; *see also* Fair Employment Practices Commission, President's Committee on Equal Employment Opportunity, unemployment
endogenous income, 80
Equal Employment Opportunity Commission, 144
Erskine, Hazel, 29, 46–47, 53, 72–74
escalation in movement goals and tactics. *See* radicalization
Evers, Medgar, 174
Ewen, Stuart, 4, 10
exogenous income, of black organizations: data on, 79–126; decline during 1966, 90; definition and calculation, 85; distribution among movement organizations, 89; growth during 1950s and 1960s, 88–91; organizational acceptability and, 91; summary of patterns in, 99, 126–28, 173, 199; trends, 81–99; *see also* financial support
extremists. *See* radicals

Fair Employment Practices Commission (FEPC), 23, 138, 161, 163
Fairclough, Adam, 40
Farley, Reynolds, 201–2
Farm worker's movement, 205
Farmer, James, 153, 155, 199, 202
Feagin, Joseph R., 51, 147, 199, 204
Federal Airport Act, 141
Federal Bureau of Investigation, 205
federal government: activists' mistrust of, 37, 44, 48, 140, 156; antiriot measures, 169; bureaucracy as a special interest group, 134, 135–36, 180–81; civil rights enforcement, 169; expected impact of radical flanks on, 132–33; and financial support of movement, 80, 124–25; nondiscrimination clauses in government contracts, 142, 163; protection of civil rights workers, 48, 152, 163; responsiveness: during era of direct action integrationism, 140–43, 149–66, during era of legalistic integrationism, 137–39, during era of new black radicalism, 143–49; and urban poor, 146
Fellowship of Reconciliation, 23, 24
feminism. *See* women's movement
Field Foundation, 114, 154
Fifteenth Amendment to the U.S. Constitution, 137

filibuster, 132, 144, 147
financial support: for civil rights organizations, 62, 77–128; determination of internal and external income, 85; as index of radical flank effects, 77–78, 126; for social movement organizations, 3, 8–9; sources of, 80, 81, 99–125; *see also* exogenous income, outside groups, resource mobilization theory
Fogelson, Robert M., 51, 199
Foner, Philip S., 106
Fones-Wolf, Elizabeth, 10
Food Stamp program, 146, 202
Ford Foundation, 114, 117–19, 128, 179
Ford Motor Company, 107
Foundation Library Center, 100
Foundation News, 81, 87, 100, 114–24 *passim*, 200–1
foundations: as financial supporters of movement organizations, 13, 80, 81, 93, 97, 100–1, 105, 106, 113–24, 127–28, 175–76, 201; and Voter Education Project, 154
Forman, James, 59, 69, 199
Fourteenth Amendment to the U.S. Constitution, 137
"Freedom Now" slogan, 58
Freedom Rides, 24, 36–37, 153–54, 174
Freedom Summer. *See* Mississippi Freedom Summer
Freeman, Jo, 2, 3, 197
Friedman, Leon, 197
Friends of SNCC, 104
fundraising tactics, 127; *see also* exogenous income

Galbraith, John Kenneth, 160–61, 203
Gallup polls, 45
Gamson, William A., 4–5
Gandhi, Mahatma, 24, 31

Garraty, John A., 2
Garrow, David J., 40, 41, 54, 58, 95, 197, 200, 205
Garvey, Marcus, 20, 55, 65
General Education Board, 114
General Electric, 107
General Motors Corporation, 107, 204
Georgia, University of, 152
Geschwender, James A., 70
Ghetto conditions, as movement issue, 120
Gintis, Herbert, 4, 10
Ginzberg, Eli, 110
goal attainment. *See* outcome of movement activity
Golden, Harry, 3
Goldstone, Jack A., 5, 182
Gordon, David M., 4, 10
government agencies. *See* federal government
Greeley, Andrew, 177
Greensboro, N.C., 33
Gregor, A. James, 51, 65
Gregory, Dick, 52

Hahn, Harlan, 51, 147, 199, 204
Hamilton, Charles V., 60
Hare, A. Paul, 40
Harper v. Virginia State Board of Education, 148
Harris poll, 34, 46
Harvey, James C., 141
Henderson v. U.S., 139
Henry, Charles P., 114
Hicks, Alexander, 147
Hodgson, Godfrey, 35, 36, 54, 55, 106, 165
Hollingsworth, Leslie, 202
Hough, Joseph C., Jr., 28, 76
House of Representatives, U.S., 138–39, 144
housing: foundation grants for, 179; as movement issue, 21–22, 120, 131, 139, 141, 147, 149
Howard, John R., 18–19, 65, 71

Howard University, 169
Hubbard, Howard, 40, 41, 47, 48, 53
Hughes, Langston, 18, 19, 21, 22, 140
Human Relations Councils, 201
Huntley, Chet, 19

individual contributors: black, 101, 104; as financial supporters of movement organizations, 80, 93, 96, 101–4, 174
Innis, Roy, 62–63
integration, racial: black power and the rejection of, 62, 71, 75; as moderate, 50; as organizational goal, 17, 19, 20, 26, 42, 71, 120, 170; as radical, 19, 75; white opinion of, 28–29, 45–46, 72–74, 75
interests: economic, 179–80; political, 134–37, 178–79; *see also* corporations, foundations
interposition, doctrine of, 30
Interracial Council for Business Opportunity, 201
Interreligious Foundation for Community Organization, 70
Interstate Commerce Commission, 131, 141
Isaac, Larry, 147

Jackson, Maurice, 15
Jackson, Miss., 69
Jenkins, J. Craig, 5, 8, 117, 121, 124, 197, 201, 205
Jezer, Marty, 23, 31, 40
Job Corps, 145–46
Johnson, James Weldon, 18
Johnson, Lyndon B., 49, 52, 54, 61–62, 73, 136, 145, 148, 149, 168, 202
Joseph, J. A., 114
Journey of Reconciliation, 24
Justice Department. *See* Department of Justice

Kappel, F. R., 203, 204
Karenga, Ron, 64
Kelly, William R., 147
Kennedy, John F., 36–37, 39, 44, 124–25, 135, 142, 163, 168; administration, 14, 35, 73, 133, 149–66; and antipoverty program, 145; and Birmingham crisis, 150; civil rights meetings, 164–65, 203; civil rights speeches, 160; concern over impact of racial incidents on U.S. image, 151–52; housing order, 141, 151, 162; and March on Washington, 165–66; phases of reaction to civil rights movement, 150, 156, 163; pre-presidential civil rights record, 150–51; proposals for civil rights legislation, 162–63, 164; *see also* violence
Kennedy, Robert F., 141, 152–53, 155–56, 159, 160, 161, 164–65, 202, 203, 204
Killian, Lewis, 3, 6, 7, 16, 19, 28, 34, 52–53, 69, 197, 198
King, Martin Luther, 1, 43, 202; appearance at SCLC "Freedom Rallies," 104; assassination of, 58, 96, 136; and Birmingham campaign, 38, 157–63; and black power slogan, 65; and early racial violence, 157; and economic issues, 145; and Freedom Rides, 37, 153–54; and Kennedy administration, 155; "Letter from Birmingham Jail," 159; and Malcolm X, 1, 55; and March on Washington, 39, 95, 165–66; as moderate, 96; and Montgomery Bus Boycott, 31–32; and the National Urban Coalition, 112; opposition to Vietnam War, 49, 96, 97–98; as radical, 32, 75–76, 95; and Selma campaign, 54; SNCC disillusionment with,

King, Martin Luther (*cont.*) 49; and Watts riot, 52; white opinion of, 1966, 72–73
King, Martin Luther, Library and Archives, 86–87, 200
Kluger, Richard, 21, 25, 138
Khrushchev, Nikita, 153–54
Ku Klux Klan, 28, 41, 75–76

labor movement, 2, 4, 10, 24
labor unions: as financial supporter for black organizations, 13, 80, 93, 99, 101, 106, 108–9; racial discrimination in, 18, 131, 139; relations with black movement organizations, 106
Laue, James H., 17
law and order, as issue in 1968 elections, 69
Law Students' Civil Rights Research Council, 201
Lawson, Steven F., 21, 135, 144, 197, 198, 202
Lawyers' Committee for Civil Rights Under Law, 201
LDEF. *See* NAACP Legal Defense and Educational Fund, Inc.
Leadership Conference on Civil Rights, 112
League of Revolutionary Black Workers, 70
Legal Defense and Educational Fund, Inc. *See* NAACP Legal Defense and Educational Fund, Inc.
legalistic integrationism, 20–29, 79; federal government responsiveness during era of, 137–39; as radical, 74–75, 89; rejection of, 167
legislation, civil rights, 73, 129, 137, 147, 162, 176; *see also* Civil Rights Acts of 1957, 1960, 1964, 1966, 1968
Levison, Stanley, 205
Lewis, Anthony, 155, 164–65, 202

Lewis, John, 59, 166
Lilly Endowment, 120
Linen, James A., 66
Lipsky, Michael, 5, 6, 12, 82
literacy tests, 130, 140, 143, 144
litigation, as organizational tactic, 15, 16–17, 19, 42
Little Rock, Ark., school desegregation crisis, 141, 178
lobbying, as organizational tactic, 16–17, 19, 42
Lomax, L. E., 37
London Economist, 202
Lowndes County, Ala., 54–55
Lowndes County Freedom Organization (LCFO), 55, 60
lynchings, 174
Lytle, Clifford, 106, 135, 144

McAdam, Doug, 13, 32, 80–81, 85–87, 91, 105, 154, 182, 183–85, 197, 199, 200
McCarthy, John D., 8, 9, 12, 121, 124, 178
McConahay, John B., 52, 199
McKissick, Floyd, 73
McLaurin v. Oklahoma State Regents, 21, 25, 138
Malcolm X, 1, 55–56, 59, 65
manpower training, federal grants for, 124
Marable, Manning, 58, 64
March on Washington, 23, 39, 95, 133, 150, 164, 165–66, 175, 204
Marcos, Ferdinand, 205
Marger, Martin N., 94
Marine, Gene, 56
Marshall, Burke, 155–56, 158–59, 202, 203
Marshall, Thurgood, 24, 73
Martin, Louis, 160
Marwell, Gerald, 101
Marx, Gary, 32, 198
Masotti, Louis H., 52, 67
"Maximum feasible participation," 124, 145

Medicare, 202
Meier, August, 7, 17–25 *passim*, 31–35 *passim*, 40, 43, 44, 49, 54, 61–62, 80, 86, 96, 106, 107, 138, 198
Meredith, James, 58
Merton, Robert, 4, 135
Metropolitan Applied Research Center (MARC), 112, 119, 121, 201
Michels, Robert, 135
militant. *See* radical(s)
Military Housing Act of 1949, 139
Miroff, Bruce, 150, 151, 153
Mississippi Freedom Democratic Party (MFDP), 48–49
Mississippi Freedom March, 58
Mississippi Freedom Summer, 48–49, 156, 175
Mississippi, University of, 107, 141, 178
moderate(s), 1–2, 72–73, 82, 198; dominance in movement fundraising, 90; and organizational symbiosis, 184–85; organizations, less dependent upon individual contributors, 104; relations with business interests, 107, 113; relations with political leadership, 162; typical income patterns, 82, 90, 98, 126–27; *see also* radical flank effects
moderation, tactical, 6
Monroe, N.C., 47
Montgomery Bus Boycott, 30–31, 32, 34; and radical flank effects, 79
Montgomery Improvement Association, 31
Morgan, Ruth P., 139, 141, 148
Morgan v. Virginia, 139
Morris, Aldon, 13, 32, 104, 183, 197, 198
movement success, "stepwise," 185–86

Muhammad, Elijah, 55
Mulhollan, Paige, 202
Muse, Benjamin, 16, 23, 43, 51, 52, 65–66, 67, 80, 101, 112, 197

NAACP. *See* National Association for the Advancement of Colored People
NAACP Legal Defense and Educational Fund, Inc. (LDEF), 11, 79, 137–49 *passim*, 198; activities of: 1945–1954, 75, 1955–1963, 42–43, 75, 1964–1970, 71; corporate contributions to, 111–12, 190; and direct action tactics, 38; exogenous income, 83–89, 90, 94–95, 99, 101, 127, 190; financial data on, 80–81, 100, 114–15, 199–200; foundation support for, 114–16, 190; individual contributors to, 102–4, 190; labor union contributions to, 190; as radical, 75; redefined as moderate, 75, 127
NAACP Special Contribution Fund, 117
National Advisory Commission on Civil Disorders, 51, 67, 199, 204
National Alliance of Businessmen (NAB), 112
National Association for the Advancement of Colored People (NAACP), 11, 17, 79, 97, 137–49 *passim*; activities of: pre-War years, 18–20, 1945–1954, 137–38, 1955–1963, 29–30, 42–43, 75; and COFO, 48; conflict with labor unions, 106; contrasted to National Urban League, 22; corporate financial support of, 111–12; on direct action, 24, 34, 37–38, 40–41, 50, 198; endogenous income, 100, 104, 189; exogenous income, 83–89, 90–91, 93–94, 99, 127, 189; financial data on, 81, 199–200; financial

NAACP (*cont.*)
support of SNCC, 201; foundation support of, 116–18, 122; and March on Washington, 166; and Montgomery Bus Boycott, 31; as radical, 19–21, 27–30, 75, 114, 138; redefined as moderate, 38, 71, 75, 127, 140; southern harassment of, 198; Special Contribution Fund, 117; support for establishment of Fair Employment Practices Commission, 139; Youth Councils, 37

National Catholic Conference for Inter-racial Justice, 201

National Committee Against Discrimination in Housing, 201

National Council of Churches, 48

National League on Urban Conditions. *See* National Urban League

National Opinion Research Center (NORC), 28, 45

National Scholarship Service and Fund for Negro Students, 201

National Urban Coalition, 112, 119, 201

National Urban League (NUL), 12, 79, 80, 97, 137–49 *passim*, 179; activities of: pre-War years, 17–18, 19, 1945–1954, 21–22, 26–28, 75, 1955–1963, 42, 75, 137, 1964–1970, 71; Commerce and Industry Council, 107; corporate support for, 111, 112–13, 188; on direct action, 34, 40–41, 50; early antipoverty work, 144; exogenous income, 83–89, 90–93, 99, 127, 188; federal government funding of, 124–25, 188; financial data on, 81, 100, 199–200; foundation support for, 114–16, 122, 188; individual contributors to, 102–4, 188; and March on Washington, 166; "New Thrust" program and black power, 66; relations with corporate sector, 107

National Welfare Rights Organization (NWRO): lack of corporate support for, 111; federal grants to, 124

Native Americans, 6

Navasky, Victor S., 150

Neighborhood Youth Corps, 145–46

neoconservatives, 169

"new" black radicalism, 46–74, 96; federal government responsiveness during era of, 143–49

New South, 85

Newton, Huey, 56, 63

New York Times, 66

Newark, N.J., 1967 rioting, 67

Newman, Dorothy K., 25, 106, 134, 198, 202

Nielsen, Waldemar A., 114

Nixon, Richard M., 112, 151

nonviolence: and corporate relations with legalistic integrationists, 107; decline of faith in, 46–47, 49–50, 53–57, 61, 71, 75, 156; and NAACP income, 94; as organizational philosophy, 17, 24, 26, 43; and radical flank effects, 79, 89–90, 126; *see also* direct action

North Carolina Agricultural and Technical College, 33

NUL. *See* National Urban League

Nye, Russel B., 2, 3

Oakland, Calif., 56

Oberschall, Anthony, 3, 8, 13, 80, 101, 105

O'Dell, Jack, 205

Office of Economic Opportunity, 124, 145–46

Organization of African Unity, 59

organizational infrastructure, 3, 25

outcome of movement activity, 9–10
outside groups, 2–3, 8, 12, 62, 77; see also churches, corporations, elites, exogenous income, financial support, foundations, individual contributors, labor unions
outside financial support, as index of movement acceptability, 13

Parks, Rosa, 31
Parris, Guichard, 18, 21–22, 28, 41, 42, 49, 66, 80, 86, 106, 107, 140
Part III powers. See Attorney General, civil rights enforcement powers
Patterson, James, 107
Peck, James, 24, 31, 37
Perrow, Charles, 5, 8, 135
"Philadelphia Plan," 136
philanthropy. See foundations
Pine Ridge reservation, 6
Pinkney, Alfonso, 101
Piven, Frances F., 5, 9, 13, 124, 146–47, 150, 154, 183–85, 202
Plessy v. Ferguson, 19
police brutality, 41, 136, 152, 163
political climate, as factor in movement outcome, 171, 176–77, 205
political process theory, 2
poll tax, 130, 138, 141, 144, 148
Poor People's Campaign, 75
poverty, as a movement issue, 115, 120, 121, 144–47
Powledge, F., 16, 40, 41, 107, 136, 197
preferential treatment of blacks, 169
President's Committee on Equal Employment Opportunity, 141
Pressman, Jeffrey L., 135
professional movement organizations, 183, 197
Progressive Era, 4, 10

Project Head Start, 145–46
public accommodations: as movement issue, 24, 38, 42, 131, 139, 142, 148, 157, 163; provisions of Civil Rights Act of 1964, 143
public and federally-assisted housing, 131, 141
public opinion on civil rights, 107, (1945–1954) 28–29, (1955–1963) 44–46, (1964–1970) 72–74, 75, 172–73; see also radical flank effects, negative; radical flank effects, positive

Quotations from Chairman Mao Tse-tung, 56

radical(s), 1–2; black organizations, dependence upon small contributors, 101; black organizations, typical income patterns, 82, 91, 96, 97–98, 126–27; and organizational symbiosis, 184–85; redefined as moderates, 7; see also radicalization
radical flank effects, 2–11, 77, 80; in black collective action, expected timing, 79; in black collective action, summary of findings, 172–73; defined, 2, 172; and economic interests, 179–80; factors leading to positive and negative, 180–82; expected impacts on government policies, 132, 143; and political interests, 134, 178–79; simultaneous opposing, 10–11, 176; thresholds, 149
radical flank effects, negative: on access to decision-makers, 9; on awareness and recognition, 6; and black power slogan, 65, 94; defined, 3, 167; on movement outcome, 10, 169–70; on outside financial support, 8, 77–79, 81–82, 126; on public opinion, 7–8; see also backlash

radical flank effects, positive: on access to decision-makers, 9, 107, 112; on awareness and recognition, 6; vs. co-optation, 184–86; defined, 3–4, 167; on federal government responsiveness to movement demands, 133, 142, 143, 148–49, 166–71; on foundation support for moderate organizations, 115, 122, 124; as link between competing theories, 5; on movement outcome, 9–10; on outside financial support, 8, 77–79, 81–82, 90–91, 98, 101, 113, 126–28; on public opinion, 7–8, 75; in southern cities, 107

radicalism, black, 16–17, 26–29, 57, 166; defined, 197; and financial support of moderate organizations, 89–90, 94; ideological, 16, 26; "new," 46–74, 97, 167; shifts over time, 11, 21, 26, 30, 41–46, 50, 70–76, 140, 168, 172, 198; tactical, 6, 16, 26, 46, 71–72, 162, 167

radicalization, in black collective action, 1–2, 11, 14; and corporate urban affairs efforts, 111; differential reactions to, 178–80; and moderate organizational income, 78; and political crises during Kennedy administration, 152–53, 161, 165

Raines, Howell, 197
Ramirez, G., 4, 10
Randolph, A. Philip, 19, 23, 39, 112
Reagan, Ronald, 202, 205
Reedy, George, 202
Reeves, Thomas C., 114
repression, as factor in movement successes, 174–75
Republic of New Africa (RNA), 16, 20, 61, 69, 71
resource mobilization. *See* exogenous income

resource mobilization theory, 2, 5, 8, 12, 77, 80, 182, 197, 199
restrictive covenants, 131, 139
Reuther, Walter, 106, 203–4
Revolutionary Action Movement (RAM), 61, 68–69, 72
revolutionary black nationalism, 67–70, 71, 133, 170
Rhind, Flora M., 114
Right to Life movement. *See* antiabortion movement
"riot ideology," 65
riots, xiii, 1, 21, 57, 199; and corporate interests, 179–80; and defeat of 1966 civil rights bill, 169; of early twentieth century, 204; and federal government responsiveness to movement demands, 133, 143, 170, 173; and foundation grant priorities, 121; Kennedy administration fears of, 157; and moderate organizational income, 78–79, 90, 93–94, 95–96, 98, 113; of 1963–1966, 48, 50–53; of 1967–1968, 67, 147; "protest interpretation" of, 181; response of moderate civil rights leaders to, 52–53, 182; segregation as cause of, 164; welfare programs, 147
Rockefeller, John D., 114
Rockefeller Brothers Fund, 114
Rockefeller Foundation, 119
Roof, Wade C., 202
Rudwick, Elliot M., 7, 17–25 *passim*, 31–34 *passim*, 40, 43, 49, 54, 61–62, 80, 86, 96, 106, 107, 204
Rustin, Bayard, 36, 39, 65–66

satyagraha, 24, 31
Schneidler, Joseph, 6
school desegregation. *See* education
Schram, Sanford F., 147
SCLC. *See* Southern Christian Leadership Conference

Scott, R. L., 3, 65
Seale, Bobby, 56
Sears, David O., 52, 199
self-help, as organizational philosophy, 15, 17, 19, 26
Selma, Ala., xi, 41, 54, 133, 136, 145, 174
Selznick, Phillip, 135
Senate, U.S., 138–39, 144, 147
Senate Permanent Committee on Investigation, 51, 67
separate-but-equal doctrine, 19, 25, 138; *see also Plessy v. Ferguson*
separatism, as an organizational philosophy, 17, 50, 57–66, 72, 171; *see also* black nationalism, revolutionary black nationalism
Sheatsley, Paul B., 28–29, 45–46, 177
Shelley v. Kraemer, 21, 139
shootouts, between black militants and authorities, 69
Simkins, Dr. George, 34
sit-ins, 24, 33–35; business reaction to, 107; Kennedy endorsement of, 151; and radical flank effects, 79, 98, 133
Skolnick, Jerome H., 29, 45–46, 51
"small money" funding sources, 101, 105, 127; *see also* individual contributors, churches, labor unions
Smith v. Allwright, 21
Smyth, Mabel M., 201–202
SNCC. *See* Student Nonviolent Coordinating Committee
Sobel, Lester A., 112, 146, 157, 159
Somoza, Anastasio, 205
Sorensen, Annmette, 202
Sorensen, Theodore C., 150, 202, 203
Southern Christian Leadership Conference (SCLC), 12, 79; activities of: 1955–1963, 43–44, 75, 140–49 *passim*, 1964–1970, 70–71; American Foundation on Nonviolence, 117; and Birmingham campaign, 38, 157–63; and COFO, 48; controversy over communists in, 205; direct-mail fundraising, 200; exogenous income, 83–89, 95–96, 98–99, 101, 127, 193; financial data on, 81, 100, 200; formation of, 31; foundation support for, 117; Freedom Rallies, 104; labor union and church contributions to, 193; and sit-ins, 34; Southern Christian Leadership Foundation, 117
Southern Christian Leadership Foundation. *See* Southern Christian Leadership Conference
Southern Regional Council (SRC), 12, 79, 80; activities of: 1945–1954, 22–23, 27, 1955–1963, 38, 1964–1970, 71; church contributions, 105, 191–92; exogenous income, 83–89, 93, 127, 191–92; financial data on, 81, 100, 114–15, 199–200; foundation support of, 114–16, 191–92; individual contributors to, 102–4, 191–92; labor union support of, 191–92; and the Voter Education Project, 154
Southern resistance to desegregation, 29–30, 178–79; *see also* anti–civil rights countermovement
Spring, Joel, 10
SRC. *See* Southern Regional Council
St. James, Warren D., 19, 80
Standard Oil, 107
Stern Family Fund, 114, 154
Student Nonviolent Coordinating Committee (SNCC), 12, 35–36, 40, 57, 70, 140–49 *passim*; activities of: 1960–1963, 44, 1964–1968, 48; and Black Panther Party, 60–61; and black

230 SNCC (cont.)
power, 59–61, 75; church contributions to, 105, 195; criticism of white participation in, 49–50, 60; exogenous income, 83–89, 97, 98, 101, 126–27, 175, 195, 201; financial data on, 81, 100, 200; "Friends of SNCC" groups, 104; individual contributions to, 195; internal divisions after 1964, 49; lack of corporate contributions to, 111; and March on Washington, 165; payroll, 198–99; as radical, 36, 60, 70, 76, 97, 126; radicalization of, 57, 61, 71, 75; and violent self-defense, 53–54; and voter education project, 154–55; see also Mississippi Freedom Democratic Party, Mississippi Freedom Summer, Voter Education Project, voter registration

Subcabinet Group on Civil Rights, 155
Sundquist, James D., 141, 142
Swank, Duane, 147
Sweatt v. Painter, 21, 25, 138
symbiosis, organizational, 185–86

Taconic Foundation, 125, 154
Taeuber, Alma F., 202
Taeuber, Karl E., 202
Taylor, D. Garth, 177
third parties, 77, 82; see also outside groups
Thirteenth Amendment to the U.S. Constitution, 137
This is CORE, 32
transportation, as movement issue, 24, 131, 139; see also Freedom Rides, public accommodations
Turbett, J. Patrick, 147
Turner, Ralph, 181
Tuttle, William M., 19
Twenty-fourth Amendment to the U.S. Constitution, 144

unemployment: as a movement issue, 120; federal jobs programs, 131
United Auto Workers, 106
United Nations, 59
United Negro College Fund: corporate support of, 111, 112; foundation support of, 118–19, 122, 201
United States Information Agency, 152
United States Steel, 107
universities, race-related foundation grants to, 119, 121–22
Urban America, 201
urban disorders. *See* riots
urban guerrillas, 26, 61, 62; see also revolutionary black nationalism
US, 64

Vander Zanden, J. W., 50
Van Valey, Thomas L., 202
Variable-sum goals, 71
Vietnam War, 49, 69, 96, 127, 170
Violence, 2, 72, 199, 202; against blacks, 48, 53–54, 152, 174–75, 198, 204; in Birmingham, 39, 50, 179; and black power, 59; business reaction to, 107, 110–11, 136; Kennedy administration fear of, 159–62, 163, 164, 166, 174–75, 179; as movement tactic, 15, 16, 26; and radical flank effects, 79, 98, 101, 126, 171, 173; see also revolutionary black nationalism, riots, urban guerrillas, violent self-defense
violent self-defense: in ghettos, 55–57; in South, 53–56
visibility, of black organizations, 20
Volunteers in Service to America (VISTA), 145
Von Eschen, Donald, 40
Voter Education Project, 150, 154–57, 162
voter registration, 35, 44, 48, 125,

135, 150, 151, 154–55; *see also* Voter Education Project
voting rights: federal law and policy on, 138, 140, 144, 148, 163; as movement issue, 51, 120, 130; provisions of Civil Rights Act of 1964, 143
Voting Rights Act of 1965, 52, 54–55, 130, 132, 136, 143, 144, 167

Walker, Jack, 9, 32, 40, 58, 64, 107
Wall Street Journal, 64
Wallace, George, 158
War on Poverty, 61, 73, 124, 135–36, 145, 148, 170
Warren, Earl, 26
Washington, Booker T., 17
Washington, D.C., 147; *see also* March on Washington
Waskow, Arthur, 204
Watts, Los Angeles, 1965 rioting, 51–52, 133
Weisskopf, Thomas E., 4, 10
Welch, Susan, 147
welfare, federal policy, 134; expansion of programs, 145
Wheeler, John, 112
White, Lee, 160, 203
White Citizens' Councils, 30, 76
White House Conference on Civil Rights, 59
White liberals, 27, 165; and black power slogan, 65; as contributors to black collective action, 99, 101, 177; mistrust of, 49, 59, 62
White participation in civil rights movement: black disapproval of, 49–50, 60, 61; as factor in movement successes, 175
White primary, 198
Wilcox, Jerome E., 202
Wildavsky, Aaron B., 135
Wilkins, Roy, 43, 55, 68, 163; and black power slogan, 65; and National Urban Coalition, 112; white opinion of, 1966, 73
Williams, G. Mennen, 160–61, 203
Williams, Robert R., 47, 68–69
Wisconsin, University of, 200
Wofford, Harris, 150–51, 153, 155–56, 157, 162, 202
Wolff, Miles, 32, 34
Wolk, Allan, 137
women's movement, 2, 3–4, 7, 197
Woodward, C. Vann, 137

Young, Whitney, 42, 66, 68, 73

Zald, Mayer, 8, 9, 12, 96, 121, 124, 178
zero-sum goals, 71
Zieger, Robert H., 2
Zinn, Howard, 150

Black Radicals and the Civil Rights Mainstream, 1954–1970 was designed by Sheila Hart; composed by Tseng Information Systems, Inc., Durham, North Carolina; and printed and bound by Braun-Brumfield, Inc., Ann Arbor, Michigan. The book was set in 10/12 Palatino with Franklin Gothic Condensed display and printed on 60-lb. Glatfelter.

www.ingramcontent.com/pod-product-compliance
Lightning Source LLC
Chambersburg PA
CBHW022216090526
44584CB00012BB/569